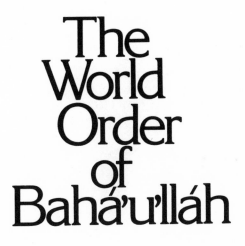

The
World
Order
of
Bahá'u'lláh

By Shoghi Effendi:

GOD PASSES BY
THE ADVENT OF DIVINE JUSTICE
THE PROMISED DAY IS COME

Collections of Letters and Messages:

MESSAGES TO THE BAHÁ'Í WORLD
CITADEL OF FAITH
BAHÁ'Í ADMINISTRATION

Translations:

THE DAWN-BREAKERS
THE KITÁB-I-ÍQÁN
EPISTLE TO THE SON OF THE WOLF
GLEANINGS FROM THE WRITINGS OF BAHÁ'U'LLÁH
PRAYERS AND MEDITATIONS BY BAHÁ'U'LLÁH
THE HIDDEN WORDS OF BAHÁ'U'LLÁH

The World Order of Bahá'u'lláh

SELECTED LETTERS
BY
SHOGHI EFFENDI

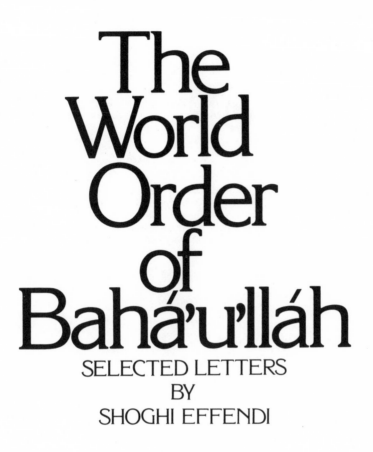

BAHÁ'Í PUBLISHING TRUST
WILMETTE, ILLINOIS

The World Order of Bahá'u'lláh *was first*
published in 1938, a second printing being issued in 1944.
A revised edition with a new preface was published in 1955,
of which three printings subsequently appeared.
This second revised edition contains
a number of corrections.

Second revised edition 1974

Reprinted 1980

ISBN 0-87743-031-4 (cloth)
ISBN 0-87743-004-7 (paper)
Library of Congress Catalog Card No. 56-17685

Printed in the United States of America

INTRODUCTION

The general communications written to the American Bahá'í community by the Guardian of the Faith between 1922 and 1929 explained and encouraged the development of the administrative institutions created by Bahá'u'lláh and promulgated by 'Abdu'l-Bahá in His Will and Testament. These letters have been published in a volume entitled "Bahá'í Administration," the source of information on the institutions of Local and National Spiritual Assemblies, the Annual Convention, and the nature of those relationships organically uniting Bahá'ís in their collective worship and activity.

The letters now collected and published under the title of "The World Order of Bahá'u'lláh" have a different aim and a far larger scope. These later communications unfold a clear vision of the relation between the Bahá'í community and the entire process of social evolution under the Dispensation of Bahá'u'lláh. The vital distinction between the Bahá'í community and the sects and congregations of former religions had already been made apparent, but the present volume establishes the Bahá'í Administrative Order as the nucleus and pattern of the world civilization emerging under divine inspiration at this focal point of human history. While, therefore, it represents a continuance of the Guardian's special task of teaching and guiding the Bahá'ís throughout the development of a rapidly maturing Faith, the volume discloses the full degree to which Bahá'u'lláh's Message applies to the world of humanity and not merely to those who are believers at this time. The title and subtitles were not part of the original text, but have been added with Shoghi Effendi's approval for the convenience of the reader.

In "The World Order of Bahá'u'lláh" we are enabled to perceive the significance of the new dimension which Bahá'u'lláh gave to religion in this era: the supremacy of Divine Law in civilization, fulfilling that supremacy which in previous Dispensations religion had exercised over individual souls. Shoghi Effendi's exposition of the Teachings, his unique realization of the ultimate aim and purpose of Bahá'u'lláh's Revelation, are no static commentary upon a sacred text but the very essence of world statesmanship evoked in the hour of man's direst need. No longer do the Bahá'ís require 'Abdu'l-Bahá's written Testament to prove the existence of the Guardianship—the successive communications from Shoghi Effendi, and especially those devoted to the subject of World Order, in themselves contain the highest demonstration that Bahá'u'lláh's Spirit continues to bless His Cause and assure its victory in the reconciliation of the peoples of earth and their union in "one Faith and one Order."

For those who have inclined to believe that even the realization of the mighty dream of the "return of Christ" would mean nothing more than the vindication of personal spirituality and individual righteousness, the idea of religion giving a law to the nation is the most revolutionary conception which can enter the mind of man. "For Bahá'u'lláh, we should readily recognize, has not only imbued mankind with a new and regenerating Spirit. He has not merely enunciated certain universal principles, or propounded a particular philosophy, however potent, sound and universal these may be. In addition to these He, as well as 'Abdu'l-Bahá after Him, has, unlike the Dispensations of the past, clearly and specifically laid down a set of Laws, established definite institutions, and provided for the essentials of a Divine Economy. These are destined to be a pattern for future society, a supreme instrument for the establishment of the Most Great Peace, and the one agency for the unification of the world, and the proclamation of the reign of righteousness and justice upon the earth." . . . "Does not the very operation of the world-unifying forces that are at work in this age necessitate that He Who is the Bearer of the Message of God in this day should not only reaffirm that self-same exalted standard of individual conduct inculcated by the Prophets gone before Him, but embody in His appeal, to all governments and peoples, the essentials of that social code, that Divine Economy, which must guide humanity's concerted efforts in establishing that all-embracing federation which is to signalize the advent of the Kingdom of God on this earth?"

Such words as these, charged with the potency of a Faith that is not merely a written book but the very dynamic Spirit transforming the life of the entire world, make "The World Order of Bahá'u'lláh" a work of consummate importance to every sincere seeker and not to Bahá'ís alone. In the light of the existing international chaos, they reveal the most significant Truth of this era, namely that the old conception of religion, which separated spirituality from the fundamental functions of civilization, compelling men to abide by conflicting principles of faith, of politics and of economics, has been forever destroyed. The command, "Render unto God that which is of God, and unto Cæsar that which is of Cæsar," has been annulled by the law of the oneness of humanity revealed by Bahá'u'lláh.

"Leaders of religion, exponents of political theories, governors of human institutions, who at present are witnessing with perplexity and dismay the bankruptcy of their ideas, and the disintegration of their handiwork, would do well to turn their gaze to the Revelation of Bahá'u'lláh, and to meditate upon the World Order which, lying enshrined in His teachings, is slowly and imperceptibly rising amid the welter and chaos of present-day civilization."

HORACE HOLLEY

CONTENTS

The world's equilibrium hath been upset through the vibrating influence of this most great, this new World Order.

BAHÁ'U'LLÁH

PREFACE TO 1955 EDITION

Seventeen fateful years have passed since the publication of the first edition of *The World Order of Bahá'u'lláh*. Neither the disasters of the second World War nor the increasing menace of the post-war period can challenge Shoghi Effendi's convictions, nor invalidate his thesis, nor deny his ultimate hopes expressed in these letters written between 1929 and 1936. On the contrary, his presentation of the world mission of the Bahá'í Faith acquires added force from the very failure of human philosophy and statesmanship to attain security for mankind. The reader has in these pages access to a public document addressed to the people of spiritual faith in all races, all nations and all creeds. Recognition and acceptance, however, calls for an act of faith since these basic truths have as yet no endorsement comparable in public influence with the massive prejudices which still command the loyalty of partisan minds.

The fundamental thesis developed in this work has been carried farther in two later works by the Guardian of the Faith.

In a text dated December 25, 1938, Shoghi Effendi unfolded the mighty theme, *The Advent of Divine Justice*, hailing the ultimate victory of world unity after the peoples have been purged and purified by intense ordeals. Recognizing that the Bahá'ís have established their administrative order, the Guardian holds aloft the great teaching missions which that order is destined to undertake. The text is intimately identified with the Bahá'í community, but that community is associated with a goal representing the best interests of humanity itself.

The second work, *The Promised Day Is Come*, dated March 28, 1941, related the history of the Nineteenth and early Twentieth centuries to the Báb, Bahá'u'lláh and 'Abdu'l-Bahá, Who exemplified the expression of the Divine Will. The destiny of an era is determined by its reception of the Prophets. When the Word of God is denied, resisted and effort made to destroy its potency, man places himself in opposition to God. From that opposition flow the wars and revolutions which become the instruments by which a non-believing generation inflicts dire punishment upon itself.

The Promised Day Is Come brings the note of dramatic climax to the Guardian's discussion of the Faith of Bahá'u'lláh and the world in which its high mystery is unveiled.

For the reader who seeks understanding of the historic background in which the Bahá'í Faith arose and fulfilled its destiny and some knowledge of the establishment of Bahá'í institutions in East and West, Shoghi Effendi's *God Passes By* provides the authentic record of events and elucidates their meaning. This work, in fact, stands unique in the annals of religion as a history of the Prophet written soon after His passing by the Head of its community, with access to all documents and materials and complete understanding of its nature and purpose.

Consideration of *The World Order of Bahá'u'lláh*, therefore, opens the door to the most effective expression of spiritual statesmanship available in the world today.

HORACE HOLLEY

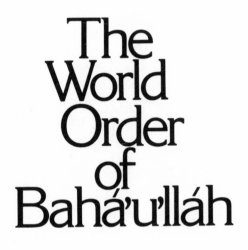

The
World
Order
of
Bahá'u'lláh

THE WORLD ORDER OF BAHÁ'U'LLÁH

*To the members of the National Spiritual Assembly of the Bahá'ís
of the United States and Canada.*

Dearly-beloved co-workers:

I have been acquainted by the perusal of your latest communications with the nature of the doubts that have been publicly expressed,
by one who is wholly misinformed as to the true precepts of the
Cause, regarding the validity of institutions that stand inextricably
interwoven with the Faith of Bahá'u'lláh. Not that I for a moment
view such faint misgivings in the light of an open challenge to the
structure that embodies the Faith, nor is it because I question in the
least the unyielding tenacity of the faith of the American believers,
if I venture to dwell upon what seems to me appropriate observations at the present stage of the evolution of our beloved Cause. I
am indeed inclined to welcome these expressed apprehensions inasmuch as they afford me an opportunity to familiarize the elected
representatives of the believers with the origin and the character of
the institutions which stand at the very basis of the World Order
ushered in by Bahá'u'lláh. We should feel truly thankful for such
futile attempts to undermine our beloved Faith—attempts that pro-
trude their ugly face from time to time, seem for a while able to
create a breach in the ranks of the faithful, recede finally into the
obscurity of oblivion, and are thought of no more. Such incidents
we should regard as the interpositions of Providence, designed to
fortify our faith, to clarify our vision, and to deepen our understanding of the essentials of His Divine Revelation.

Sources of the Bahá'í World Order

It would, however, be helpful and instructive to bear in mind
certain basic principles with reference to the Will and Testament
of 'Abdu'l-Bahá, which together with the Kitáb-i-Aqdas, constitutes
the chief depository wherein are enshrined those priceless elements
of that Divine Civilization, the establishment of which is the pri-

mary mission of the Bahá'í Faith. A study of the provisions of these sacred documents will reveal the close relationship that exists between them, as well as the identity of purpose and method which they inculcate. Far from regarding their specific provisions as incompatible and contradictory in spirit, every fair-minded inquirer will readily admit that they are not only complementary, but that they mutually confirm one another, and are inseparable parts of one complete unit. A comparison of their contents with the rest of Bahá'í sacred Writings will similarly establish the conformity of whatever they contain with the spirit as well as the letter of the authenticated writings and sayings of Bahá'u'lláh and 'Abdu'l-Bahá. In fact, he who reads the Aqdas with care and diligence will not find it hard to discover that the Most Holy Book itself anticipates in a number of passages the institutions which 'Abdu'l-Bahá ordains in His Will. By leaving certain matters unspecified and unregulated in His Book of Laws, Bahá'u'lláh seems to have deliberately left a gap in the general scheme of Bahá'í Dispensation, which the unequivocal provisions of the Master's Will has filled. To attempt to divorce the one from the other, to insinuate that the Teachings of Bahá'u'lláh have not been upheld, in their entirety and with absolute integrity, by what 'Abdu'l-Bahá has revealed in His Will, is an unpardonable affront to the unswerving fidelity that has characterized the life and labors of our beloved Master.

I will not attempt in the least to assert or demonstrate the authenticity of the Will and Testament of 'Abdu'l-Bahá, for that in itself would betray an apprehension on my part as to the unanimous confidence of the believers in the genuineness of the last written wishes of our departed Master. I will only confine my observations to those issues which may assist them to appreciate the essential unity that underlies the spiritual, the humanitarian, and the administrative principles enunciated by the Author and the Interpreter of the Bahá'í Faith.

I am at a loss to explain that strange mentality that inclines to uphold as the sole criterion of the truth of the Bahá'í Teachings what is admittedly only an obscure and unauthenticated translation of an oral statement made by 'Abdu'l-Bahá, in defiance and total disregard of the available text of all of His universally recognized writings. I truly deplore the unfortunate distortions that have resulted in days past from the incapacity of the interpreter to grasp the meaning of 'Abdu'l-Bahá, and from his incompetence to render adequately such truths as have been revealed to him by the Master's statements. Much of the confusion that has obscured the understanding of the believers should be attributed to this double error involved in the inexact rendering of an only partially understood statement. Not infrequently has the interpreter even failed to convey the exact purport of the inquirer's specific questions, and, by his deficiency of understanding and expression in conveying the answer of 'Abdu'l-Bahá, has been responsible for reports wholly at variance with the true spirit and purpose of the Cause. It was chiefly in view of the misleading nature of the reports of the informal conversations of 'Abdu'l-Bahá with visiting pilgrims, that I have insistently urged the believers of the West to regard such statements as merely personal impressions of the sayings of their Master, and to quote and consider as authentic only such translations as are based upon the authenticated text of His recorded utterances in the original tongue.

It should be remembered by every follower of the Cause that the system of Bahá'í administration is not an innovation imposed arbitrarily upon the Bahá'ís of the world since the Master's passing, but derives its authority from the Will and Testament of 'Abdu'l-Bahá, is specifically prescribed in unnumbered Tablets, and rests in some of its essential features upon the explicit provisions of the Kitáb-i-Aqdas. It thus unifies and correlates the principles separately laid down by Bahá'u'lláh and 'Abdu'l-Bahá, and is indissolubly bound with the essential verities of the Faith. To dissociate the administrative principles of the Cause from the purely spiritual and humanitarian teachings would be tantamount to a mutilation of the body of the Cause, a separation that can only result in the disintegration of its component parts, and the extinction of the Faith itself.

Local and National Houses of Justice

It should be carefully borne in mind that the local as well as the international Houses of Justice have been expressly enjoined by the Kitáb-i-Aqdas; that the institution of the National Spiritual Assembly, as an intermediary body, and referred to in the Master's Will as the "Secondary House of Justice," has the express sanction of 'Abdu'l-Bahá; and that the method to be pursued for the election of the International and National Houses of Justice has been set forth by Him in His Will, as well as in a number of His Tablets. Moreover, the institutions of the local and national Funds, that are now the necessary adjuncts to all local and national spiritual assemblies, have not only been established by 'Abdu'l-Bahá in the Tablets He revealed to the Bahá'ís of the Orient, but their importance and necessity have been repeatedly emphasized by Him in His utterances and writings. The concentration of authority in the hands of the elected representatives of the believers; the necessity of the submission of every adherent of the Faith to the considered judgment of Bahá'í Assemblies; His preference for unanimity in decision; the decisive character of the majority vote; and even the desirability for the exercise of close supervision over all Bahá'í publications, have been sedulously instilled by 'Abdu'l-Bahá, as evidenced by His authenticated and widely-scattered Tablets. To accept His broad and humanitarian Teachings on one hand, and to reject and dismiss with neglectful indifference His more challenging and distinguishing precepts, would be an act of manifest disloyalty to that which He has cherished most in His life.

That the Spiritual Assemblies of today will be replaced in time by the Houses of Justice, and are to all intents and purposes identical and not separate bodies, is abundantly confirmed by 'Abdu'l-Bahá Himself. He has in fact in a Tablet addressed to the members of the first Chicago Spiritual Assembly, the first elected Bahá'í body instituted in the United States, referred to them as the members of the "House of Justice" for that city, and has thus with His own pen established beyond any doubt the identity of the present Bahá'í Spiritual Assemblies with the Houses of Justice referred to by Bahá'u'lláh. For reasons which are not difficult to discover, it has been found advisable to bestow upon the elected representatives of Bahá'í communities throughout the world the temporary appellation of Spiritual Assemblies, a term which, as the position and aims of the Bahá'í Faith are better understood and more fully recognized, will gradually be superseded by the permanent and more appropriate designation of House of Justice. Not only will the present-day Spiritual Assemblies be styled differently in future, but they will be enabled also to add to their present functions those powers, duties, and prerogatives necessitated by the recognition of the Faith of Bahá'u'lláh, not merely as one of the recognized religious systems of the world, but as the State Religion of an independent and Sovereign Power. And as the Bahá'í Faith permeates the masses of the peoples of East and West, and its truth is embraced by the majority of the peoples of a number of the Sovereign States of the world, will the Universal House of Justice attain the plenitude of its power, and exercise, as the supreme organ of the Bahá'í Commonwealth, all the rights, the duties, and responsibilities incumbent upon the world's future super-state.

It must be pointed out, however, in this connection that, contrary to what has been confidently asserted, the establishment of the Supreme House of Justice is in no way dependent upon the adoption of the Bahá'í Faith by the mass of the peoples of the world, nor does it presuppose its acceptance by the majority of the inhabitants of any one country. In fact, 'Abdu'l-Bahá, Himself, in one of His earliest Tablets, contemplated the possibility of the formation of the Universal House of Justice in His own lifetime, and but for the unfavorable circumstances prevailing under the Turkish régime, would have, in all probability, taken the preliminary steps for its establishment. It will be evident, therefore, that given favorable circumstances, under which the Bahá'ís of Persia and of the adjoining countries under Soviet rule, may be enabled to elect their national representatives, in accordance with the guiding principles laid down in 'Abdu'l-Bahá's writings, the only remaining obstacle in the way of the definite formation of the International House of Justice will have been removed. For upon the National Houses of Justice of the East and the West devolves the task, in conformity with the explicit provisions of the Will, of electing directly the members of the International House of Justice. Not until they are themselves fully representative of the rank and file of the believers in their respective countries, not until they have acquired the weight and the experience that will enable them to function vigorously in the organic life of the Cause, can they approach their sacred task, and provide the spiritual basis for the constitution of so august a body in the Bahá'í world.

The Institution of Guardianship

It must be also clearly understood by every believer that the institution of Guardianship does not under any circumstances abrogate, or even in the slightest degree detract from, the powers granted to the Universal House of Justice by Bahá'u'lláh in the Kitáb-i-Aqdas, and repeatedly and solemnly confirmed by 'Abdu'l-Bahá in His Will. It does not constitute in any manner a contradiction to the Will and Writings of Bahá'u'lláh, nor does it nullify any of His revealed instructions. It enhances the prestige of that exalted assembly, stabilizes its supreme position, safeguards its unity, assures the continuity of its labors, without presuming in the slightest to infringe upon the inviolability of its clearly-defined sphere of jurisdiction. We stand indeed too close to so monumental a document to claim for ourselves a complete understanding of all its implications, or to presume to have grasped the manifold mysteries it undoubtedly contains. Only future generations can comprehend the value and the significance attached to this Divine Masterpiece, which the hand of the Master-builder of the world has designed for the unification and the triumph of the world-wide Faith of Bahá'u'lláh. Only those who come after us will be in a position to realize the value of the surprisingly strong emphasis that has been placed on the institution of the House of Justice and of the Guardianship. They only will appreciate the significance of the vigorous language employed by 'Abdu'l-Bahá with reference to the band of Covenant-breakers that has opposed Him in His days. To them alone will be revealed the suitability of the institutions initiated by 'Abdu'l-Bahá to the character of the future society which is to emerge out of the chaos and confusion of the present age. In this connection, I cannot but feel amused at the preposterous and fantastic idea that Muḥammad-'Alí, the prime mover and the focal center of unyielding hostility to the person of 'Abdu'l-Bahá, should have freely associated himself with the members of the family of 'Abdu'l-Bahá in the forging of a will which in the words of the writer herself, is but a "recital of the plottings" in which for thirty years Muḥammad-'Alí has been busily engaged. To such a hopeless victim of confused ideas, I feel I can best reply by a genuine expression of compassion and pity, mingled with my hopes for her deliverance from so profound a delusion. It was in view of the aforesaid observations, that I have, after the unfortunate and unavoidable delay occasioned by my ill health and absence from the Holy Land during the Master's passing, hesitated to resort to the indiscriminate circulation of the Will, realizing full well that it was primarily directed to the recognized believers, and only indirectly concerned the larger body of the friends and sympathizers of the Cause.

The Animating Purpose of Bahá'í Institutions

And now, it behooves us to reflect on the animating purpose and the primary functions of these divinely-established institutions, the sacred character and the universal efficacy of which can be demonstrated only by the spirit they diffuse and the work they actually achieve. I need not dwell upon what I have already reiterated and emphasized that the administration of the Cause is to be conceived as an instrument and not a substitute for the Faith of Bahá'u'lláh, that it should be regarded as a channel through which His promised blessings may flow, that it should guard against such rigidity as would clog and fetter the liberating forces released by His Revelation. I need not enlarge at the present moment upon what I have stated in the past, that contributions to the local and national Funds are of a purely voluntary character; that no coercion or solicitation of funds is to be tolerated in the Cause; that general appeals addressed to the communities as a body should be the only form in which the financial requirements of the Faith are to be met; that the financial support accorded to a very few workers in the teaching and administrative fields is of a temporary nature; that the present restrictions imposed on the publication of Bahá'í literature will be definitely abolished; that the World Unity activity is being carried out as an experiment to test the efficacy of the indirect method of teaching; that the whole machinery of assemblies, of committees and conventions is to be regarded as a means, and not an end in itself; that they will rise or fall according to their capacity to further the interests, to coördinate the activities, to apply the principles, to embody the ideals and execute the purpose of the Bahá'í Faith. Who, I may ask, when viewing the international character of the Cause, its far-flung ramifications, the increasing complexity of its affairs, the diversity of its adherents, and the state of confusion that assails on every side the infant Faith of God, can for a moment question the necessity of some sort of administrative machinery that will insure, amid the storm and stress of a struggling civilization, the unity of the Faith, the preservation of its identity, and the protection of its interests? To repudiate the validity of the assemblies of the elected ministers of the Faith of Bahá'u'lláh would be to reject those countless Tablets of Bahá'u'lláh and 'Abdu'l-Bahá, wherein they have extolled their privileges and duties, emphasized the glory of their mission, revealed the immensity of their task, and warned them of the attacks they must needs expect from the unwisdom of their friends as well as from the malice of their enemies. It is surely for those to whose hands so priceless a heritage has been committed to prayerfully watch lest the tool should supersede the Faith itself, lest undue concern for the minute details arising from the administration of the Cause obscure the vision of its promoters, lest partiality, ambition, and worldliness tend in the course of time to becloud the radiance, stain the purity, and impair the effectiveness of the Faith of Bahá'u'lláh.

Situation in Egypt

I have already referred in my previous communications of January 10, 1926, and February 12, 1927, to the perplexing yet highly significant situation that has arisen in Egypt as a result of the final judgment of the Muslim ecclesiastical court in that country pronounced against our Egyptian brethren, denouncing them as heretics, expelling them from their midst, and refusing them the application and benefits of the Muslim Law. I have also acquainted you with the difficulties with which they are faced, and the plans which they have conceived, in order to obtain from the Egyptian civil authorities a recognition of the independent status of their Faith. It must be explained, however, that in the Muslim countries of the Near and Middle East, with the exception of Turkey which has lately abolished all ecclesiastical courts under its rule, every recognized religious community has, in matters of personal status such as marriage, divorce and inheritance, its own ecclesiastical court, totally independent of the civil and criminal tribunals, there being in such instances no civil code promulgated by the government and embracing all the different religious communities. Hitherto regarded as a sect of Islám, the Bahá'ís of Egypt, who for the most part are of Muslim origin, and unable therefore to refer for purposes of marriage and divorce to the recognized religious tribunals of any other denomination, find themselves in consequence in a delicate and anomalous position. They have naturally resolved to refer their case to the Egyptian Government, and have prepared for this purpose a petition to be addressed to the head of the Egyptian Cabinet. In this document they have set forth the motives compelling them to seek recognition from their rulers, have asserted their readiness and their qualifications to exercise the functions of an independent Bahá'í court, have assured them of their implicit obedience and loyalty to the State, and of their abstinence from interference in the politics of their country. They have also decided to accompany the text of their petition with a copy of the judgment of the Court, with selections from Bahá'í writings, and with the document that sets forth the principles of their national constitution which, with few exceptions, is identical with the Declaration and By-laws promulgated by your Assembly.

I have insisted that the provisions of their constitution should, in all its details, conform to the text of the Declaration of Trust and By-laws which you have established, endeavoring thereby to preserve the uniformity which I feel is essential in all Bahá'í National Constitutions. I would like, therefore, in this connection to request of you what I have already intimated to them, that whatever amendments you may decide to introduce in the text of the Declaration and By-laws should be duly communicated to me, that I may take the necessary steps for the introduction of similar changes in the text of all other National Bahá'í Constitutions.

It will be readily admitted that in view of the peculiar privileges granted to recognized religious Communities in the Islamic countries of the Near and Middle East, the request which is to be submitted by the Bahá'í Egyptian National Assembly to the Government of Egypt is more substantial and far-reaching than what has already been granted by the Federal Authorities to your Assembly. For their petition is chiefly concerned with a formal request for recognition by the highest civil authorities in Egypt of the Egyptian National Spiritual Assembly as a recognized and independent Bahá'í court, free and able to execute and apply in all matters of personal status such laws and ordinances as have been promulgated by Bahá'u'lláh in the Kitáb-i-Aqdas.

I have asked them to approach informally the authorities concerned, and to make the fullest possible inquiry as a preliminary measure to the formal presentation of their historic petition. Any assistance which your Assembly, after careful deliberation, may find it advisable to offer to the valiant promoters of the Faith in that land will be deeply appreciated, and will serve to confirm the solidarity that characterizes the Bahá'í Communities of East and West. Whatever the outcome of this mighty issue—and none can fail to appreciate the incalculable possibilities of the present situation—we can rest assured that the guiding Hand that has released these forces will, in His inscrutable wisdom and by His omnipotent power, continue to shape and direct their course for the glory, the ultimate emancipation, and the unqualified recognition of His Faith.

. . . .

Your true brother,

SHOGHI.

Haifa, Palestine.
February 27, 1929.

THE WORLD ORDER OF BAHÁ'U'LLÁH
FURTHER CONSIDERATIONS

THE WORLD ORDER OF BAHÁ'U'LLÁH
FURTHER CONSIDERATIONS

*To the beloved of the Lord and the handmaids of the Merciful
throughout the West.*

Dearly-beloved co-workers:

Amid the reports that have of late reached the Holy Land, most
of which witness to the triumphant march of the Cause, a few seem
to betray a certain apprehension regarding the validity of the institutions which stand inseparably associated with the Faith of Bahá'-
u'lláh. These expressed misgivings appear to be actuated by certain
whisperings which have emanated from quarters which are either
wholly misinformed regarding the fundamentals of the Bahá'í Revelation, or which deliberately contrive to sow the seeds of dissension in
the hearts of the faithful.

A Blessing in Disguise

Viewed in the light of past experience, the inevitable result of
such futile attempts, however persistent and malicious they may be,
is to contribute to a wider and deeper recognition by believers and
unbelievers alike of the distinguishing features of the Faith proclaimed by Bahá'u'lláh. These challenging criticisms, whether or not
dictated by malice, cannot but serve to galvanize the souls of its
ardent supporters, and to consolidate the ranks of its faithful promoters. They will purge the Faith from those pernicious elements
whose continued association with the believers tends to discredit the
fair name of the Cause, and to tarnish the purity of its spirit. We
should welcome, therefore, not only the open attacks which its
avowed enemies persistently launch against it, but should also view
as a blessing in disguise every storm of mischief with which they
who apostatize their faith or claim to be its faithful exponents
assail it from time to time. Instead of undermining the Faith, such
assaults, both from within and from without, reinforce its foundations, and excite the intensity of its flame. Designed to becloud its
radiance, they proclaim to all the world the exalted character of its

15

precepts, the completeness of its unity, the uniqueness of its position, and the pervasiveness of its influence.

I do not feel for one moment that such clamor, mostly attributable to impotent rage against the resistless march of the Cause of God, can ever distress the valiant warriors of the Faith. For these heroic souls, whether they be contending in America's impregnable stronghold, or struggling in the heart of Europe, and across the seas as far as the continent of Australasia, have already abundantly demonstrated the tenacity of their Faith and the abiding value of their conviction.

Distinguishing Features of Bahá'í World Order

I feel it, however, incumbent upon me by virtue of the responsibility attached to the Guardianship of the Faith, to dwell more fully upon the essential character and the distinguishing features of that world order as conceived and proclaimed by Bahá'u'lláh. I feel impelled, at the present stage of the evolution of the Bahá'í Revelation, to state candidly and without any reservation, whatever I regard may tend to insure the preservation of the integrity of the nascent institutions of the Faith. I strongly feel the urge to elucidate certain facts, which would at once reveal to every fair-minded observer the unique character of that Divine Civilization the foundations of which the unerring hand of Bahá'u'lláh has laid, and the essential elements of which the Will and Testament of 'Abdu'l-Bahá has disclosed. I consider it my duty to warn every beginner in the Faith that the promised glories of the Sovereignty which the Bahá'í teachings foreshadow, can be revealed only in the fullness of time, that the implications of the Aqdas and the Will of 'Abdu'l-Bahá, as the twin repositories of the constituent elements of that Sovereignty, are too far-reaching for this generation to grasp and fully appreciate. I cannot refrain from appealing to them who stand identified with the Faith to disregard the prevailing notions and the fleeting fashions of the day, and to realize as never before that the exploded theories and the tottering institutions of present-day civilization must needs appear in sharp contrast with those God-given institutions which are destined to arise upon their ruin. I pray that they may realize with all their heart and soul the ineffable glory of their calling, the overwhelming responsibility of their mission, and the astounding immensity of their task.

For let every earnest upholder of the Cause of Bahá'u'lláh realize that the storms which this struggling Faith of God must needs encounter, as the process of the disintegration of society advances, shall be fiercer than any which it has already experienced. Let him be aware that so soon as the full measure of the stupendous claim of the Faith of Bahá'u'lláh comes to be recognized by those time-honored and powerful strongholds of orthodoxy, whose deliberate aim is to maintain their stranglehold over the thoughts and consciences of men, this infant Faith will have to contend with enemies more powerful and more insidious than the cruellest torture-mongers and the most fanatical clerics who have afflicted it in the past. What foes may not in the course of the convulsions that shall seize a dying civilization be brought into existence, who will reinforce the indignities which have already been heaped upon it!

The Onslaught of All Peoples and Kindreds

We have only to refer to the warnings uttered by 'Abdu'l-Bahá in order to realize the extent and character of the forces that are destined to contest with God's holy Faith. In the darkest moments of His life, under 'Abdu'l-Hamíd's régime, when He stood ready to be deported to the most inhospitable regions of Northern Africa, and at a time when the auspicious light of the Bahá'í Revelation had only begun to break upon the West, He, in His parting message to the cousin of the Báb, uttered these prophetic and ominous words: *"How great, how very great is the Cause! How very fierce the onslaught of all the peoples and kindreds of the earth. Ere long shall the clamor of the multitude throughout Africa, throughout America, the cry of the European and of the Turk, the groaning of India and China, be heard from far and near. One and all, they shall arise with all their power to resist His Cause. Then shall the knights of the Lord, assisted by His grace from on high, strengthened by faith, aided by the power of understanding, and reinforced by the legions of the Covenant, arise and make manifest the truth of the verse: 'Behold the confusion that hath befallen the tribes of the defeated!' "*

Stupendous as is the struggle which His words foreshadow, they also testify to the complete victory which the upholders of the Greatest Name are destined eventually to achieve. Peoples, nations, adherents of divers faiths, will jointly and successively arise to shatter its unity, to sap its force, and to degrade its holy name. They will assail not only the spirit which it inculcates, but the administration which is the channel, the instrument, the embodiment of that spirit. For as the authority with which Bahá'u'lláh has invested the future Bahá'í Commonwealth becomes more and more apparent, the fiercer shall be the challenge which from every quarter will be thrown at the verities it enshrines.

Difference Between Bahá'í Faith and Ecclesiastical Organizations

It behooves us, dear friends, to endeavor not only to familiarize ourselves with the essential features of this supreme Handiwork of Bahá'u'lláh, but also to grasp the fundamental difference existing between this world-embracing, divinely-appointed Order and the chief ecclesiastical organizations of the world, whether they pertain to the Church of Christ, or to the ordinances of the Muḥammadan Dispensation.

For those whose priceless privilege is to guard over, administer the affairs, and advance the interests of these Bahá'í institutions will have, sooner or later, to face this searching question: "Where and how does this Order established by Bahá'u'lláh, which to outward seeming is but a replica of the institutions established in Christianity and Islám, differ from them? Are not the twin institutions of the House of Justice and of the Guardianship, the institution of the Hands of the Cause of God, the institution of the national and local Assemblies, the institution of the Mashriqu'l-Adhkár, but different names for the institutions of the Papacy and the Caliphate, with all their attending ecclesiastical orders which the Christians and Moslems uphold and advocate? What can possibly be the agency that can safeguard these Bahá'í institutions, so strikingly resemblant, in some of their features, to those which have been reared by the Fathers of the Church and the Apostles of Muḥammad, from witnessing the deterioration in character, the breach of unity, and the extinction of influence, which have befallen all organized religious hierarchies? Why should they not eventually suffer the self-same fate that has overtaken the institutions which the successors of Christ and Muhammad have reared?"

Upon the answer given to these challenging questions will, in a great measure, depend the success of the efforts which believers in every land are now exerting for the establishment of God's kingdom upon the earth. Few will fail to recognize that the Spirit breathed by Bahá'u'lláh upon the world, and which is manifesting itself with varying degrees of intensity through the efforts consciously displayed by His avowed supporters and indirectly through certain humanitarian organizations, can never permeate and exercise an abiding influence upon mankind unless and until it incarnates itself in a visible Order, which would bear His name, wholly identify itself with His principles, and function in conformity with His laws. That Bahá'u'lláh in His Book of Aqdas, and later 'Abdu'l-Bahá in His Will—a document which confirms, supplements, and correlates the provisions of the Aqdas—have set forth in their entirety those essential elements for the constitution of the world Bahá'í Commonwealth, no one who has read them will deny. According to these divinely-ordained administrative principles, the Dispensation of Bahá'u'lláh—the Ark of human salvation—must needs be modeled. From them, all future blessings must flow, and upon them its inviolable authority must ultimately rest.

For Bahá'u'lláh, we should readily recognize, has not only imbued mankind with a new and regenerating Spirit. He has not merely enunciated certain universal principles, or propounded a particular philosophy, however potent, sound and universal these may be. In addition to these He, as well as 'Abdu'l-Bahá after Him, has, unlike the Dispensations of the past, clearly and specifically laid down a set of Laws, established definite institutions, and provided for the essentials of a Divine Economy. These are destined to be a pattern for future society, a supreme instrument for the establishment of the Most Great Peace, and the one agency for the unification of the world, and the proclamation of the reign of righteousness and justice upon the earth. Not only have They revealed all the directions required for the practical realization of those ideals which the Prophets of God have visualized, and which from time immemorial have inflamed the imagination of seers and poets in every age. They have also, in unequivocal and emphatic language, appointed those twin institutions of the House of Justice and of the Guardianship as their chosen Successors, destined to apply the principles, promulgate the laws, protect the institutions, adapt loyally and intelligently the Faith to the requirements of progressive society, and consummate the incorruptible inheritance which the Founders of the Faith have bequeathed to the world.

Should we look back upon the past, were we to search out the Gospel and the Qur'án, we will readily recognize that neither the Christian nor the Islamic Dispensations can offer a parallel either to the system of Divine Economy so thoroughly established by Bahá'u'lláh, or to the safeguards which He has provided for its preservation and advancement. Therein, I am profoundly convinced, lies the answer to those questions to which I have already referred.

None, I feel, will question the fact that the fundamental reason why the unity of the Church of Christ was irretrievably shattered, and its influence was in the course of time undermined, was that the Edifice which the Fathers of the Church reared after the passing of His First Apostle was an Edifice that rested in nowise upon the explicit directions of Christ Himself. The authority and features of their administration were wholly inferred, and indirectly derived, with more or less justification, from certain vague and fragmentary references which they found scattered amongst His utterances as recorded in the Gospel. Not one of the sacraments of the Church; not one of the rites and ceremonies which the Christian Fathers have elaborately devised and ostentatiously observed; not one of the elements of the severe discipline they rigorously imposed upon the primitive Christians; none of these reposed on the direct authority of Christ, or emanated from His specific utterances. Not one of these did Christ conceive, none did He specifically invest with sufficient authority to either interpret His Word, or to add to what He had not specifically enjoined.

For this reason, in later generations, voices were raised in protest against the self-appointed Authority which arrogated to itself privileges and powers which did not emanate from the clear text of the Gospel of Jesus Christ, and which constituted a grave departure from the spirit which that Gospel did inculcate. They argued with force and justification that the canons promulgated by the Councils of the Church were not divinely-appointed laws, but were merely human devices which did not even rest upon the actual utterances of Jesus. Their contention centered around the fact that the vague and inconclusive words, addressed by Christ to Peter, "Thou art Peter, and upon this rock I will build my Church," could never justify the extreme measures, the elaborate ceremonials, the fettering creeds and dogmas, with which His successors have gradually burdened and obscured His Faith. Had it been possible for the Church Fathers, whose unwarranted authority was thus fiercely assailed from every side, to refute the denunciations heaped upon them by quoting specific utterances of Christ regarding the future administration of His Church, or the nature of the authority of His Successors, they would surely have been capable of quenching the flame of controversy, and preserving the unity of Christendom. The Gospel, however, the only repository of the utterances of Christ, afforded no such shelter to these harassed leaders of the Church, who found themselves helpless in the face of the pitiless onslaught of their enemy, and who eventually had to submit to the forces of schism which invaded their ranks.

In the Muḥammadan Revelation, however, although His Faith as compared with that of Christ was, so far as the administration of His Dispensation is concerned, more complete and more specific in its provisions, yet in the matter of succession, it gave no written, no binding and conclusive instructions to those whose mission was to propagate His Cause. For the text of the Qur'án, the ordinances of which regarding prayer, fasting, marriage, divorce, inheritance, pilgrimage, and the like, have after the revolution of thirteen hundred years remained intact and operative, gives no definite guidance regarding the Law of Succession, the source of all the dissensions, the controversies, and schisms which have dismembered and discredited Islám.

Not so with the Revelation of Bahá'u'lláh. Unlike the Dispensation of Christ, unlike the Dispensation of Muḥammad, unlike all the Dispensations of the past, the apostles of Bahá'u'lláh in every land, wherever they labor and toil, have before them in clear, in unequivocal and emphatic language, all the laws, the regulations, the principles, the institutions, the guidance, they require for the prosecution and consummation of their task. Both in the administrative provisions of the Bahá'í Dispensation, and in the matter of succession, as embodied in the twin institutions of the House of Justice and of the

Guardianship, the followers of Bahá'u'lláh can summon to their aid such irrefutable evidences of Divine Guidance that none can resist, that none can belittle or ignore. Therein lies the distinguishing feature of the Bahá'í Revelation. Therein lies the strength of the unity of the Faith, of the validity of a Revelation that claims not to destroy or belittle previous Revelations, but to connect, unify, and fulfill them. This is the reason why Bahá'u'lláh and 'Abdu'l-Bahá have both revealed and even insisted upon certain details in connection with the Divine Economy which they have bequeathed to us, their followers. This is why such an emphasis has been placed in their Will and Testament upon the powers and prerogatives of the ministers of their Faith.

For nothing short of the explicit directions of their Book, and the surprisingly emphatic language with which they have clothed the provisions of their Will, could possibly safeguard the Faith for which they have both so gloriously labored all their lives. Nothing short of this could protect it from the heresies and calumnies with which denominations, peoples, and governments have endeavored, and will, with increasing vigor, endeavor to assail it in future.

We should also bear in mind that the distinguishing character of the Bahá'í Revelation does not solely consist in the completeness and unquestionable validity of the Dispensation which the teachings of Bahá'u'lláh and 'Abdu'l-Bahá have established. Its excellence lies also in the fact that those elements which in past Dispensations have, without the least authority from their Founders, been a source of corruption and of incalculable harm to the Faith of God, have been strictly excluded by the clear text of Bahá'u'lláh's writings. Those unwarranted practices, in connection with the sacrament of baptism, of communion, of confession of sins, of asceticism, of priestly domination, of elaborate ceremonials, of holy war and of polygamy, have one and all been rigidly suppressed by the Pen of Bahá'u'lláh; whilst the rigidity and rigor of certain observances, such as fasting, which are necessary to the devotional life of the individual, have been considerably abated.

A Living Organism

It should also be borne in mind that the machinery of the Cause has been so fashioned, that whatever is deemed necessary to incorporate into it in order to keep it in the forefront of all progressive movements, can, according to the provisions made by Bahá'u'lláh, be safely embodied therein. To this testify the words of Bahá'u'lláh, as recorded in the Eighth Leaf of the exalted Paradise: *"It is incumbent upon the Trustees of the House of Justice to take counsel together regarding those things which have not outwardly been revealed in the Book, and to enforce that which is agreeable to them. God will verily inspire them with whatsoever He willeth, and He, verily, is the Provider, the Omniscient."* Not only has the House of Justice been invested by Bahá'u'lláh with the authority to legislate whatsoever has not been explicitly and outwardly recorded in His holy Writ, upon it has also been conferred by the Will and Testament of 'Abdu'l-Bahá the right and power to abrogate, according to the changes and requirements of the time, whatever has been already enacted and enforced by a preceding House of Justice. In this connection, He revealed the following in His Will: *"And inasmuch as the House of Justice hath power to enact laws that are not expressly recorded in the Book and bear upon daily transactions, so also it hath power to repeal the same. Thus for example, the House of Justice enacteth today a certain law and enforceth it, and a hundred years hence, circumstances having profoundly changed and the conditions having altered, another House of Justice will then have power, according to the exigencies of the time, to alter that law. This it can do because that law formeth no part of the divine explicit text. The House of Justice is both the initiator and the abrogator of its own laws."* Such is the immutability of His revealed Word. Such is the elasticity which characterizes the functions of His appointed ministers. The first preserves the identity of His Faith, and guards the integrity of His law. The second enables it, even as a living organism, to expand and adapt itself to the needs and requirements of an ever-changing society.

Dear friends! Feeble though our Faith may now appear in the eyes of men, who either denounce it as an offshoot of Islám, or contemptuously ignore it as one more of those obscure sects that abound in the West, this priceless gem of Divine Revelation, now still in its embryonic state, shall evolve within the shell of His law, and shall forge ahead, undivided and unimpaired, till it embraces the whole of mankind. Only those who have already recognized the supreme station of Bahá'u'lláh, only those whose hearts have been touched by His love, and have become familiar with the potency of His spirit, can adequately appreciate the value of this Divine Economy—His inestimable gift to mankind.

Leaders of religion, exponents of political theories, governors of human institutions, who at present are witnessing with perplexity and dismay the bankruptcy of their ideas, and the disintegration of their handiwork, would do well to turn their gaze to the Revelation of Bahá'u'lláh, and to meditate upon the World Order which, lying enshrined in His teachings, is slowly and imperceptibly rising amid the welter and chaos of present-day civilization. They need have no doubt or anxiety regarding the nature, the origin or validity of the institutions which the adherents of the Faith are building up throughout the world. For these lie embedded in the teachings themselves, unadulterated and unobscured by unwarrantable inferences, or unauthorized interpretations of His Word.

How pressing and sacred the responsibility that now weighs upon those who are already acquainted with these teachings! How glorious the task of those who are called upon to vindicate their truth, and demonstrate their practicability to an unbelieving world! Nothing short of an immovable conviction in their divine origin, and their uniqueness in the annals of religion; nothing short of an unwavering purpose to execute and apply them to the administrative machinery of the Cause, can be sufficient to establish their reality, and insure their success. How vast is the Revelation of Bahá'u'lláh! How great the magnitude of His blessings showered upon humanity in this day! And yet, how poor, how inadequate our conception of their significance and glory! This generation stands too close to so colossal a Revelation to appreciate, in their full measure, the infinite possibilities of His Faith, the unprecedented character of His Cause, and the mysterious dispensations of His Providence.

In the Íqán, Bahá'u'lláh, wishing to emphasize the transcendent character of this new Day of God, reinforces the strength of His argument by His reference to the text of a correct and authorized tradition, which reveals the following: *"Knowledge is twenty and seven letters. All that the Prophets have revealed are two letters thereof. No man thus far hath known more than these two letters.*

But when the Qá'im shall arise, He will cause the remaining twenty and five letters to be made manifest." And then immediately follow these confirming and illuminating words of Bahá'u'lláh: *"Consider: He hath declared knowledge to consist of twenty and seven letters, and regarded all the prophets, from Adam even unto Muḥammad, the 'seal,' as expounders of only two letters thereof. He also saith that the Qá'im will reveal all the remaining twenty and five letters. Behold from this utterance how great and lofty is His station! His rank excelleth that of all the prophets, and His revelation transcendeth the comprehension and understanding of all their chosen ones. A revelation, of which the prophets of God, His saints and chosen ones have either not been informed or which, in pursuance of God's inscrutable decree, they have not disclosed—such a revelation, these vile and villainous people have sought to measure with their own deficient minds, their own deficient learning and understanding."*

In another passage of the same Book, Bahá'u'lláh, referring to the transformation effected by every Revelation in the ways, thoughts and manners of the people, reveals these words: *"Is not the object of every Revelation to effect a transformation in the whole character of mankind, a transformation that shall manifest itself, both outwardly and inwardly, that shall affect both its inner life and external conditions? For if the character of mankind be not changed, the futility of God's universal Manifestation would be apparent."*

Did not Christ Himself, addressing His disciples, utter these words: *"I have yet many things to say unto you, but ye cannot bear them now. Howbeit when He, the Spirit of Truth, is come, He will guide you into all truth"?*

From the text of this recognized tradition, as well as from the words of Christ, as attested by the Gospel, every unprejudiced observer will readily apprehend the magnitude of the Faith which Bahá'u'lláh has revealed, and recognize the staggering weight of the claim He has advanced. No wonder if 'Abdu'l-Bahá has portrayed in such lurid colors the fierceness of the agitation that shall center in the days to come round the nascent institutions of the Faith. We can now but faintly discern the beginnings of that turmoil which the rise and ascendancy of the Cause of God is destined to cast in the world.

The Greatest Drama of the World's Spiritual History

Whether in the ferocious and insidious campaign of repression and cruelty which the rulers of Russia have launched against the upholders of the Faith under their rule; whether in the unyielding animosity with which the Shiites of Islám are trampling upon the sacred rights of the adherents of the Cause in connection with Bahá'u'lláh's house in Baghdád; whether in the impotent rage which has impelled the ecclesiastical leaders of the Sunnite sect of Islám to expel our Egyptian brethren from their midst—in all of these we can perceive the manifestations of the relentless hate which peoples, religions, and governments entertain for so pure, so innocent, so glorious a Faith.

Ours is the duty to ponder these things in our heart, to strive to widen our vision, and to deepen our comprehension of this Cause, and to arise, resolutely and unreservedly, to play our part, however small, in this greatest drama of the world's spiritual history.

Your brother and co-worker,

SHOGHI.

Haifa, Palestine,
March 21, 1930.

THE GOAL OF A NEW WORLD ORDER

THE GOAL OF A NEW WORLD ORDER

Fellow-believers in the Faith of Bahá'u'lláh:

The inexorable march of recent events has carried humanity so near to the goal foreshadowed by Bahá'u'lláh that no responsible follower of His Faith, viewing on all sides the distressing evidences of the world's travail, can remain unmoved at the thought of its approaching deliverance.

It would not seem inappropriate, at a time when we are commemorating the world over the termination of the first decade since 'Abdu'l-Bahá's sudden removal from our midst, to ponder, in the light of the teachings bequeathed by Him to the world, such events as have tended to hasten the gradual emergence of the World Order anticipated by Bahá'u'lláh.

Ten years ago, this very day, there flashed upon the world the news of the passing of Him Who alone, through the ennobling influence of His love, strength and wisdom, could have proved its stay and solace in the many afflictions it was destined to suffer.

How well we, the little band of His avowed supporters who lay claim to have recognized the Light that shone within Him, can still remember His repeated allusions, in the evening of His earthly life, to the tribulation and turmoil with which an unregenerate humanity was to be increasingly afflicted. How poignantly some of us can recall His pregnant remarks, in the presence of the pilgrims and visitors who thronged His doors on the morrow of the jubilant celebrations that greeted the termination of the World War—a war, which by the horrors it evoked, the losses it entailed and the complications it engendered, was destined to exert so far-reaching an influence on the fortunes of mankind. How serenely, yet how powerfully, He stressed the cruel deception which a Pact, hailed by peoples and nations as the embodiment of triumphant justice and the unfailing instrument of an abiding peace, held in store for an unrepented humanity. Peace, Peace, how often we heard Him remark, the

lips of potentates and peoples unceasingly proclaim, whereas the
fire of unquenched hatreds still smoulders in their hearts. How often
we heard Him raise His voice, whilst the tumult of triumphant enthusiasm was still at its height and long before the faintest misgivings could have been felt or expressed, confidently declaring that the
Document, extolled as the Charter of a liberated humanity, con-
tained within itself seeds of such bitter deception as would further
enslave the world. How abundant are now the evidences that attest
the perspicacity of His unerring judgment!

Ten years of unceasing turmoil, so laden with anguish, so
fraught with incalculable consequences to the future of civilization,
have brought the world to the verge of a calamity too awful to
contemplate. Sad indeed is the contrast between the manifestations
of confident enthusiasm in which the Plenipotentiaries at Versailles
so freely indulged and the cry of unconcealed distress which victors
and vanquished alike are now raising in the hour of bitter delusion.

A War-Weary World

Neither the force which the framers and guarantors of the
Peace Treaties have mustered, nor the lofty ideals which originally
animated the author of the Covenant of the League of Nations,
have proved a sufficient bulwark against the forces of internal dis-
ruption with which a structure so laboriously contrived had been
consistently assailed. Neither the provisions of the so-called Settlement which the victorious Powers have sought to impose, nor the
machinery of an institution which America's illustrious and far-
seeing President had conceived, have proved, either in conception or
practice, adequate instruments to ensure the integrity of the Order
they had striven to establish. *"The ills from which the world now
suffers,"* wrote 'Abdu'l-Bahá in January, 1920, *"will multiply; the
gloom which envelops it will deepen. The Balkans will remain dis-
contented. Its restlessness will increase. The vanquished Powers will
continue to agitate. They will resort to every measure that may
rekindle the flame of war. Movements, newly-born and world-wide
in their range, will exert their utmost effort for the advancement of
their designs. The Movement of the Left will acquire great importance. Its influence will spread."*

Economic distress, since those words were written, together with political confusion, financial upheavals, religious restlessness and racial animosities, seem to have conspired to add immeasurably to the burdens under which an impoverished, a war-weary world is groaning. Such has been the cumulative effect of these successive crises, following one another with such bewildering rapidity, that the very foundations of society are trembling. The world, to whichever continent we turn our gaze, to however remote a region our survey may extend, is everywhere assailed by forces it can neither explain nor control.

Europe, hitherto regarded as the cradle of a highly-vaunted civilization, as the torch-bearer of liberty and the mainspring of the forces of world industry and commerce, stands bewildered and paralyzed at the sight of so tremendous an upheaval. Long-cherished ideals in the political no less than in the economic sphere of human activity are being severely tested under the pressure of reactionary forces on one hand and of an insidious and persistent radicalism on the other. From the heart of Asia distant rumblings, ominous and insistent, portend the steady onslaught of a creed which, by its negation of God, His Laws and Principles, threatens to disrupt the foundations of human society. The clamor of a nascent nationalism, coupled with a recrudescence of skepticism and unbelief, come as added misfortunes to a continent hitherto regarded as the symbol of age-long stability and undisturbed resignation. From darkest Africa the first stirrings of a conscious and determined revolt against the aims and methods of political and economic imperialism can be increasingly discerned, adding their share to the growing vicissitudes of a troubled age. Not even America, which until very recently prided itself on its traditional policy of aloofness and the self-contained character of its economy, the invulnerability of its institutions and the evidences of its growing prosperity and prestige, has been able to resist the impelling forces that have swept her into the vortex of an economic hurricane that now threatens to impair the basis of her own industrial and economic life. Even far-away Australia, which, owing to its remoteness from the storm-centers of Europe, would have been expected to be immune from the trials and torments of an ailing continent, has been caught in this whirlpool of passion and strife, impotent to extricate herself from their ensnaring influence.

The Signs of Impending Chaos

Never indeed have there been such widespread and basic upheavals, whether in the social, economic or political spheres of human
activity as those now going on in different parts of the world. Never
have there been so many and varied sources of danger as those that
now threaten the structure of society. The following words of
Bahá'u'lláh are indeed significant as we pause to reflect upon the
present state of a strangely disordered world: *"How long will
humanity persist in its waywardness? How long will injustice continue? How long is chaos and confusion to reign amongst men?
How long will discord agitate the face of society? The winds of
despair are, alas, blowing from every direction, and the strife that
divides and afflicts the human race is daily increasing. The signs of
impending convulsions and chaos can now be discerned, inasmuch as
the prevailing order appears to be lamentably defective."*

The disquieting influence of over thirty million souls living under
minority conditions throughout the continent of Europe; the vast
and ever-swelling army of the unemployed with its crushing burden
and demoralizing influence on governments and peoples; the wicked,
unbridled race of armaments swallowing an ever-increasing share of
the substance of already impoverished nations; the utter demoral-
ization from which the international financial markets are now
increasingly suffering; the onslaught of secularism invading what
has hitherto been regarded as the impregnable strongholds of Christian and Muslim orthodoxy—these stand out as the gravest symp-
toms that bode ill for the future stability of the structure of modern
civilization. Little wonder if one of Europe's preëminent thinkers,
honored for his wisdom and restraint, should have been forced to
make so bold an assertion: "The world is passing through the
gravest crisis in the history of civilization." "We stand," writes
another, "before either a world catastrophe, or perhaps before the
dawn of a greater era of truth and wisdom." "It is in such times,"
he adds, "that religions have perished and are born."

Might we not already discern, as we scan the political horizon,
the alignment of those forces that are dividing afresh the continent
of Europe into camps of potential combatants, determined upon a
contest that may mark, unlike the last war, the end of an epoch, a

vast epoch, in the history of human evolution? Are we, the privileged custodians of a priceless Faith, called upon to witness a cataclysmical change, politically as fundamental and spiritually as beneficent as that which precipitated the fall of the Roman Empire in the West? Might it not happen—every vigilant adherent of the Faith of Bahá'u'lláh might well pause to reflect—that out of this world eruption there may stream forces of such spiritual energy as shall recall, nay eclipse, the splendor of those signs and wonders that accompanied the establishment of the Faith of Jesus Christ? Might there not emerge out of the agony of a shaken world a religious revival of such scope and power as to even transcend the potency of those world-directing forces with which the Religions of the Past have, at fixed intervals and according to an inscrutable Wisdom, revived the fortunes of declining ages and peoples? Might not the bankruptcy of this present, this highly-vaunted materialistic civilization, in itself clear away the choking weeds that now hinder the unfoldment and future efflorescence of God's struggling Faith?

Let Bahá'u'lláh Himself shed the illumination of His words upon our path as we steer our course amid the pitfalls and miseries of this troubled age. More than fifty years ago, in a world far removed from the ills and trials that now torment it, there flowed from His Pen these prophetic words: *"The world is in travail and its agitation waxeth day by day. Its face is turned towards waywardness and unbelief. Such shall be its plight that to disclose it now would not be meet and seemly. Its perversity will long continue. And when the appointed hour is come, there shall suddenly appear that which shall cause the limbs of mankind to quake. Then and only then will the Divine Standard be unfurled and the Nightingale of Paradise warble its melody."*

The Impotence of Statesmanship

Dearly-beloved friends! Humanity, whether viewed in the light of man's individual conduct or in the existing relationships between organized communities and nations, has, alas, strayed too far and suffered too great a decline to be redeemed through the unaided efforts of the best among its recognized rulers and statesmen—however disinterested their motives, however concerted their action, however unsparing in their zeal and devotion to its cause. No scheme which the calculations of the highest statesmanship may yet devise; no doctrine which the most distinguished exponents of economic theory may hope to advance; no principle which the most ardent of moralists may strive to inculcate, can provide, in the last resort, adequate foundations upon which the future of a distracted world can be built. No appeal for mutual tolerance which the worldly-wise might raise, however compelling and insistent, can calm its passions or help restore its vigor. Nor would any general scheme of mere organized international coöperation, in whatever sphere of human activity, however ingenious in conception, or extensive in scope, succeed in removing the root cause of the evil that has so rudely upset the equilibrium of present-day society. Not even, I venture to assert, would the very act of devising the machinery required for the political and economic unification of the world—a principle that has been increasingly advocated in recent times—provide in itself the antidote against the poison that is steadily undermining the vigor of organized peoples and nations. What else, might we not confidently affirm, but the unreserved acceptance of the Divine Program enunciated, with such simplicity and force as far back as sixty years ago, by Bahá'u'lláh, embodying in its essentials God's divinely appointed scheme for the unification of mankind in this age, coupled with an indomitable conviction in the unfailing efficacy of each and all of its provisions, is eventually capable of withstanding the forces of internal disintegration which, if unchecked, must needs continue to eat into the vitals of a despairing society. It is towards this goal—the goal of a new World Order, Divine in origin, all-embracing in scope, equitable in principle, challenging in its features—that a harassed humanity must strive.

To claim to have grasped all the implications of Bahá'u'lláh's prodigious scheme for world-wide human solidarity, or to have fathomed its import, would be presumptuous on the part of even the declared supporters of His Faith. To attempt to visualize it in all its possibilities, to estimate its future benefits, to picture its glory, would be premature at even so advanced a stage in the evolution of mankind.

The Guiding Principles of World Order

All we can reasonably venture to attempt is to strive to obtain a glimpse of the first streaks of the promised Dawn that must, in the fullness of time, chase away the gloom that has encircled humanity. All we can do is to point out, in their broadest outlines, what appears to us to be the guiding principles underlying the World Order of Bahá'u'lláh, as amplified and enunciated by 'Abdu'l-Bahá, the Center of His Covenant with all mankind and the appointed Interpreter and Expounder of His Word.

That the unrest and suffering afflicting the mass of mankind are in no small measure the direct consequences of the World War and are attributable to the unwisdom and shortsightedness of the framers of the Peace Treaties only a biased mind can refuse to admit. That the financial obligations contracted in the course of the war, as well as the imposition of a staggering burden of reparations upon the vanquished, have, to a very great extent, been responsible for the maldistribution and consequent shortage of the world's monetary gold supply, which in turn has, to a very great measure, accentuated the phenomenal fall in prices and thereby relentlessly increased the burdens of impoverished countries, no impartial mind would question. That inter-governmental debts have imposed a severe strain on the masses of the people in Europe, have upset the equilibrium of national budgets, have crippled national industries, and led to an increase in the number of the unemployed, is no less apparent to an unprejudiced observer. That the spirit of vindictiveness, of suspicion, of fear and rivalry, engendered by the war, and which the provisions of the Peace Treaties have served to perpetuate and foster, has led to an enormous increase of national competitive armaments, involving during the last year the aggregate expenditure of no less than a thousand million pounds, which in turn has accentuated the effects of the world-wide depression, is a truth that even the most superficial observer will readily admit. That a narrow and brutal nationalism, which the post-war theory of self-determination has served to reinforce, has been chiefly responsible for the policy of high and prohibitive tariffs, so injurious to the healthy flow of international trade and to the mechanism of international finance, is a fact which few would venture to dispute.

It would be idle, however, to contend that the war, with all the losses it involved, the passions it aroused and the grievances it left behind, has solely been responsible for the unprecedented confusion into which almost every section of the civilized world is plunged at present. Is it not a fact—and this is the central idea I desire to emphasize—that the fundamental cause of this world unrest is attributable, not so much to the consequences of what must sooner or later come to be regarded as a transitory dislocation in the affairs of a continually changing world, but rather to the failure of those into whose hands the immediate destinies of peoples and nations have been committed, to adjust their system of economic and political institutions to the imperative needs of a rapidly evolving age? Are not these intermittent crises that convulse present-day society due primarily to the lamentable inability of the world's recognized leaders to read aright the signs of the times, to rid themselves once for all of their preconceived ideas and fettering creeds, and to reshape the machinery of their respective governments according to those standards that are implicit in Bahá'u'lláh's supreme declaration of the Oneness of Mankind—the chief and distinguishing feature of the Faith He proclaimed? For the principle of the Oneness of Mankind, the cornerstone of Bahá'u'lláh's world-embracing dominion, implies nothing more nor less than the enforcement of His scheme for the unification of the world—the scheme to which we have already referred. *"In every Dispensation,"* writes 'Abdu'l-Bahá, *"the light of Divine Guidance has been focussed upon one central theme. . . . In this wondrous Revelation, this glorious century, the foundation of the Faith of God and the distinguishing feature of His Law is the consciousness of the Oneness of Mankind."*

How pathetic indeed are the efforts of those leaders of human institutions who, in utter disregard of the spirit of the age, are striving to adjust national processes, suited to the ancient days of self-contained nations, to an age which must either achieve the unity of the world, as adumbrated by Bahá'u'lláh, or perish. At so critical an hour in the history of civilization it behooves the leaders of all the nations of the world, great and small, whether in the East or in the West, whether victors or vanquished, to give heed to the clarion call of Bahá'u'lláh and, thoroughly imbued with a sense of world solidarity, the *sine quâ non* of loyalty to His Cause, arise manfully to carry out in its entirety the one remedial scheme He, the Divine Physician, has prescribed for an ailing humanity. Let them discard, once for all, every preconceived idea, every national prejudice, and give heed to the sublime counsel of 'Abdu'l-Bahá, the authorized Expounder of His teachings. You can best serve your country, was 'Abdu'l-Bahá's rejoinder to a high official in the service of the federal government of the United States of America, who had questioned Him as to the best manner in which he could promote the interests of his government and people, if you strive, in your capacity as a citizen of the world, to assist in the eventual application of the principle of federalism underlying the government of your own country to the relationships now existing between the peoples and nations of the world.

In "The Secret of Divine Civilization" ("The Mysterious Forces of Civilization"), 'Abdu'l-Bahá's outstanding contribution to the future reorganization of the world, we read the following:

"True civilization will unfurl its banner in the midmost heart of the world whenever a certain number of its distinguished and high-minded sovereigns—the shining exemplars of devotion and determination—shall, for the good and happiness of all mankind, arise, with firm resolve and clear vision, to establish the Cause of Universal Peace. They must make the Cause of Peace the object of general consultation, and seek by every means in their power to establish a Union of the nations of the world. They must conclude a binding treaty and establish a covenant, the provisions of which shall be sound, inviolable and definite. They must proclaim it to all the world and obtain for it the sanction of all the human race. This supreme and noble undertaking—the real source of the peace and well-being of all the world—should be regarded as sacred by all that dwell on earth. All the forces of humanity must be mobilized to ensure the stability and permanence of this Most Great Covenant. In this all-embracing Pact the limits and frontiers of each and every nation should be clearly fixed, the principles underlying the relations of governments towards one another definitely laid down, and all international agreements and obligations ascertained. In like manner, the size of the armaments of every government should be

strictly limited, for if the preparations for war and the military forces of any nation should be allowed to increase, they will arouse the suspicion of others. The fundamental principle underlying this solemn Pact should be so fixed that if any government later violate any one of its provisions, all the governments on earth should arise to reduce it to utter submission, nay the human race as a whole should resolve, with every power at its disposal, to destroy that government. Should this greatest of all remedies be applied to the sick body of the world, it will assuredly recover from its ills and will remain eternally safe and secure."

"A few," He further adds, *"unaware of the power latent in human endeavor, consider this matter as highly impracticable, nay even beyond the scope of man's utmost efforts. Such is not the case, however. On the contrary, thanks to the unfailing grace of God, the loving-kindness of His favored ones, the unrivaled endeavors of wise and capable souls, and the thoughts and ideas of the peerless leaders of this age, nothing whatsoever can be regarded as unattainable. Endeavor, ceaseless endeavor, is required. Nothing short of an indomitable determination can possibly achieve it. Many a cause which past ages have regarded as purely visionary, yet in this day has become most easy and practicable. Why should this most great and lofty Cause—the day-star of the firmament of true civilization and the cause of the glory, the advancement, the well-being and the success of all humanity—be regarded as impossible of achievement? Surely the day will come when its beauteous light shall shed illumination upon the assemblage of man."*

Seven Lights of Unity

In one of His Tablets 'Abdu'l-Bahá, elucidating further His noble theme, reveals the following:

"In cycles gone by, though harmony was established, yet, owing to the absence of means, the unity of all mankind could not have been achieved. Continents remained widely divided, nay even among the peoples of one and the same continent association and interchange of thought were well nigh impossible. Consequently intercourse, understanding and unity amongst all the peoples and kindreds of the earth were unattainable. In this day, however, means of communication have multiplied, and the five continents of the earth have

*virtually merged into one. . . . In like manner all the members of
the human family, whether peoples or governments, cities or villages,
have become increasingly interdependent. For none is self-sufficiency
any longer possible, inasmuch as political ties unite all peoples and
nations, and the bonds of trade and industry, of agriculture and
education, are being strengthened every day. Hence the unity of all
mankind can in this day be achieved. Verily this is none other but
one of the wonders of this wondrous age, this glorious century. Of
this past ages have been deprived, for this century—the century of
light—has been endowed with unique and unprecedented glory,
power and illumination. Hence the miraculous unfolding of a fresh
marvel every day. Eventually it will be seen how bright its candles
will burn in the assemblage of man.*

*"Behold how its light is now dawning upon the world's darkened
horizon. The first candle is unity in the political realm, the early
glimmerings of which can now be discerned. The second candle is
unity of thought in world undertakings, the consummation of which
will ere long be witnessed. The third candle is unity in freedom
which will surely come to pass. The fourth candle is unity in religion
which is the corner-stone of the foundation itself, and which, by the
power of God, will be revealed in all its splendor. The fifth candle
is the unity of nations—a unity which in this century will be securely
established, causing all the peoples of the world to regard themselves
as citizens of one common fatherland. The sixth candle is unity of
races, making of all that dwell on earth peoples and kindreds of one
race. The seventh candle is unity of language, i.e., the choice of a
universal tongue in which all peoples will be instructed and con-
verse. Each and every one of these will inevitably come to pass,
inasmuch as the power of the Kingdom of God will aid and assist in
their realization."*

A World Super-State

Over sixty years ago, in His Tablet to Queen Victoria, Bahá-
'u'lláh, addressing "the concourse of the rulers of the earth," revealed the following:

*"Take ye counsel together, and let your concern be only for that
which profiteth mankind and bettereth the condition thereof. . . .
Regard the world as the human body which, though created whole*

and perfect, has been afflicted, through divers causes, with grave ills and maladies. Not for one day did it rest, nay its sicknesses waxed more severe, as it fell under the treatment of unskilled physicians who have spurred on the steed of their worldly desires and have erred grievously. And if at one time, through the care of an able physician, a member of that body was healed, the rest remained afflicted as before. Thus informeth you the All-Knowing, the All-Wise. . . . That which the Lord hath ordained as the sovereign remedy and mightiest instrument for the healing of all the world is the union of all its peoples in one universal Cause, one common Faith. This can in no wise be achieved except through the power of a skilled, an all-powerful and inspired Physician. This verily is the truth, and all else naught but error."

In a further passage Bahá'u'lláh adds these words:

"We see you adding every year unto your expenditures and laying the burden thereof on the people whom ye rule; this verily is naught but grievous injustice. Fear the sighs and tears of this Wronged One, and burden not your peoples beyond that which they can endure. . . . Be reconciled among yourselves, that ye may need armaments no more save in a measure to safeguard your territories and dominions. Be united, O concourse of the sovereigns of the world, for thereby will the tempest of discord be stilled amongst you and your peoples find rest. Should any one among you take up arms against another, rise ye all against him, for this is naught but manifest justice."

What else could these weighty words signify if they did not point to the inevitable curtailment of unfettered national sovereignty as an indispensable preliminary to the formation of the future Commonwealth of all the nations of the world? Some form of a world super-state must needs be evolved, in whose favor all the nations of the world will have willingly ceded every claim to make war, certain rights to impose taxation and all rights to maintain armaments, except for purposes of maintaining internal order within their respective dominions. Such a state will have to include within its orbit an international executive adequate to enforce supreme and unchallengeable authority on every recalcitrant member of the com-wealth; a world parliament whose members shall be elected by the people in their respective countries and whose election shall be confirmed by their respective governments; and a supreme tribunal whose judgment will have a binding effect even in such cases where the parties concerned did not voluntarily agree to submit their case to its consideration. A world community in which all economic barriers will have been permanently demolished and the interdependence of Capital and Labor definitely recognized; in which the clamor of religious fanaticism and strife will have been forever stilled; in which the flame of racial animosity will have been finally extinguished; in which a single code of international law—the product of the considered judgment of the world's federated representatives—shall have as its sanction the instant and coercive intervention of the combined forces of the federated units; and finally a world community in which the fury of a capricious and militant nationalism will have been transmuted into an abiding consciousness of world citizenship—such indeed, appears, in its broadest outline, the Order anticipated by Bahá'u'lláh, an Order that shall come to be regarded as the fairest fruit of a slowly maturing age.

"*The Tabernacle of Unity,*" Bahá'u'lláh proclaims in His message to all mankind, "*has been raised; regard ye not one another as strangers. . . . Of one tree are all ye the fruit and of one bough the leaves. . . . The world is but one country and mankind its citizens. . . . Let not a man glory in that he loves his country; let him rather glory in this, that he loves his kind.*"

Unity in Diversity

Let there be no misgivings as to the animating purpose of the world-wide Law of Bahá'u'lláh. Far from aiming at the subversion of the existing foundations of society, it seeks to broaden its basis, to remold its institutions in a manner consonant with the needs of an ever-changing world. It can conflict with no legitimate allegiances, nor can it undermine essential loyalties. Its purpose is neither to stifle the flame of a sane and intelligent patriotism in men's hearts, nor to abolish the system of national autonomy so essential if the evils of excessive centralization are to be avoided. It does not ignore, nor does it attempt to suppress, the diversity of ethnical origins, of climate, of history, of language and tradition, of thought and habit, that differentiate the peoples and nations of the world. It calls for a wider loyalty, for a larger aspiration than any that has animated

the human race. It insists upon the subordination of national im-
pulses and interests to the imperative claims of a unified world. It
repudiates excessive centralization on one hand, and disclaims all
attempts at uniformity on the other. Its watchword is unity in
diversity such as 'Abdu'l-Bahá Himself has explained:

*"Consider the flowers of a garden. Though differing in kind,
color, form and shape, yet, inasmuch as they are refreshed by the
waters of one spring, revived by the breath of one wind, invigorated
by the rays of one sun, this diversity increaseth their charm and
addeth unto their beauty. How unpleasing to the eye if all the flowers
and plants, the leaves and blossoms, the fruit, the branches and the
trees of that garden were all of the same shape and color! Diversity
of hues, form and shape enricheth and adorneth the garden, and
heighteneth the effect thereof. In like manner, when divers shades of
thought, temperament and character, are brought together under the
power and influence of one central agency, the beauty and glory of
human perfection will be revealed and made manifest. Naught but
the celestial potency of the Word of God, which ruleth and transcendeth the realities of all things, is capable of harmonizing the
divergent thoughts, sentiments, ideas and convictions of the children
of men."*

The call of Bahá'u'lláh is primarily directed against all forms of
provincialism, all insularities and prejudices. If long-cherished ideals
and time-honored institutions, if certain social assumptions and religious formulae have ceased to promote the welfare of the generality of mankind, if they no longer minister to the needs of a continually evolving humanity, let them be swept away and relegated to the
limbo of obsolescent and forgotten doctrines. Why should these, in
a world subject to the immutable law of change and decay, be exempt
from the deterioration that must needs overtake every human institution? For legal standards, political and economic theories are
solely designed to safeguard the interests of humanity as a whole,
and not humanity to be crucified for the preservation of the integrity
of any particular law or doctrine.

The Principle of Oneness

Let there be no mistake. The principle of the Oneness of Mankind—the pivot round which all the teachings of Bahá'u'lláh revolve

—is no mere outburst of ignorant emotionalism or an expression of vague and pious hope. Its appeal is not to be merely identified with a reawakening of the spirit of brotherhood and good-will among men, nor does it aim solely at the fostering of harmonious coöperation among individual peoples and nations. Its implications are deeper, its claims greater than any which the Prophets of old were allowed to advance. Its message is applicable not only to the individual, but concerns itself primarily with the nature of those essential relationships that must bind all the states and nations as members of one human family. It does not constitute merely the enunciation of an ideal, but stands inseparably associated with an institution adequate to embody its truth, demonstrate its validity, and perpetuate its influence. It implies an organic change in the structure of present-day society, a change such as the world has not yet experienced. It constitutes a challenge, at once bold and universal, to outworn shibboleths of national creeds—creeds that have had their day and which must, in the ordinary course of events as shaped and controlled by Providence, give way to a new gospel, fundamentally different from, and infinitely superior to, what the world has already conceived. It calls for no less than the reconstruction and the demilitarization of the whole civilized world—a world organically unified in all the essential aspects of its life, its political machinery, its spiritual aspiration, its trade and finance, its script and language, and yet infinite in the diversity of the national characteristics of its federated units.

It represents the consummation of human evolution—an evolution that has had its earliest beginnings in the birth of family life, its subsequent development in the achievement of tribal solidarity, leading in turn to the constitution of the city-state, and expanding later into the institution of independent and sovereign nations.

The principle of the Oneness of Mankind, as proclaimed by Bahá'u'lláh, carries with it no more and no less than a solemn assertion that attainment to this final stage in this stupendous evolution is not only necessary but inevitable, that its realization is fast approaching, and that nothing short of a power that is born of God can succeed in establishing it.

So marvellous a conception finds its earliest manifestations in the efforts consciously exerted and the modest beginnings already achieved by the declared adherents of the Faith of Bahá'u'lláh who, conscious of the sublimity of their calling and initiated into the ennobling principles of His Administration, are forging ahead to establish His Kingdom on this earth. It has its indirect manifestations in the gradual diffusion of the spirit of world solidarity which is spontaneously arising out of the welter of a disorganized society.

It would be stimulating to follow the history of the growth and development of this lofty conception which must increasingly engage the attention of the responsible custodians of the destinies of peoples and nations. To the states and principalities just emerging from the welter of the great Napoleonic upheaval, whose chief preoccupation was either to recover their rights to an independent existence or to achieve their national unity, the conception of world solidarity seemed not only remote but inconceivable. It was not until the forces of nationalism had succeeded in overthrowing the foundations of the Holy Alliance that had sought to curb their rising power, that the possibility of a world order, transcending in its range the political institutions these nations had established, came to be seriously entertained. It was not until after the World War that these exponents of arrogant nationalism came to regard such an order as the object of a pernicious doctrine tending to sap that essential loyalty upon which the continued existence of their national life depended. With a vigor that recalled the energy with which the members of the Holy Alliance sought to stifle the spirit of a rising nationalism among the peoples liberated from the Napoleonic yoke, these champions of an unfettered national sovereignty, in their turn, have labored and are still laboring to discredit principles upon which their own salvation must ultimately depend.

The fierce opposition which greeted the abortive scheme of the Geneva Protocol; the ridicule poured upon the proposal for a United States of Europe which was subsequently advanced, and the failure of the general scheme for the economic union of Europe, may appear as setbacks to the efforts which a handful of foresighted people are earnestly exerting to advance this noble ideal. And yet, are we not justified in deriving fresh encouragement when we observe that the very consideration of such proposals is in itself an evidence of their steady growth in the minds and hearts of men? In the organized attempts that are being made to discredit so exalted a conception are we not witnessing the repetition, on a larger scale, of those stirring struggles and fierce controversies that preceded the birth, and assisted in the reconstruction, of the unified nations of the West?

The Federation of Mankind

To take but one instance. How confident were the assertions made in the days preceding the unification of the states of the North American continent regarding the insuperable barriers that stood in the way of their ultimate federation! Was it not widely and emphatically declared that the conflicting interests, the mutual distrust, the differences of government and habit that divided the states were such as no force, whether spiritual or temporal, could ever hope to harmonize or control? And yet how different were the conditions prevailing a hundred and fifty years ago from those that characterize present-day society! It would indeed be no exaggeration to say that the absence of those facilities which modern scientific progress has placed at the service of humanity in our time made of the problem of welding the American states into a single federation, similar though they were in certain traditions, a task infinitely more complex than that which confronts a divided humanity in its efforts to achieve the unification of all mankind.

Who knows that for so exalted a conception to take shape a suffering more intense than any it has yet experienced will have to be inflicted upon humanity? Could anything less than the fire of a civil war with all its violence and vicissitudes—a war that nearly rent the great American Republic—have welded the states, not only into a Union of independent units, but into a Nation, in spite of all the ethnic differences that characterized its component parts? That so fundamental a revolution, involving such far-reaching changes in the structure of society, can be achieved through the ordinary processes of diplomacy and education seems highly improbable. We have but to turn our gaze to humanity's blood-stained history to realize that nothing short of intense mental as well as physical agony has been able to precipitate those epoch-making changes that constitute the greatest landmarks in the history of human civilization.

The Fire of Ordeal

Great and far-reaching as have been those changes in the past, they cannot appear, when viewed in their proper perspective, except as subsidiary adjustments preluding that transformation of unparalleled majesty and scope which humanity is in this age bound to undergo. That the forces of a world catastrophe can alone precipitate such a new phase of human thought is, alas, becoming increasingly apparent. That nothing short of the fire of a severe ordeal, unparalleled in its intensity, can fuse and weld the discordant entities that constitute the elements of present-day civilization, into the integral components of the world commonwealth of the future, is a truth which future events will increasingly demonstrate.

The prophetic voice of Bahá'u'lláh warning, in the concluding passages of the Hidden Words, *"the peoples of the world"* that *"an unforeseen calamity is following them and that grievous retribution awaiteth them"* throws indeed a lurid light upon the immediate fortunes of sorrowing humanity. Nothing but a fiery ordeal, out of which humanity will emerge, chastened and prepared, can succeed in implanting that sense of responsibility which the leaders of a newborn age must arise to shoulder.

I would again direct your attention to those ominous words of Bahá'u'lláh which I have already quoted: *"And when the appointed hour is come, there shall suddenly appear that which shall cause the limbs of mankind to quake."*

Has not 'Abdu'l-Bahá Himself asserted in unequivocal language that *"another war, fiercer than the last, will assuredly break out"?*

Upon the consummation of this colossal, this unspeakably glorious enterprise—an enterprise that baffled the resources of Roman statesmanship and which Napoleon's desperate efforts failed to achieve—will depend the ultimate realization of that millennium of which poets of all ages have sung and seers have long dreamed. Upon it will depend the fulfillment of the prophecies uttered by the Prophets of old when swords shall be beaten into ploughshares and the lion and the lamb lie down together. It alone can usher in the Kingdom of the Heavenly Father as anticipated by the Faith of Jesus Christ. It alone can lay the foundation for the New World Order visualized by Bahá'u'lláh—a World Order that shall reflect, however dimly, upon this earthly plane, the ineffable splendors of the 'Abhá Kingdom.

One word more in conclusion. The proclamation of the Oneness of Mankind—the head corner-stone of Bahá'u'lláh's all-embracing dominion—can under no circumstances be compared with such expressions of pious hope as have been uttered in the past. His is not merely a call which He raised, alone and unaided, in the face of the relentless and combined opposition of two of the most powerful Oriental potentates of His day—while Himself an exile and prisoner in their hands. It implies at once a warning and a promise—a warning that in it lies the sole means for the salvation of a greatly suffering world, a promise that its realization is at hand.

Uttered at a time when its possibility had not yet been seriously envisaged in any part of the world, it has, by virtue of that celestial potency which the Spirit of Bahá'u'lláh has breathed into it, come at last to be regarded, by an increasing number of thoughtful men, not only as an approaching possibility, but as the necessary outcome of the forces now operating in the world.

The Mouthpiece of God

Surely the world, contracted and transformed into a single highly complex organism by the marvellous progress achieved in the realm of physical science, by the world-wide expansion of commerce and industry, and struggling, under the pressure of world economic forces, amidst the pitfalls of a materialistic civilization, stands in dire need of a restatement of the Truth underlying all the Revelations of the past in a language suited to its essential requirements. And what voice other than that of Bahá'u'lláh—the Mouthpiece of God for this age—is capable of effecting a transformation of society as radical as that which He has already accomplished in the hearts of those men and women, so diversified and seemingly irreconcilable, who constitute the body of His declared followers throughout the world?

That such a mighty conception is fast budding out in the minds of men, that voices are being raised in its support, that its salient features must fast crystallize in the consciousness of those who are in authority, few indeed can doubt. That its modest beginnings have already taken shape in the world-wide Administration with which the adherents of the Faith of Bahá'u'lláh stand associated only those whose hearts are tainted by prejudice can fail to perceive.

Ours, dearly-beloved co-workers, is the paramount duty to continue, with undimmed vision and unabated zeal, to assist in the final erection of that Edifice the foundations of which Bahá'u'lláh has laid in our hearts, to derive added hope and strength from the general trend of recent events, however dark their immediate effects, and to pray with unremitting fervor that He may hasten the approach of the realization of that Wondrous Vision which constitutes the brightest emanation of His Mind and the fairest fruit of the fairest civilization the world has yet seen.

Might not the hundredth anniversary of the Declaration of the Faith of Bahá'u'lláh mark the inauguration of so vast an era in human history?

Your true brother,
SHOGHI

Haifa, Palestine,
November 28, 1931

THE GOLDEN AGE OF THE
CAUSE OF BAHÁ'U'LLÁH

THE GOLDEN AGE OF THE CAUSE OF BAHÁ'U'LLÁH

To the beloved of God and the handmaids of the Merciful through out the United States and Canada.

Friends and fellow-defenders of the Faith of Bahá'u'lláh:

Significant as have been the changes that have lately overtaken a swiftly awakening humanity at this transitional phase of its checkered history, the steady consolidation of the institutions which the administrators of the Faith of Bahá'u'lláh are, in every land, toiling to establish should appear no less remarkable to even those who are as yet imperfectly acquainted with the obstacles they have had to surmount or the meagre resources on which they could rely.

That a Faith which, ten years ago, was severely shaken by the sudden removal of an incomparable Master should have, in the face of tremendous obstacles, maintained its unity, resisted the malignant onslaught of its ill-wishers, silenced its calumniators, broadened the basis of its far-flung administration, and raised upon it institutions symbolizing its ideals of worship and service, should be deemed sufficient evidence of the invincible power with which the Almighty has chosen to invest it from the moment of its inception.

That the Cause associated with the name of Bahá'u'lláh feeds itself upon those hidden springs of celestial strength which no force of human personality, whatever its glamour, can replace; that its reliance is solely upon that mystic Source with which no worldly advantage, be it wealth, fame, or learning can compare; that it propagates itself by ways mysterious and utterly at variance with

51

the standards accepted by the generality of mankind, will, if not already apparent, become increasingly manifest as it forges ahead towards fresh conquests in its struggle for the spiritual regeneration of mankind.

Indeed, how could it, unsupported as it has ever been by the counsels and the resources of the wise, the rich, and the learned in the land of its birth, have succeeded in breaking asunder the shackles that weighed upon it at the hour of its birth, in emerging unscathed from the storms that agitated its infancy, had not its animating breath been quickened by that spirit which is born of God, and on which all success, wherever and however it be sought, must ultimately depend?

It is not necessary for me to recall, even in their briefest outline, the heart-rending details of that appalling tragedy which marked the birth-pangs of our beloved Faith, enacted in a land notorious for its unrestrained fanaticisms, its crass ignorance, its unbridled cruelty. Nor do I need to expatiate on the valor, the sublime fortitude, that defied the cruel torture-mongers of that race, or stress the number, or emphasize the purity of the lives, of those who died willingly that their Cause might live and prosper. Nor is it necessary to dwell upon the indignation which those atrocities evoked, and the feelings of unqualified admiration that surged, in the breasts of countless men and women, in regions remote from the scene of those indescribable cruelties. Suffice it to say that upon these heroes of Bahá'u'lláh's native land was bestowed the inestimable privilege of sealing with their life-blood the early triumphs of their cherished Faith, and of paving the way for its approaching victory. In the blood of the unnumbered martyrs of Persia lay the seed of the Divinely-appointed Administration which, though transplanted from its native soil, is now budding out, under your loving care, into a new order, destined to overshadow all mankind.

America's Contribution to the Cause

For great as have been the attainments and unforgettable the services of the pioneers of the heroic age of the Cause in Persia, the contribution which their spiritual descendants, the American believers, the champion-builders of the organic structure of the Cause, are now making towards the fulfillment of the Plan which must usher in the golden age of the Cause is no less meritorious in this strenuous period of its history. Few, if any, I venture to assert, among these privileged framers and custodians of the constitution of the Faith of Bahá'u'lláh are even dimly aware of the preponderating rôle which the North American continent is destined to play in the future orientation of their world-embracing Cause. Nor does any appreciable number among them seem sufficiently conscious of the decisive influence which they already exercise in the direction and management of its affairs.

"*The continent of America,*" wrote 'Abdu'l-Bahá in February, 1917, "*is, in the eyes of the one true God, the land wherein the splendors of His light shall be revealed, where the mysteries of His Faith shall be unveiled, where the righteous will abide, and the free assemble.*"

That the supporters of the Cause of Bahá'u'lláh, throughout the United States and Canada, are increasingly demonstrating the truth of this solemn affirmation is evident to even a casual observer of the record of their manifold services, whether in their individual capacities or through their concerted endeavors. The manifestations of spontaneous loyalty which marked their response to the expressed wishes of a departed Master; the generosity with which they have, on more than one occasion, arisen to lend a helping hand to the needy and harassed among their brethren in Persia; the vigor with which they have resisted the shameless attacks which unrelenting enemies, both from within and without, have, with increasing frequency, launched against them; the example which the body of their national representatives have set to their sister Assemblies in fashioning the instruments essential to the effective discharge of their collective duties; their successful intervention on behalf of their persecuted fellow-workers in Russia; the moral support they have extended to their Egyptian fellow-disciples at a most critical stage in their struggle for emancipation from the fetters of Islamic orthodoxy; the historic services rendered by those intrepid pioneers who, faithful to the call of 'Abdu'l-Bahá, forsook their homes to plant, in the uttermost corners of the globe, the standard of His Faith; and, last but not least, the magnificence of their self-sacrifice, culminating in the completion of the super-structure of the Mashriqu'l-Adhkár—these stand out each as an eloquent testimony to the indomitable character of the faith Bahá'u'lláh has kindled in their hearts.

Who, contemplating so splendid a record of service, can doubt that these faithful stewards of the redeeming grace of God have preserved, undivided and unimpaired, the priceless heritage entrusted to their charge? Have they not, one might well reflect, in ways which only future historians will indicate, approached the high standard that characterized those deeds of imperishable renown accomplished by those that have gone before them?

Not by the material resources which the members of this infant community can now summon to their aid; not by the numerical strength of its present-day supporters; nor by any direct tangible benefits its votaries can as yet confer upon the multitude of the needy and the disconsolate among their countrymen, should its potentialities be tested or its worth determined. Nowhere but in the purity of its precepts, the sublimity of its standards, the integrity of its laws, the reasonableness of its claims, the comprehensiveness of its scope, the universality of its program, the flexibility of its institutions, the lives of its founders, the heroism of its martyrs, and the transforming power of its influence, should the unprejudiced observer seek to obtain the true criterion that can enable him to fathom its mysteries or to estimate its virtue.

Decline of Mortal Dominion

How unfair, how irrelevant, to venture any comparison between the slow and gradual consolidation of the Faith proclaimed by Bahá'u'lláh and those man-created movements which, having their origin in human desires and with their hopes centered on mortal dominion, must inevitably decline and perish! Springing from a finite mind, begotten of human fancy, and oftentimes the product of ill-conceived designs, such movements succeed, by reason of their novelty, their appeal to man's baser instincts and their dependence upon the resources of a sordid world, in dazzling for a time the eyes of men, only to plunge finally from the heights of their meteoric career into the darkness of oblivion, dissolved by the very forces that had assisted in their creation.

Not so with the Revelation of Bahá'u'lláh. Born in an environment of appalling degradation, springing from a soil steeped in age-long corruptions, hatreds and prejudice, inculcating principles irreconcilable with the accepted standards of the times, and faced from the beginning with the relentless enmity of government, church and people, this nascent Faith of God has, by virtue of the celestial potency with which it has been endowed, succeeded, in less than four score years and ten, in emancipating itself from the galling chains of Islamic domination, in proclaiming the self-sufficiency of its ideals and the independent integrity of its laws, in planting its banner in no less than forty of the most advanced countries of the world, in establishing its outposts in lands beyond the farthest seas, in consecrating its religious edifices in the midmost heart of the Asiatic and American continents, in inducing two of the most powerful governments of the West to ratify the instruments essential to its administrative activities, in obtaining from royalty befitting tributes to the excellence of its teachings, and, finally, in forcing its grievances upon the attention of the representatives of the highest Tribunal in the civilized world, and in securing from its members written affirmations that are tantamount to a tacit recognition of its religious status and to an express declaration of the justice of its cause.

Circumscribed though its power as a social force may as yet appear, and however obvious may seem the present ineffectiveness of its world-embracing program, we, who stand identified with its blessed name, cannot but marvel at the measure of its achievements if we but compare them with the modest accomplishments that have marked the rise of the Dispensations of the past. Where else, if not in the Revelation of Bahá'u'lláh, can the unbiased student of comparative religion cite instances of a claim as stupendous as that which the Author of that Faith advanced, foes as relentless as those which He faced, a devotion more sublime than that which He kindled, a life as eventful and as enthralling as that which He led? Has Christianity or Islám, has any Dispensation that preceded them, offered instances of such combinations of courage and restraint, of magnanimity and power, of broad-mindedness and loyalty, as those which characterized the conduct of the heroes of the Faith of Bahá'u'lláh? Where else do we find evidences of a transformation as swift, as complete, and as sudden, as those effected in the lives of the apostles of the Báb? Few, indeed, are the instances recorded in any of the authenticated annals of the religions of the past of a self-abnegation as complete, a constancy as firm, a magnanimity as sublime, a loyalty as uncompromising, as those which bore witness to the character of that immortal band which stands identified with this Divine Revelation—this latest and most compelling manifestation of the love and the omnipotence of the Almighty!

Contrast with Religions of the Past

We may vainly search in the records of the earliest beginnings of any of the recognized religions of the past for episodes as thrilling in their details, or as far-reaching in their consequences, as those that illumine the pages of the history of this Faith. The almost incredible circumstances attending the martyrdom of that youthful Prince of Glory; the forces of barbaric repression which this tragedy subsequently released; the manifestations of unsurpassed heroism to which it gave rise; the exhortations and warnings which have streamed from the pen of the Divine Prisoner in His Epistles to the potentates of the Church and the monarchs and rulers of the world; the undaunted loyalty with which our brethren are battling in Muslim countries with the forces of religious orthodoxy —these may be reckoned as the most outstanding features of what the world will come to recognize as the greatest drama in the world's spiritual history.

I need not recall, in this connection, the unfortunate episodes that have, admittedly, and to a very great extent, marred the early history of both Judaism and Islám. Nor is it necessary to stress the damaging effect of the excesses, the rivalries and divisions, the fanatical outbursts and acts of ingratitude that are associated with the early development of the people of Israel and with the militant career of the ruthless pioneers of the Faith of Muḥammad.

It would be sufficient for my purpose to call attention to the great number of those who, in the first two centuries of the Christian era, "purchased an ignominious life by betraying the holy Scriptures into the hands of the infidels," the scandalous conduct of those bishops who were thereby branded as traitors, the discord of the African Church, the gradual infiltration into Christian doc-

trine of the principles of the Mithraic cult, of the Alexandrian
school of thought, of the precepts of Zoroastrianism and of Grecian
philosophy, and the adoption by the churches of Greece and of Asia
of the institutions of provincial synods of a model which they
borrowed from the representative councils of their respective
countries.

How great was the obstinacy with which the Jewish converts
among the early Christians adhered to the ceremonies of their an-
cestors, and how fervent their eagerness to impose them on the
Gentiles! Were not the first fifteen bishops of Jerusalem all circum-
cised Jews, and had not the congregation over which they presided
united the laws of Moses with the doctrine of Christ? Is it not a
fact that no more than a twentieth part of the subjects of the Roman
Empire had enlisted themselves under the standard of Christ before
the conversion of Constantine? Was not the ruin of the Temple,
in the city of Jerusalem, and of the public religion of the Jews,
severely felt by the so-called Nazarenes, who persevered, above a
century, in the practice of the Mosaic Law?

How striking the contrast when we remember, in the light of
the afore-mentioned facts, the number of those followers of
Bahá'u'lláh who, in Persia and the adjoining countries, had enlisted
at the time of His Ascension as the convinced supporters of His
Faith! How encouraging to observe the undeviating loyalty with
which His valiant followers are guarding the purity and integrity
of His clear and unequivocal teachings! How edifying the spectacle
of those who are battling with the forces of a firmly intrenched
orthodoxy in their struggle to emancipate themselves from the
fetters of an outworn creed! How inspiring the conduct of those
Muslim followers of Bahá'u'lláh who view, not with regret or
apathy, but with feelings of unconcealed satisfaction, the deserved
chastisement which the Almighty has inflicted upon those twin
institutions of the Sultanate and the Caliphate, those engines of
despotism and sworn enemies of the Cause of God!

Fundamental Principle of Religious Truth

Let no one, however, mistake my purpose. The Revelation, of
which Bahá'u'lláh is the source and center, abrogates none of the
religions that have preceded it, nor does it attempt, in the slightest

degree, to distort their features or to belittle their value. It disclaims any intention of dwarfing any of the Prophets of the past, or of whittling down the eternal verity of their teachings. It can, in no wise, conflict with the spirit that animates their claims, nor does it seek to undermine the basis of any man's allegiance to their cause. Its declared, its primary purpose is to enable every adherent of these Faiths to obtain a fuller understanding of the religion with which he stands identified, and to acquire a clearer apprehension of its purpose. It is neither eclectic in the presentation of its truths, nor arrogant in the affirmation of its claims. Its teachings revolve around the fundamental principle that religious truth is not absolute but relative, that Divine Revelation is progressive, not final. Unequivocally and without the least reservation it proclaims all established religions to be divine in origin, identical in their aims, complementary in their functions, continuous in their purpose, indispensable in their value to mankind.

"*All the Prophets of God,*" asserts Bahá'u'lláh in the Kitáb-i-Íqán, "*abide in the same tabernacle, soar in the same heaven, are seated upon the same throne, utter the same speech, and proclaim the same Faith.*" From the "*beginning that hath no beginning,*" these Exponents of the Unity of God and Channels of His incessant utterance have shed the light of the invisible Beauty upon mankind, and will continue, to the "*end that hath no end,*" to vouchsafe fresh revelations of His might and additional experiences of His inconceivable glory. To contend that any particular religion is final, that "*all Revelation is ended, that the portals of Divine mercy are closed, that from the daysprings of eternal holiness no sun shall rise again, that the ocean of everlasting bounty is forever stilled, and that out of the Tabernacle of ancient glory the Messengers of God have ceased to be made manifest*" would indeed be nothing less than sheer blasphemy.

"*They differ,*" explains Bahá'u'lláh in that same epistle, "*only in the intensity of their revelation and the comparative potency of their light.*" And this, not by reason of any inherent incapacity of any one of them to reveal in a fuller measure the glory of the Message with which He has been entrusted, but rather because of the immaturity and unpreparedness of the age He lived in to apprehend and absorb the full potentialities latent in that Faith.

"Know of a certainty," explains Bahá'u'lláh, *"that in every Dispensation the light of Divine Revelation has been vouchsafed to men in direct proportion to their spiritual capacity. Consider the sun. How feeble its rays the moment it appears above the horizon. How gradually its warmth and potency increase as it approaches its zenith, enabling meanwhile all created things to adapt themselves to the growing intensity of its light. How steadily it declines until it reaches its setting-point. Were it, all of a sudden, to manifest the energies latent within it, it would, no doubt, cause injury to all created things. . . . In like manner, if the Sun of Truth were suddenly to reveal, at the earliest stages of its manifestation, the full measure of the potencies which the providence of the Almighty has bestowed upon it, the earth of human understanding would waste away and be consumed; for men's hearts would neither sustain the intensity of its revelation, nor be able to mirror forth the radiance of its light. Dismayed and overpowered, they would cease to exist."*

It is for this reason, and this reason only, that those who have recognized the Light of God in this age, claim no finality for the Revelation with which they stand identified, nor arrogate to the Faith they have embraced powers and attributes intrinsically superior to, or essentially different from, those which have characterized any of the religious systems that preceded it.

Does not Bahá'u'lláh Himself allude to the progressiveness of Divine Revelation and to the limitations which an inscrutable Wisdom has chosen to impose upon Him? What else can this passage of the Hidden Words imply, if not that He Who revealed it disclaimed finality for the Revelation entrusted to Him by the Almighty? *"O Son of Justice! In the night-season the beauty of the immortal Being hath repaired from the emerald height of fidelity unto the Sadratu'l-Muntahá, and wept with such a weeping that the concourse on high and the dwellers of the realms above wailed at His lamenting. Whereupon there was asked, Why the wailing and weeping? He made reply: As bidden I waited expectant upon the hill of faithfulness, yet inhaled not from them that dwell on earth the fragrance of fidelity. Then summoned to return I beheld, and lo! certain doves of holiness were sore tried within the claws of the dogs of earth. Thereupon the Maid of Heaven hastened forth, unveiled, and resplendent, from Her mystic mansion, and asked of their names, and all were told but one. And when urged, the first Letter thereof was uttered, whereupon the dwellers of the celestial chambers rushed forth out of their habitation of glory. And whilst the second letter was pronounced they fell down, one and all, upon the dust. At that moment a Voice was heard from the inmost shrine: 'Thus far and no farther.' Verily we bear witness to that which they have done and now are doing."*

"The Revelation of which I am the bearer," Bahá'u'lláh explicitly declares, *"is adapted to humanity's spiritual receptiveness and capacity; otherwise, the Light that shines within me can neither wax nor wane. Whatever I manifest is nothing more or less than the measure of the Divine glory which God has bidden me reveal."*

If the Light that is now streaming forth upon an increasingly responsive humanity with a radiance that bids fair to eclipse the splendor of such triumphs as the forces of religion have achieved in days past; if the signs and tokens which proclaimed its advent have been, in many respects, unique in the annals of past Revelations; if its votaries have evinced traits and qualities unexampled in the spiritual history of mankind; these should be attributed not to a superior merit which the Faith of Bahá'u'lláh, as a Revelation isolated and alien from any previous Dispensation, might possess, but rather should be viewed and explained as the inevitable outcome of the forces that have made of this present age an age infinitely more advanced, more receptive, and more insistent to receive an ampler measure of Divine Guidance than has hitherto been vouchsafed to mankind.

Necessity for a Fresh Revelation

Dearly beloved friends: Who, contemplating the helplessness, the fears and miseries of humanity in this day, can any longer question the necessity for a fresh revelation of the quickening power of God's redemptive love and guidance? Who, witnessing on one hand the stupendous advance achieved in the realm of human knowledge, of power, of skill and inventiveness, and viewing on the other the unprecedented character of the sufferings that afflict, and the dangers that beset, present-day society, can be so blind as to doubt that the hour has at last struck for the advent of a new Revelation, for a re-statement of the Divine Purpose, and for the consequent revival of those spiritual forces that have, at fixed intervals, rehabilitated the fortunes of human society? Does not the very operation of the world-unifying forces that are at work in this age necessitate that He Who is the Bearer of the Message of God in this day should not only reaffirm that self-same exalted standard of individual conduct inculcated by the Prophets gone before Him, but embody in His appeal, to all governments and peoples, the essentials of that social code, that Divine Economy, which must guide humanity's concerted efforts in establishing that all-embracing federation which is to signalize the advent of the Kingdom of God on this earth?

May we not, therefore, recognizing as we do the necessity for such a revelation of God's redeeming power, meditate upon the supreme grandeur of the System unfolded by the hand of Bahá'u'lláh in this day? May we not pause, pressed though we be by the daily preoccupations which the ever-widening range of the administrative activities of His Faith must involve, to reflect upon the sanctity of the responsibilities it is our privilege to shoulder?

The Station of the Báb

Not only in the character of the revelation of Bahá'u'lláh, however stupendous be His claim, does the greatness of this Dispensation reside. For among the distinguishing features of His Faith ranks, as a further evidence of its uniqueness, the fundamental truth that in the person of its Forerunner, the Báb, every follower of Bahá'u'lláh recognizes not merely an inspired annunciator but a direct Manifestation of God. It is their firm belief that, no matter how short the duration of His Dispensation, and however brief the period of the operation of His laws, the Báb had been endowed with a potency such as no founder of any of the past religions was, in the providence of the Almighty, allowed to possess. That He was not merely the precursor of the Revelation of Bahá'u'lláh, that He was more than a divinely-inspired personage, that His was the station of an independent, self-sufficient Manifestation of God, is abundantly demonstrated by Himself, is affirmed in unmistakable terms by Bahá'u'lláh, and is finally attested by the Will and Testament of 'Abdu'l-Bahá.

Nowhere but in the Kitáb-i-Íqán, Bahá'u'lláh's masterly exposition of the one unifying truth underlying all the Revelations of the past, can we obtain a clearer apprehension of the potency of those forces inherent in that Preliminary Manifestation with which His own Faith stands indissolubly associated. Expatiating upon the unfathomed import of the signs and tokens that have accompanied the Revelation proclaimed by the Báb, the promised Qá'im, He recalls these prophetic words: *"Knowledge is twenty and seven letters. All that the Prophets have revealed are two letters thereof. No man thus far hath known more than these two letters. But when the Qá'im shall arise, He will cause the remaining twenty and five letters to be made manifest."* "Behold," adds Bahá'u'lláh, *"how great and lofty is His station!"* "Of His Revelation," He further adds, *"the Prophets of God, His saints and chosen ones, have either not been informed, or in pursuance of God's inscrutable Decree, they have not disclosed."*

And yet, immeasurably exalted as is the station of the Báb, and marvellous as have been the happenings that have signalized the advent of His Cause, so wondrous a Revelation cannot but pale before the effulgence of that Orb of unsurpassed splendor Whose rise He foretold and whose superiority He readily acknowledged. We have but to turn to the writings of the Báb Himself in order to estimate the significance of that Quintessence of Light of which He, with all the majesty of His power, was but its humble and chosen Precursor.

Again and again the Báb admits, in glowing and unequivocal language, the preëminent character of a Faith destined to be made manifest after Him and to supersede His Cause. *"The germ,"* He asserts in the Persian Bayán, the chief and best-preserved repository of His laws, *"that holds within itself the potentialities of the Revelation that is to come is endowed with a potency superior to the combined forces of all those who follow me."* "Of all the tributes," the Báb repeatedly proclaims in His writings, *"I have paid to Him Who is to come after Me, the greatest is this, My written confession, that no words of Mine can adequately describe Him, nor can any reference to Him in my Book, the Bayán, do justice to His Cause."* Addressing Siyyid Yaḥyáy-i-Dárábí, surnamed Vaḥíd, the most learned and influential among his followers, He says: *"By the righteousness of Him Whose power causeth the seed to germinate and Who breatheth the spirit of life into all things, were I to be assured that in the*

day of His Manifestation thou wilt deny Him, I would unhesi-
tatingly disown thee and repudiate thy faith. . . . If, on the other
hand, I be told that a Christian, who beareth no allegiance to My
Faith, will believe in Him, the same will I regard as the apple of
Mine eye."

The Outpouring of Divine Grace

"If all the peoples of the world," Bahá'u'lláh Himself affirms,
"be invested with the powers and attributes destined for the Letters
of the Living, the chosen disciples of the Báb, whose station is ten
thousand times more glorious than any which the apostles of old
have attained, and if they, one and all, should, swift as the twinkling
of an eye, hesitate to recognize the Light of my Revelation, their
faith shall be of no avail, and they shall be accounted among the
infidels." "So tremendous," He writes, *"is the outpouring of Divine*
grace in this Dispensation that if mortal hands could be swift enough
to record them, within the space of a single day and night, there
would stream verses of such number as to be equivalent to the whole
of the Persian Bayán."

Such, dearly-beloved friends, is the effusion of celestial grace
vouchsafed by the Almighty to this age, this most illumined century! We stand too close to so colossal a Revelation to expect in
this, the first century of its era, to arrive at a just estimate of its
towering grandeur, its infinite possibilities, its transcendent beauty.
Small though our present numbers may be, however limited our
capacities, or circumscribed our influence, we, into whose hands so
pure, so tender, so precious a heritage has been entrusted, should
at all times strive, with unrelaxing vigilance, to abstain from any
thoughts, words, or deeds, that might tend to dim its brilliance, or
injure its growth. How tremendous our responsibility; how delicate
and laborious our task!

Dear friends: Clear and emphatic as are the instructions which
our departed Master has reiterated in countless Tablets bequeathed
by Him to His followers throughout the world, a few, owing to the
restricted influence of the Cause in the West, have been purposely
withheld from the body of His occidental disciples, who, despite
their numerical inferiority, are now exercising such a preponderating influence in the direction and administration of its affairs.
I feel it, therefore, incumbent upon me to stress, now that the time

is ripe, the importance of an instruction which, at the present stage of the evolution of our Faith, should be increasingly emphasized, irrespective of its application to the East or to the West. And this principle is no other than that which involves the non-participation by the adherents of the Faith of Bahá'u'lláh, whether in their individual capacities or collectively as local or national Assemblies, in any form of activity that might be interpreted, either directly or indirectly, as an interference in the political affairs of any particular government. Whether it be in the publications which they initiate and supervise; or in their official and public deliberations; or in the posts they occupy and the services they render; or in the communications they address to their fellow-disciples; or in their dealings with men of eminence and authority; or in their affiliations with kindred societies and organizations, it is, I am firmly convinced, their first and sacred obligation to abstain from any word or deed that might be construed as a violation of this vital principle. Theirs is the duty to demonstrate, on one hand, their unqualified loyalty and obedience to whatever is the considered judgment of their respective governments.

The Divine Polity

Let them refrain from associating themselves, whether by word or by deed, with the political pursuits of their respective nations, with the policies of their governments and the schemes and programs of parties and factions. In such controversies they should assign no blame, take no side, further no design, and identify themselves with no system prejudicial to the best interests of that worldwide Fellowship which it is their aim to guard and foster. Let them beware lest they allow themselves to become the tools of unscrupulous politicians, or to be entrapped by the treacherous devices of the plotters and the perfidious among their countrymen. Let them so shape their lives and regulate their conduct that no charge of secrecy, of fraud, of bribery or of intimidation may, however ill-founded, be brought against them. Let them rise above all particularism and partisanship, above the vain disputes, the petty calculations, the transient passions that agitate the face, and engage the attention, of a changing world. It is their duty to strive to distinguish, as clearly as they possibly can, and if needed with the aid of their elected representatives, such posts and functions as are either diplomatic or political from those that are purely administrative in character, and which under no circumstances are affected by the changes and chances that political activities and party government, in every land, must necessarily involve. Let them affirm their unyielding determination to stand, firmly and unreservedly, for the way of Bahá'u'lláh, to avoid the entanglements and bickerings inseparable from the pursuits of the politician, and to become worthy agencies of that Divine Polity which incarnates God's immutable Purpose for all men.

It should be made unmistakably clear that such an attitude implies neither the slightest indifference to the cause and interests of their own country, nor involves any insubordination on their part to the authority of recognized and established governments. Nor does it constitute a repudiation of their sacred obligation to promote, in the most effective manner, the best interests of their government and people. It indicates the desire cherished by every true and loyal follower of Bahá'u'lláh to serve, in an unselfish, unostentatious and patriotic fashion, the highest interests of the country to which he belongs, and in a way that would entail no departure from the high standards of integrity and truthfulness associated with the teachings of his Faith.

As the number of the Bahá'í communities in various parts of the world multiplies and their power, as a social force, becomes increasingly apparent, they will no doubt find themselves increasingly subjected to the pressure which men of authority and influence, in the political domain, will exercise in the hope of obtaining the support they require for the advancement of their aims. These communities will, moreover, feel a growing need of the good-will and the assistance of their respective governments in their efforts to widen the scope, and to consolidate the foundations, of the institutions committed to their charge. Let them beware lest, in their eagerness to further the aims of their beloved Cause, they should be led unwittingly to bargain with their Faith, to compromise with their essential principles, or to sacrifice, in return for any material advantage which their institutions may derive, the integrity of their spiritual ideals. Let them proclaim that in whatever country they reside, and however advanced their institutions, or profound their desire to enforce the laws, and apply the principles, enunciated by Bahá'u'lláh, they will, unhesitatingly, subordinate the operation of such laws and the application of such principles to the requirements and legal enactments of their respective governments. Theirs is not the purpose, while endeavoring to conduct and perfect the administrative affairs of their Faith, to violate, under any circumstances, the provisions of their country's constitution, much less to allow the machinery of their administration to supersede the government of their respective countries.

It should also be borne in mind that the very extension of the activities in which we are engaged, and the variety of the communities which labor under divers forms of government, so essentially different in their standards, policies, and methods, make it absolutely essential for all those who are the declared members of any one of these communities to avoid any action that might, by arousing the suspicion or exciting the antagonism of any one government, involve their brethren in fresh persecutions or complicate the nature of their task. How else, might I ask, could such a far-flung Faith, which transcends political and social boundaries, which includes within its pale so great a variety of races and nations, which will have to rely increasingly, as it forges ahead, on the good-will and support of the diversified and contending governments of the earth—how else could such a Faith succeed in preserving its unity, in safeguarding its interests, and in ensuring the steady and peaceful development of its institutions?

Such an attitude, however, is not dictated by considerations of selfish expediency, but is actuated, first and foremost, by the broad principle that the followers of Bahá'u'lláh will, under no circumstances, suffer themselves to be involved, whether as individuals or in their collective capacities, in matters that would entail the slightest departure from the fundamental verities and ideals of their Faith. Neither the charges which the uninformed and the malicious may be led to bring against them, nor the allurements of honors and rewards, will ever induce them to surrender their trust or to deviate from their path. Let their words proclaim, and their conduct testify, that they who follow Bahá'u'lláh, in whatever land they reside, are actuated by no selfish ambition, that they neither thirst for power, nor mind any wave of unpopularity, of distrust or criticism, which a strict adherence to their standards might provoke.

Difficult and delicate though be our task, the sustaining power of Bahá'u'lláh and of His Divine guidance will assuredly assist us if we follow steadfastly in His way, and strive to uphold the integrity of His laws. The light of His redeeming grace, which no earthly power can obscure, will if we persevere, illuminate our path, as we steer our course amid the snares and pitfalls of a troubled age, and will enable us to discharge our duties in a manner that would redound to the glory and the honor of His blessed Name.

Our Beloved Temple

And finally, dearly-beloved brethren, let me once more direct your attention to the pressing claims of the Mashriqu'l-Adhkár, our beloved Temple. Need I remind you of the imperative necessity of carrying out to a successful conclusion, while there is yet time, the great enterprise to which, before the eyes of a watching world, we stand committed? Need I stress the great damage which further delay in the prosecution of this divinely-appointed task must, even in these critical and unforeseen circumstances, inflict upon the prestige of our beloved Cause? I am, I can assure you, acutely conscious of the stringency of the circumstances with which you are faced, the embarrassments under which you labor, the cares with which you are burdened, the pressing urgency of the demands that are being incessantly made upon your depleted resources. I am, however, still more profoundly aware of the unprecedented character of the opportunity which it is your privilege to seize and utilize. I am aware of the incalculable blessings that must await the termination of a collective enterprise which, by the range and quality of the sacrifices it entailed, deserves to be ranked among the most outstanding examples of Bahá'í solidarity ever since those deeds of brilliant heroism immortalized the memory of the heroes of Nayríz, of Zanján, and of Ṭabarsí. I appeal to you, therefore, friends and fellow-disciples of Bahá'u'lláh, for a more abundant measure of self-sacrifice, for a higher standard of concerted effort, for a still more compelling evidence of the reality of the faith that glows within you.

And in this fervent plea, my voice is once more reinforced by the passionate, and perhaps, the last, entreaty, of the Greatest Holy Leaf, whose spirit, now hovering on the edge of the Great Beyond, longs to carry on its flight to the Abhá Kingdom, and into the presence of a Divine, an almighty Father, an assurance of the joyous consummation of an enterprise, the progress of which has so greatly brightened the closing days of her earthly life. That the American believers, those stout-hearted pioneers of the Faith of Bahá'u'lláh, will unanimously respond, with that same spontaneous generosity, that same measure of self-sacrifice, as have characterized their response to her appeals in the past, no one who is familiar with the vitality of their faith can possibly question.

Would to God that by the end of the spring of the year 1933 the multitudes who, from the remote corners of the globe, will throng the grounds of the Great Fair to be held in the neighborhood of that hallowed shrine may, as a result of your sustained spirit of self-sacrifice, be privileged to gaze on the arrayed splendor of its dome—a dome that shall stand as a flaming beacon and a symbol of hope amidst the gloom of a despairing world.

Your true brother,
SHOGHI

Haifa, Palestine,
March 21, 1932

AMERICA AND THE MOST GREAT PEACE

AMERICA AND
THE MOST GREAT PEACE

To the beloved of the Lord and the handmaids of the Merciful throughout the United States and Canada.

Friends and fellow-promoters of the Faith of God:

Forty years will have elapsed ere the close of this coming summer since the name of Bahá'u'lláh was first mentioned on the American continent. Strange indeed must appear to every observer, pondering in his heart the significance of so great a landmark in the spiritual history of the great American Republic, the circumstances which have attended this first public reference to the Author of our beloved Faith. Stranger still must seem the associations which the brief words uttered on that historic occasion must have evoked in the minds of those who heard them.

Of pomp and circumstance, of any manifestations of public rejoicing or of popular applause, there were none to greet this first intimation * to America's citizens of the existence and purpose of the Revelation proclaimed by Bahá'u'lláh. Nor did he who was its chosen instrument profess himself a believer in the indwelling potency of the tidings he conveyed, or suspect the magnitude of the forces which so cursory a mention was destined to release.

Announced through the mouth of an avowed supporter of that narrow ecclesiasticism which the Faith itself has challenged and seeks to extirpate, characterized at the moment of its birth as an obscure offshoot of a contemptible creed, the Message of the Most Great Name, fed by streams of unceasing trial and warmed by the sunshine of 'Abdu'l-Bahá's tender care, has succeeded in driving its roots deep into America's genial soil, has in less than

---

* In an address by Dr. Henry H. Jessup at the Parliament of Religions, Columbian Exposition, Chicago, 1893.—*Editor.*

half a century sent out its shoots and tendrils as far as the remotest corners of the globe, and now stands, clothed in the majesty of the consecrated Edifice it has reared in the heart of that continent, determined to proclaim its right and vindicate its capacity to redeem a stricken people. Unsupported by any of the advantages which talent, rank and riches can confer, the community of the American believers, despite its tender age, its numerical strength, its limited experience, has by virtue of the inspired wisdom, the united will, the incorruptible loyalty of its administrators and teachers achieved the distinction of an undisputed leadership among its sister communities of East and West in hastening the advent of the Golden Age anticipated by Bahá'u'lláh.

And yet how grave the crises which this infant, this blessed, community has weathered in the course of its checkered history! How slow and painful the process that gradually brought it forth from the obscurity of unmitigated neglect to the broad daylight of public recognition! How severe the shocks which the ranks of its devoted adherents have sustained through the defection of the faint in heart, the malice of the mischief-maker, the treachery of the proud and the ambitious! What storms of ridicule, of abuse and of calumny its representatives have had to face in their staunch support of the integrity, and their valiant defense of the fair name, of the Faith they had espoused! How persistent the vicissitudes and disconcerting the reverses with which its privileged members, young and old alike, individually and collectively, have had to contend in their heroic endeavors to scale the heights which a loving Master had summoned them to attain!

Many and powerful have been its enemies who, as soon as they discovered the evidences of the growing ascendancy of its declared supporters, have vied with one another in hurling at its face the vilest imputations and in pouring out upon the Object of its devotion the vials of their fiercest wrath. How often have these sneered at the scantiness of its resources and the seeming stagnation of its life! How bitterly they ridiculed its origins and, misconceiving its purpose, dismissed it as a useless appendage of an expiring creed! Have they not in their written attacks stigmatized the heroic person of the Forerunner of so holy a Revelation as a coward recanter, a perverted apostate, and denounced the entire range of

His voluminous writings as the idle chatter of a thoughtless man? Have they not chosen to ascribe to its divine Founder the basest motives which an unscrupulous plotter and usurper can conceive, and regarded the Center of His Covenant as the embodiment of ruthless tyranny, a stirrer of mischief, and a notorious exponent of expediency and fraud? Its world-unifying principles these impotent enemies of a steadily-rising Faith have time and again denounced as fundamentally defective, have pronounced its all-embracing program as utterly fantastic, and regarded its vision of the future as chimerical and positively deceitful. The fundamental verities that constitute its doctrine its foolish ill-wishers have represented as a cloak of idle dogma, its administrative machinery they have refused to differentiate from the soul of the Faith itself, and the mysteries it reveres and upholds they have identified with sheer superstition. The principle of unification which it advocates and with which it stands identified they have misconceived as a shallow attempt at uniformity, its repeated assertions of the reality of supernatural agencies they have condemned as a vain belief in magic, and the glory of its idealism they have rejected as mere utopia. Every process of purification whereby an inscrutable Wisdom chose from time to time to purge the body of His chosen followers of the defilement of the undesirable and the unworthy, these victims of an unrelenting jealousy have hailed as a symptom of the invading forces of schism which were soon to sap its strength, vitiate its vitality, and complete its ruin.

Dearly-beloved friends! It is not for me, nor does it seem within the competence of any one of the present generation, to trace the exact and full history of the rise and gradual consolidation of this invincible arm, this mighty organ, of a continually advancing Cause. It would be premature at this early stage of its evolution, to attempt an exhaustive analysis, or to arrive at a just estimate, of the impelling forces that have urged it forward to occupy so exalted a place among the various instruments which the Hand of Omnipotence has fashioned, and is now perfecting, for the execution of His divine Purpose. Future historians of this mighty Revelation, endowed with pens abler than any which its present-day supporters can claim to possess, will no doubt transmit to posterity a masterly exposition of the origins of those forces which, through a remarkable swing of the pendulum, have caused the administrative center of the Faith to gravitate, away from its cradle, to the shores of the American continent and towards its very heart—the present mainspring and chief bulwark of its fast evolving institutions. On them will devolve the task of recording the history, and of estimating the significance, of so radical a revolution in the fortunes of a slowly maturing Faith. Theirs will be the opportunity to extol the virtues and to immortalize the memory of those men and women who have participated in its accomplishment. Theirs will be the privilege of evaluating the share which each of these champion-builders of the World Order of Bahá'u'lláh has had in ushering in that golden Millennium, the promise of which lies enshrined in His teachings.

Does not the history of primitive Christianity and of the rise of Islám, each in its own way, offer a striking parallel to this strange phenomenon the beginnings of which we are now witnessing in this, the first century of the Bahá'í Era? Has not the Divine Impulse which gave birth to each of these great religious systems been driven, through the operation of those forces which the irresistible growth of the Faith itself had released, to seek away from the land of its birth and in more propitious climes a ready field and a more adequate medium for the incarnation of its spirit and the propagation of its cause? Have not the Asiatic churches of Jerusalem, of Antioch and of Alexandria, consisting chiefly of those Jewish converts, whose character and temperament inclined them to sympathize with the traditional ceremonies of the Mosaic Dispensation, been forced as they steadily declined to recognize the growing ascendancy of their Greek and Roman brethren? Have they not been compelled to acknowledge the superior valor and the trained efficiency which have enabled these standard-bearers of the Cause of Jesus Christ to erect the symbols of His world-wide dominion on the ruins of a collapsing Empire? Has not the animating spirit of Islám been constrained, under the pressure of similar circumstances, to abandon the inhospitable wastes of its Arabian Home, the theatre of its greatest sufferings and exploits, to yield in a distant land the fairest fruit of its slowly maturing civilization?

"From the beginning of time until the present day," 'Abdu'l-

Bahá Himself affirms, *"the light of Divine Revelation hath risen in the East and shed its radiance upon the West. The illumination thus shed hath, however, acquired in the West an extraordinary brilliancy. Consider the Faith proclaimed by Jesus. Though it first appeared in the East, yet not until its light had been shed upon the West did the full measure of its potentialities become manifest." "The day is approaching,"* He, in another passage, assures us, *"when ye shall witness how, through the splendor of the Faith of Bahá'u'lláh, the West will have replaced the East, radiating the light of Divine Guidance." "In the books of the Prophets,"* He again asserts, *"certain glad-tidings are recorded which are absolutely true and free from doubt. The East hath ever been the dawning-place of the Sun of Truth. In the East all the Prophets of God have appeared . . . The West hath acquired illumination from the East but in some respects the reflection of the light hath been greater in the Occident. This is specially true of Christianity. Jesus Christ appeared in Palestine and His teachings were founded in that country. Although the doors of the Kingdom were first opened in that land and the bestowals of God were spread broadcast from its center, the people of the West have embraced and promulgated Christianity more fully than the people of the East."*

Little wonder that from the same unerring pen there should have flowed, after 'Abdu'l-Bahá's memorable visit to the West, these often-quoted words, the significance of which it would be impossible for me to overrate: *"The continent of America,"* He announced in a Tablet unveiling His Divine Plan to the believers residing in the North-Eastern States of the American Republic, *"is in the eyes of the one true God the land wherein the splendors of His light shall be revealed, where the mysteries of His Faith shall be unveiled, where the righteous will abide and the free assemble." "May this American democracy,"* He Himself, while in America, was heard to remark, *"be the first nation to establish the foundation of international agreement. May it be the first nation to proclaim the unity of mankind. May it be the first to unfurl the standard of the 'Most Great Peace' . . . The American people are indeed worthy of being the first to build the tabernacle of the great peace and proclaim the oneness of mankind . . . May America become the distributing center of spiritual enlightenment and all the world receive this heavenly blessing. For America has developed powers and capacities greater and more wonderful than other nations . . . May the inhabitants of this country become like angels of heaven with faces turned continually toward God. May all of them become servants of the omnipotent One. May they rise from their present material attainments to such a height that heavenly illumination may stream from this center to all the peoples of the world . . . This American nation is equipped and empowered to accomplish that which will adorn the pages of history, to become the envy of the world and be blest in both the East and the West for the triumph of its people . . . The American continent gives signs and evidences of very great advancement. Its future is even more promising, for its influence and illumination are far-reaching. It will lead all nations spiritually."*

Would it seem extravagant, in the light of so sublime an utterance, to expect that in the midst of so enviable a region of the earth and out of the agony and wreckage of an unprecedented crisis there should burst forth a spiritual renaissance which, as it propagates itself through the instrumentality of the American believers, will rehabilitate the fortunes of a decadent age? It was 'Abdu'l-Bahá Himself, His most intimate associates testify, Who, on more than one occasion, intimated that the establishment of His Father's Faith in the North American continent ranked as the most outstanding among the threefold aims which, as He conceived it, constituted the principal objective of His ministry. It was He Who, in the heyday of His life and almost immediately after His Father's ascension, conceived the idea of inaugurating His mission by enlisting the inhabitants of so promising a country under the banner of Bahá'u'lláh. He it was Who in His unerring wisdom and out of the abundance of His heart chose to bestow on His favored disciples, to the very last day of His life, the tokens of His unfailing solicitude and to overwhelm them with the marks of His special favor. It was He Who, in His declining years, as soon as delivered from the shackles of a long and cruel incarceration, decided to visit the land which had remained for so many years the object of His infinite care and love. It was He Who, through the power of His presence and the charm of His utterance, infused into the entire body of His followers those sentiments and principles which could alone sustain them amidst the trials which the very prosecution of their task would inevitably engender. Was He not, through the several functions which He exercised whilst He dwelt amongst them, whether in the laying of the corner-stone of their House of Worship, or in the Feast which He offered them and at which He chose to serve them in person, or in the emphasis which He on a more solemn occasion placed on the implications of His spiritual station—was He not, thereby, deliberately bequeathing to them all the essentials of that spiritual heritage which He knew they would ably safeguard and by their deeds continually enrich? And finally who can doubt that in the Divine Plan which, in the evening of His life, He unveiled to their eyes He was investing them with that spiritual primacy on which they could rely in the fulfillment of their high destiny?

"*O ye apostles of Bahá'u'lláh!*" He thus addresses them in one of His Tablets, "*May my life be sacrificed for you! . . . Behold the portals which Bahá'u'lláh hath opened before you! Consider how exalted and lofty is the station you are destined to attain; how unique the favors with which you have been endowed.*" "*My thoughts,*" He tells them in another passage, "*are turned towards you, and my heart leaps within me at your mention. Could ye know how my soul glows with your love, so great a happiness would flood your hearts as to cause you to become enamored with each other.*" "*The full measure of your success,*" He declares in another Tablet, "*is as yet unrevealed, its significance still unapprehended. Ere long ye will, with your own eyes, witness how brilliantly every one of you, even as a shining star, will radiate in the firmament of your country the light of Divine Guidance and will bestow upon its people the glory of an everlasting life.*" "*The range of your future achievements,*" He once more affirms, "*still remains undisclosed. I fervently hope that in the near future the whole earth may be stirred and shaken by the results of your achievements.*" "*The Almighty,*" He assures them, "*will no doubt grant you the help of His grace, will invest you with the tokens of His might, and will endue your souls with the sustaining power of His holy Spirit.*" "*Be not concerned,*" He admonishes them, "*with the smallness of your numbers, neither be oppressed by the multitude of an unbelieving world . . . Exert yourselves; your mission is unspeakably glorious. Should success crown your enterprise, America will assuredly evolve into a center from which waves of spiritual power will emanate, and the throne of the Kingdom of God will, in the plentitude of its majesty and glory, be firmly established."*

"*The hope which 'Abdu'l-Bahá cherishes for you,*" He thus urges them, "*is that the same success which has attended your efforts in America may crown your endeavors in other parts of the world, that through you the fame of the Cause of God may be diffused throughout the East and the West and the advent of the Kingdom of the Lord of Hosts be proclaimed in all the five continents of the globe . . . Thus far ye have been untiring in your labors. Let your exertions, henceforth, increase a thousandfold. Summon the people in these countries, capitals, islands, assemblies and churches to enter the Abhá Kingdom. The scope of your exertions must needs be extended. The wider its range, the more striking will be the evidences of Divine assistance . . . Oh! that I could travel, even though on foot and in the utmost poverty, to these regions and, raising the call of Yá Bahá'u'l-Abhá in cities, villages, mountains, deserts and oceans, promote the Divine teachings! This, alas, I cannot do! How intensely I deplore it! Please God, ye may achieve it.*" And finally, as if to crown all His previous utterances, is this solemn affirmation embodying His vision of America's spiritual destiny: "*The moment this Divine Message is carried forward by the American believers from the shores of America and is propagated through the continents of Europe, of Asia, of Africa and of Australasia, and as far as the islands of the Pacific, this community will find itself securely established upon the throne of an everlasting dominion. Then will all the peoples of the world witness that this community is spiritually illumined and divinely guided. Then will the whole earth resound with the praises of its majesty and greatness.*"

It is in the light of these above-quoted words of 'Abdu'l-Bahá that every thoughtful and conscientious believer should ponder the significance of this momentous utterance of Bahá'u'lláh: "*In the East the light of His Revelation hath broken; in the West have appeared the signs of His dominion. Ponder this in your hearts, O people, and be not of those who have turned a deaf ear to the admonitions of Him Who is the Almighty, the All-Praised . . .*

Should they attempt to conceal its light on the continent, it will assuredly rear its head in the midmost heart of the ocean, and, raising its voice, proclaim: 'I am the life-giver of the world!'"

Dearly-beloved friends! Can our eyes be so dim as to fail to recognize in the anguish and turmoil which, greater than in any other country and in a manner unprecedented in its history, are now afflicting the American nation, evidences of the beginnings of that spiritual renaissance which these pregnant words of 'Abdu'l-Bahá so clearly foreshadow? The throes and twinges of agony which the soul of a nation in travail is now beginning to experience abundantly proclaim it. Contrast the sad plight of the nations of the earth, and in particular this great Republic of the West, with the rising fortunes of that handful of its citizens, whose mission, if they be faithful to their trust, is to heal its wounds, restore its confidence and revive its shattered hopes. Contrast the dreadful convulsions, the internecine conflicts, the petty disputes, the outworn controversies, the interminable revolutions that agitate the masses, with the calm new light of Peace and of Truth which envelops, guides and sustains those valiant inheritors of the law and love of Bahá'u'lláh. Compare the disintegrating institutions, the discredited statesmanship, the exploded theories, the appalling degradation, the follies and furies, the shifts, shams and compromises that characterize the present age, with the steady consolidation, the holy discipline, the unity and cohesiveness, the assured conviction, the uncompromising loyalty, the heroic self-sacrifice that constitute the hallmark of these faithful stewards and harbingers of the golden age of the Faith of Bahá'u'lláh.

Small wonder that these prophetic words should have been revealed by 'Abdu'l-Bahá: *"The East,"* He assures us, *"hath verily been illumined with the light of the Kingdom. Ere long will this same light shed a still greater illumination upon the West. Then will the hearts of its people be vivified through the potency of the teachings of God and their souls be set aglow by the undying fire of His love." "The prestige of the Faith of God,"* He asserts, *"has immensely increased. Its greatness is now manifest. The day is approaching when it will have cast a tremendous tumult in men's hearts. Rejoice, therefore, O denizens of America, rejoice with exceeding gladness!"*

Most prized and best-beloved brethren! As we look back upon the forty years which have passed since the auspicious rays of the Bahá'í Revelation first warmed and illuminated the American continent we find that they may well fall into four distinct periods, each culminating in an event of such significance as to constitute a milestone along the road leading the American believers towards their promised victory. The first of these four decades (1893-1903), characterized by a process of slow and steady fermentation, may be said to have culminated in the historic pilgrimages undertaken by 'Abdu'l-Bahá's American disciples to the shrine of Bahá'u'lláh. The ten years which followed (1903-1913), so full of the tests and trials which agitated, cleansed and energized the body of the earliest pioneers of the Faith in that land, had as their happy climax 'Abdu'l-Bahá's memorable visit to America. The third period (1913-1923), a period of quiet and uninterrupted consolidation, had as its inevitable result the birth of that divinely-appointed Administration, the foundations of which the Will of a departed Master had unmistakably established. The remaining ten years (1923-1933), distinguished throughout by further internal development, as well as by a notable expansion of the international activities of a growing community, witnessed the completion of the superstructure of the Mashriqu'l-Adhkár—the Administration's mighty bulwark, the symbol of its strength and the sign of its future glory.

Each of these successive periods would seem to have contributed its distinct share in enriching the spiritual life of that community, and in preparing its members for the discharge of the tremendous responsibilities of their unique mission. The pilgrimages which its foremost representatives were moved to undertake in that earliest period of its history fired the souls of its members with a love and zeal which no amount of adversity could quench. The tests and tribulations it subsequently suffered enabled those who survived them to obtain a grasp of the implications of their faith that no opposition, however determined and well-organized, could ever hope to weaken. The institutions which its tried and tested adherents later on established furnished their promoters with that poise and stability which the increase of their numbers and the ceaseless extension of their activities urgently demanded. And finally the Temple which the exponents of an already firmly established Administration were inspired to erect gave them the vision which neither the storms of internal disorder nor the whirlwinds of international commotion could possibly obscure.

It would take me too long to attempt even a brief description of the first stirrings which the introduction of the Bahá'í Revelation into the New World, as conceived, initiated and directed by our beloved Master, immediately created. Nor does space permit me to narrate the circumstances attending the epoch-making visit of the first American pilgrims to Bahá'u'lláh's hallowed shrine, to relate the deeds which signalized the return of these bearers of a new-born Gospel to their native country, or to assess the immediate consequences of their achievements. No word of mine would suffice to express how instantly the revelation of 'Abdu'l-Bahá's hopes, expectations and purpose for an awakened continent, electrified the minds and hearts of those who were privileged to hear Him, who were made the recipients of His inestimable blessings and the chosen repositories of His confidence and trust. I can never hope to interpret adequately the feelings that surged within those heroic hearts as they sat at their Master's feet, beneath the shelter of His prison-house, eager to absorb and intent to preserve the effusions of His divine Wisdom. I can never pay sufficient tribute to that spirit of unyielding determination which the impact of a magnetic personality and the spell of a mighty utterance kindled in the entire company of these returning pilgrims, these consecrated heralds of the Covenant of God, at so decisive an epoch of their history. The memory of such names as Lua, Chase, MacNutt, Dealy, Goodall, Dodge, Farmer and Brittingham—to mention only a few of that immortal galaxy now gathered to the glory of Bahá'u'lláh—will for ever remain associated with the rise and establishment of His Faith in the American continent, and will continue to shed on its annals a lustre that time can never dim.

It was through these pilgrimages, as they succeeded one another in the years immediately following the ascension of Bahá'u'lláh, that the splendor of the Covenant, beclouded for a time by the apparent ascendancy of its Arch-Breaker, emerged triumphant amidst the vicissitudes which had afflicted it. It was through the arrival of these pilgrims, and these alone, that the gloom which had enveloped the disconsolate members of 'Abdu'l-Bahá's family was finally dispelled. Through the agency of these successive visitors the Greatest Holy Leaf, who alone with her Brother among the members of her Father's household had to confront the rebellion of almost the entire company of her relatives and associates, found that consolation which so powerfully sustained her till the very close of her life. By the forces which this little band of returning pilgrims was able to release in the heart of that continent the death-knell of every scheme initiated by the would-be wrecker of the Cause of God was sounded.

The Tablets which were subsequently revealed by the untiring pen of 'Abdu'l-Bahá, embodying in passionate and unequivocal language His instructions and counsels, His appeals and comments, His hopes and wishes, His fears and warnings, soon began to be translated, published and circulated throughout the length and breadth of the North American continent, providing the ever-widening circle of the first believers with that spiritual sustenance which could alone enable them to survive the severe trials they were soon to experience.

The hour of an unprecedented crisis was, however, inexorably approaching. Evidences of dissension, actuated by pride and ambition, were beginning to obscure the radiance and retard the growth of the newly-born community which the apostolic teachers of that continent had labored to establish. He who had been instrumental in inaugurating so splendid an era in the history of the Faith, on whom the Center of Bahá'u'lláh's Covenant had conferred the titles of "Bahá's Peter," of the "Shepherd of God's Flocks," of the "Conqueror of America," upon whom had been bestowed the unique privilege of helping 'Abdu'l-Bahá lay the foundation-stone of the Báb's Mausoleum on Mt. Carmel—such a man, blinded by his extraordinary success and aspiring after an uncontrolled domination over the beliefs and activities of his fellow-disciples, insolently raised the standard of revolt. Seceding from 'Abdu'l-Bahá and allying himself with the Arch-Enemy of the Faith of God, this deluded apostate sought, by perverting the teachings and directing a campaign of unrelenting vilification against the person of 'Abdu'l-Bahá, to undermine the faith of those believers whom he had during no less than eight years, so strenuously toiled to convert. By the tracts he published, through the active collaboration of the emissaries of his chief Ally, and reinforced by the efforts which the Cnristian ecclesiastical enemies of the Bahá'í Revelation were beginning to exert, he succeeded in dealing the nascent Faith of God a blow from which it could only slowly and painfully recover.

I need not dwell on the immediate effects of this serious yet transitory cleavage in the ranks of the American adherents of the Cause of Bahá'u'lláh. Nor do I need to expatiate on the character of the defamatory writings that poured upon them. Nor does it seem necessary to recount the measures to which an ever-vigilant Master resorted in order to assuage and eventually to dissipate their apprehensions. It is for the future historian to appraise the value of the mission of each of the four chosen messengers of 'Abdu'l-Bahá who, in rapid succession, were dispatched by Him to pacify and reinvigorate that troubled community. His will be the task of tracing, in the work which these deputies of 'Abdu'l-Bahá were commissioned to undertake, the beginnings of that vast Administration, the corner-stone of which these messengers were instructed to lay—an Administration whose symbolic Edifice He, at a later time, was to found in person and whose basis and scope the provisions of His Will were destined to widen.

Suffice it to say that at this stage of its evolution the activities of an invincible Faith had assumed such dimensions as to force on the one hand its enemies to devise fresh weapons for their projected assaults, and on the other to encourage its supreme Promoter to instruct its followers, through qualified representatives and teachers, in the rudiments of an Administration which, as it evolved, would at once incarnate, safeguard and foster its spirit. The works of such stubborn assailants as those of Vatralsky, Wilson, Jessup and Richardson vie with one another in their futile attempts to stain its purity, to arrest its march and compel its surrender. To the charges of Nihilism, of heresy, of Muḥammadan Gnosticism, of immorality, of Occultism and Communism so freely leveled against them, the undismayed victims of such outrageous denunciations, acting under the instructions of 'Abdu'l-Bahá, retorted by initiating a series of activities which by their very nature were to be the precursors of permanent, officially recognized administrative institutions. The inauguration of Chicago's first House of Spirituality designated by 'Abdu'l-Bahá as that city's "House of

Justice"; the establishment of the Bahá'í Publishing Society; the founding of the Green Acre Fellowship; the publication of the Star of the West; the holding of the first Bahá'í National Convention, synchronizing with the transference of the sacred remains of the Báb to its final resting-place on Mt. Carmel; the incorporation of the Bahá'í Temple Unity and the formation of the Executive Committee of the Mashriqu'l-Adhkár—these stand out as the most conspicuous accomplishments of the American believers which have immortalized the memory of the most turbulent period of their history. Launched through these very acts into the troublesome seas of ceaseless tribulation, piloted by the mighty arm of 'Abdu'l-Bahá and manned by the bold initiative and abundant vitality of a band of sorely-tried disciples, the Ark of Bahá'u'lláh's Covenant has, ever since those days, been steadily pursuing its course contemptuous of the storms of bitter misfortune that have raged, and which must continue to assail it, as it forges ahead towards the promised haven of undisturbed security and peace.

Unsatisfied with the achievements which crowned the concerted efforts of their elected representatives within the American continent, and emboldened by the initial success of their pioneer teachers, beyond its confines, in Great Britain, France and Germany, the community of the American believers resolved to win in distant climes fresh recruits to the advancing army of Bahá'u'lláh. Setting out from the western shores of their native land and impelled by the indomitable energy of a new-born faith, these itinerant teachers of the Gospel of Bahá'u'lláh pushed on towards the islands of the Pacific, and as far as China and Japan, determined to establish beyond the farthest seas the outposts of their beloved Faith. Both at home and abroad this community had by that time demonstrated its capacity to widen the range and consolidate the foundations of its vast endeavors. The angry voices that had been raised in protest against its rise were being drowned amid the acclamations with which the East greeted its recent victories. Those ugly features that had loomed so threateningly were gradually receding into the distance, furnishing a still wider field to these noble warriors for the exercise of their latent energies.

The Faith of Bahá'u'lláh in the continent of America had indeed been resuscitated. Phoenix-like it had risen in all its freshness,

vigor and beauty and was now, through the voice of its triumphant
exponents, insistingly calling to 'Abdu'l-Bahá, imploring Him to
undertake a journey to its shores. The first fruits of the mission
entrusted to its worthy upholders had lent such poignancy to their
call that 'Abdu'l-Bahá, Who had just been delivered from the
fetters of a galling tyranny, found Himself unable to resist. His
great, His incomparable, love for His own favored children impelled Him to respond. Their passionate entreaty had, moreover,
been reinforced by the numerous invitations which representatives
of various interested organizations, whether religious, educational
or humanitarian, had extended to Him, expressing their eagerness
to receive from His own mouth an exposition of His Father's
teachings.

Though bent with age, though suffering from ailments resulting
from the accumulated cares of fifty years of exile and captivity,
'Abdu'l-Bahá set out on His memorable journey across the seas
to the land where He might bless by His presence, and sanctify
through His deeds, the mighty acts His spirit had led His disciples
to perform. The circumstances that have attended His triumphal
progress through the chief cities of the United States and Canada
my pen is utterly incapable of describing. The joys which the announcement of His arrival evoked, the publicity which His activities
created, the forces which His utterances released, the opposition
which the implications of His teachings excited, the significant
episodes to which His words and deeds continually gave rise—
these future generations will, no doubt, minutely and befittingly
register. They will carefully delineate their features, will cherish
and preserve their memory, and will transmit unimpaired the record
of their minutest details to their descendants. It would indeed be
presumptuous on our part to attempt, at the present time, to sketch
even the bare outline of so vast, so enthralling a theme. Contemplating after the lapse of above twenty years this notable landmark
in America's spiritual history we still find ourselves compelled to
confess our inability to grasp its import or to fathom its mystery.
I have alluded in the preceding pages to a few of the more salient
features of that never-to-be-forgotten visit. These incidents, as we
look back upon them, eloquently proclaim 'Abdu'l-Bahá's specific
purpose to confer through these symbolic functions upon the first-

born of the communities of the West that spiritual primacy which was to be the birthright of the American believers.

The seeds which 'Abdu'l-Bahá's ceaseless activities so lavishly scattered had endowed the United States and Canada, nay the entire continent, with potentialities such as it had never known in its history. On the small band of His trained and beloved disciples, and through them on their descendants, He, through that visit, had bequeathed a priceless heritage—a heritage which carried with it the sacred and primary obligation to arise and carry on in that fertile field the work He had so gloriously initiated. We can dimly picture to ourselves the wishes that must have welled from His eager heart as He bade His last farewell to that promising country. An inscrutable Wisdom, we can well imagine Him remark to His disciples on the eve of His departure, has, in His infinite bounty singled out your native land for the execution of a mighty purpose. Through the agency of Bahá'u'lláh's Covenant I, as the ploughman, have been called upon since the beginning of my ministry to turn up and break its ground. The mighty confirmations that have, in the opening days of your career, rained upon you have prepared and invigorated its soil. The tribulations you subsequently were made to suffer have driven deep furrows into the field which my hands had prepared. The seeds with which I have been entrusted I have now scattered far and wide before you. Under your loving care, by your ceaseless exertions, every one of these seeds must germinate, every one must yield its destined fruit. A winter of unprecedented severity will soon be upon you. Its storm-clouds are fast gathering on the horizon. Tempestuous winds will assail you from every side. The Light of the Covenant will be obscured through my departure. These mighty blasts, this wintry desolation, shall however pass away. The dormant seed will burst into fresh activity. It shall put forth its buds, shall reveal, in mighty institutions, its leaves and blossoms. The vernal showers which the tender mercies of my heavenly Father will cause to descend upon you will enable this tender plant to spread out its branches to regions far beyond the confines of your native land. And finally the steadily mounting sun of His Revelation, shining in its meridian splendor, will enable this mighty Tree of His Faith to yield, in the fullness of time and on your soil, its golden fruit.

The implications of such a parting message could not long remain unrevealed to 'Abdu'l-Bahá's initiated disciples. No sooner had He concluded His long and arduous journey across the American and European continents than the tremendous happenings to which He had alluded began to be made manifest. A conflict, such as He had predicted, severed for a time all means of communication with those on whom He had come to place such implicit trust and from whom He was expecting so much in return. The wintry desolation, with all its havoc and carnage, pursued during four years its relentless course, while He, repairing to the quiet solitude of His residence in the close neighborhood of Bahá'u'lláh's hallowed shrine, continued to communicate His thoughts and wishes to those whom He had left behind and on whom He had conferred the unique tokens of His favor. In the immortal Tablets which, in the long hours of His communion with His dearly-beloved friends He was moved to reveal, He unfolded to their eyes His conception of their spiritual destiny, His Plan for the mission He wished them to undertake. The seeds His hands had sown He was now watering with that same care, that same love and patience, which had characterized His previous endeavors whilst He was laboring in their midst.

The clarion call which 'Abdu'l-Bahá had raised was the signal for an outburst of renewed activity which, alike in the motives it inspired and the forces it set in motion, America had scarcely experienced. Lending an unprecedented impetus to the work which the enterprising ambassadors of the Message of Bahá'u'lláh had initiated in distant lands, this mighty movement has continued to spread until the present day, has gathered momentum as it extended its ramifications over the surface of the globe, and will continue to accelerate its march until the last wishes of its original Promoter are completely fulfilled.

Forsaking home, kindred, friends and position a handful of men and women, fired with a zeal and confidence which no human agency can kindle, arose to carry out the mandate which 'Abdu'l-Bahá had issued. Sailing northward as far as Alaska, pushing on to the West Indies, penetrating the South American continent to the banks of the Amazon and across the Andes to the southernmost ends of the Argentine Republic, pressing on westward into the island of Tahiti and beyond it to the Australian continent and still beyond it as far as New Zealand and Tasmania, these intrepid heralds of the Faith of Bahá'u'lláh have succeeded by their very acts in setting to the present generation of their fellow-believers throughout the East an example which they may well emulate. Headed by their illustrious representative, who ever since the call of 'Abdu'l-Bahá was raised has been twice round the world and is still, with marvellous courage and fortitude, enriching the matchless record of her services, these men and women have been instrumental in extending, to a degree as yet unsurpassed in Bahá'í history, the sway of Bahá'u'lláh's universal dominion. In the face of almost insurmountable obstacles they have succeeded in most of the countries through which they have passed or in which they have resided, in proclaiming the teachings of their Faith, in circulating its literature, in defending its cause, in laying the basis of its institutions and in reinforcing the number of its declared supporters. It would be impossible for me to unfold in this short compass the tale of such heroic actions. Nor can any tribute of mine do justice to the spirit which has enabled these standardbearers of the Religion of God to win such laurels and to confer such distinction on the generation to which they belong.

The Cause of Bahá'u'lláh had by that time encircled the globe. Its light, born in darkest Persia, had been carried successively to the European, the African and the American continents, and was now penetrating the heart of Australia, encompassing thereby the whole earth with a girdle of shining glory. The share which such worthy, such stout-hearted, disciples have had in brightening the last days of 'Abdu'l-Bahá's earthly life He alone has truly recognized and can sufficiently estimate. The unique and eternal significance of such accomplishments the labors of the rising generation will assuredly reveal, their memory its works will befittingly preserve and extol. How deep a satisfaction 'Abdu'l-Bahá must have felt, while conscious of the approaching hour of His departure, as He witnessed the first fruits of the international services of these heroes of His Father's Faith! To their keeping He had committed a great and goodly heritage. In the twilight of His earthly life He could rest content in the serene assurance that such able hands could be relied upon to preserve its integrity and exalt its virtue.

The passing of 'Abdu'l-Bahá, so sudden in the circumstances which caused it, so dramatic in its consequences, could neither impede the operation of such a dynamic force nor obscure its purpose. Those fervid appeals, embodied in the Will and Testament of a departed Master, could not but confirm its aim, define its character and reinforce the promise of its ultimate success.

Out of the pangs of anguish which His bereaved followers have suffered, amid the heat and dust which the attacks launched by a sleepless enemy had precipitated, the Administration of Bahá'u'lláh's invincible Faith was born. The potent energies released through the ascension of the Center of His Covenant crystallized into this supreme, this infallible Organ for the accomplishment of a Divine Purpose. The Will and Testament of 'Abdu'l-Bahá unveiled its character, reaffirmed its basis, supplemented its principles, asserted its indispensability, and enumerated its chief institutions. With that self-same spontaneity which had characterized her response to the Message proclaimed by Bahá'u'lláh America had now arisen to espouse the cause of the Administration which the Will and Testament of His Son had unmistakably established. It was given to her, and to her alone, in the turbulent years following the revelation of so momentous a Document, to become the fearless champion of that Administration, the pivot of its new-born institutions and the leading promoter of its influence. To their Persian brethren, who in the heroic age of the Faith had won the crown of martyrdom, the American believers, forerunners of its golden age, were now worthily succeeding, bearing in their turn the palm of a hard-won victory. The unbroken record of their illustrious deeds had established beyond the shadow of a doubt their preponderating share in shaping the destinies of their Faith. In a world writhing with pain and declining into chaos this community— the vanguard of the liberating forces of Bahá'u'lláh—succeeded in the years following 'Abdu'l-Bahá's passing in raising high above the institutions established by its sister communities in East and West what may well constitute the chief pillar of that future House —a House which posterity will regard as the last refuge of a tottering civilization.

In the prosecution of their task neither the whisperings of the treacherous nor the virulent attacks of their avowed enemies were allowed to deflect them from their high purpose or to undermine their faith in the sublimity of their calling. The agitation provoked by him who in his incessant and sordid pursuit of earthly riches would have, but for 'Abdu'l-Bahá's warning, sullied the fair name of their Faith, had left them in the main undisturbed. Schooled by tribulation and secure within the stronghold of their fast evolving institutions they scorned his insinuations and by their unswerving loyalty were able to shatter his hopes. They refused to allow any consideration of the admitted prestige and past services of his father and of his associates to weaken their determination to ignore entirely the person whom 'Abdu'l-Bahá had so emphatically condemned. The veiled attacks with which a handful of deluded enthusiasts subsequently sought in the pages of their periodical to check the growth and blight the prospects of an infant Administration had likewise failed to achieve their purpose. The attitude which a besotted woman later on assumed, her ludicrous assertions, her boldness in flouting the Will of 'Abdu'l-Bahá and in challenging its authenticity and her attempts to subvert its principles were again powerless to produce the slightest breach in the ranks of its valiant upholders. The treacherous schemes which the ambition of a perfidious and still more recent enemy has devised and through which he is still striving to deface 'Abdu'l-Bahá's noble handiwork and corrupt its administrative principles are being once more completely frustrated. These intermittent and abortive attempts on the part of its assailants to force the surrender of the newly built stronghold of the Faith its defenders have from the very beginning utterly disdained. No matter how fierce the assaults of the enemy or skillful his stratagem they have refused to yield one jot or one tittle of their cherished convictions. His insinuations and clamor they have consistently ignored. The motives which animated his actions, the methods he steadily pursued, the precarious privileges he seemed momentarily to enjoy they could not but despise. Thriving for a time through the devices which their scheming minds had conceived and supported by the ephemeral advantages which fame, ability or fortune can confer these notorious exponents of corruption and heresy have succeeded in protruding for a time their ugly features only to sink, as rapidly as they had risen, into the mire of an ignominious end.

From the midst of these afflictive trials, reminiscent in some of their aspects of the violent storm that had accompanied the birth of the Faith in their native land, the American believers had again triumphantly emerged, their course undeflected, their fame unsullied, their heritage unimpaired. A series of magnificent accomplishments, each more significant than the previous, were to shed increasing lustre on an already illustrious record. In the dark years immediately following 'Abdu'l-Bahá's ascension their deeds shone with a radiance that made them the object of the envy and the admiration of the less privileged among their brethren. The entire community, untrammeled and supremely confident, was rising to a great and glorious opportunity. The forces that had motivated its birth, that had assisted in its rise, were now accelerating its growth, in a manner and with such rapidity that neither the pangs of a world-wide sorrow nor the unceasing convulsions of a distracted age could paralyze its efforts or retard its march.

Internally the community had embarked in a number of enterprises that were to enable it on the one hand to extend still further the scope of its spiritual jurisdiction and on the other to fashion the essential instruments for the creation and consolidation of the institutions which such an extension imperatively demanded. Externally its undertakings were inspired by the twofold objective of prosecuting, even more intensely than before, the admirable work which in each of the five continents its international teachers had initiated, and of assuming an increasing share in the handling and solution of the delicate and complex problems with which a newly-emancipated Faith was being confronted. The birth of the Administration in that continent had signalized these praiseworthy exertions. Its gradual consolidation was destined to insure their continuance and to accentuate their effectiveness.

To enumerate only the most outstanding accomplishments which, in their own country and beyond its confines, have so greatly enhanced the prestige of the American believers and have redounded to the glory and honor of the Most Great Name is all I can presently undertake, leaving to future generations the task of explaining their import and of affixing a fitting estimate to their value. To the body of their elected representatives must be attributed the honor of having been the first among their sister Assemblies of East and

West to devise, promulgate and legalize the essential instruments for the effective discharge of their collective duties—instruments which every properly constituted Bahá'í community must regard as a pattern worthy to be adopted and copied. To their efforts must likewise be ascribed the historic achievement of establishing their national endowments upon a permanent and unassailable basis and of creating the necessary agency for the formation of those subsidiary organs whose function is to administer on behalf of their trustees such possessions as these may acquire beyond the limits of their immediate jurisdiction. By the weight of their moral support so freely extended to their Egyptian brethren they were able to remove some of the most formidable obstacles which the Faith had to surmount in its struggle to enfranchise itself from the fetters of Muslim orthodoxy. Through the effective and timely intervention of these same elected representatives they were able to avert the woes and dangers which had menaced their persecuted fellow-workers in the Soviet Republics, and to ward off the rage which had threatened with immediate ruin one of the most precious and noblest of Bahá'í institutions. Nothing short of the whole-hearted assistance, whether moral or financial which the American believers, individually and collectively, were moved to extend on several occasions to the needy and harassed among their brethren in Persia could have saved these hapless victims of the consequences of the calamities that had visited them in the years following 'Abdu'l-Bahá's ascension. It was the publicity which the efforts of their American brethren had created, the protests they were led to make, the appeals and petitions they had submitted, which mitigated these sufferings and curbed the violence of the worst and most tyrannical opponents of the Faith in that land. Who else, if not one of their most distinguished representatives, has risen to force upon the attention of the highest Tribunal the world has yet seen the grievances which a Faith, robbed of one of its holiest sanctuaries, had suffered at the hand of the usurper? Who else has succeeded in securing, through patient and persistent effort, those written affirmations which proclaim the justice of a persecuted cause and tacitly recognize its right to an independent religious status? "The Commission," is the resolution passed by the Permanent Mandates Commission of the League of Nations, "recommends that the Council

should ask the British Government to make representations to the
'Iráqí Government with a view to the immediate redress of the
denial of justice from which the petitioners (the Bahá'í Spiritual
Assembly of Baghdád) have suffered." Has any one else except
an American believer been led to obtain from royalty such remarkable and repeated testimonies to the regenerating power of
the Faith of God, such striking references to the universality of
its teachings and the sublimity of its mission. "The Bahá'í teaching," such is the Queen's written testimony, "brings peace and understanding. It is like a wide embrace gathering together all those
who have long searched for words of hope. It accepts all great
Prophets gone before, it destroys no other creeds and leaves all
doors open. Saddened by the continual strife amongst believers of
many confessions and wearied of their intolerance towards each
other, I discovered in the Bahá'í teaching the real spirit of Christ
so often denied and misunderstood: Unity instead of strife, Hope
instead of condemnation, Love instead of hate, and a great reas-
surance for all men." Have not the American adherents of the
Faith of Bahá'u'lláh, through the courage displayed by one of the
most brilliant members of their community, been instrumental in
paving the way for the removal of those barriers which have, for
well-nigh a century, hampered the growth and crippled the energy
of their fellow-believers in Persia? Is it not America who, ever
mindful of 'Abdu'l-Bahá's passionate entreaty, has sent out to the
ends of the earth a steadily increasing number of its most consecrated citizens—men and women the one wish of whose lives is to
consolidate the foundations of Bahá'u'lláh's world-embracing dominion? In the northernmost capitals of Europe, in most of its
central states, throughout the Balkan Peninsula, along the shores
of the African, the Asiatic and South American continents are to
be found this day a small band of women pioneers who, single-
handed and with scanty resources, are toiling for the advent of the
Day 'Abdu'l-Bahá has foretold. Did not the attitude of the Greatest
Holy Leaf, as she approached the close of her life, bear eloquent
testimony to the incomparable share which her steadfast and self-
sacrificing lovers in that continent have had in lightening the burden
which had weighed so long and so heavily on her heart? And
finally who can be so bold as to deny that the completion of the

superstructure of the Mashriqu'l-Adhkár—the crowning glory of America's past and present achievements—has forged that mystic chain which is to link, more firmly than ever, the hearts of its champion-builders with Him Who is the Source and Center of their Faith and the Object of their truest adoration?

Fellow-believers in the American continent! Great indeed have been your past and present achievements! Immeasurably greater are the wonders which the future has in store for you! The Edifice your sacrifices have raised still remains to be clothed. The House which must needs be supported by the highest administrative institution your hands have reared, is as yet unbuilt. The provisions of the chief Repository of those laws that must govern its operation are thus far mostly undisclosed. The Standard which, if 'Abdu'l-Bahá's wishes are to be fulfilled, must be raised in your own country has yet to be unfurled. The Unity of which that standard is to be the symbol is far from being yet established. The machinery which must needs incarnate and preserve that unity is not even created. Will it be America, will it be one of the countries of Europe, who will arise to assume the leadership essential to the shaping of the destinies of this troubled age? Will America allow any of her sister communities in East or West to achieve such ascendancy as shall deprive her of that spiritual primacy with which she has been invested and which she has thus far so nobly retained? Will she not rather contribute, by a still further revelation of those inherent powers that motivate her life, to enhance the priceless heritage which the love and wisdom of a departed Master have conferred upon her?

Her past has been a testimony to the inexhaustible vitality of her faith. May not her future confirm it?

Your true brother,

SHOGHI.

Haifa, Palestine,
April 21, 1933.

THE DISPENSATION OF BAHÁ'U'LLÁH

THE DISPENSATION
OF BAHÁ'U'LLÁH

*To the beloved of God and the handmaids of the Merciful through-
out the West.*

Fellow-laborers in the Divine Vineyard:

On the 23rd of May of this auspicious year the Bahá'í world
will celebrate the 90th anniversary of the founding of the Faith of
Bahá'u'lláh. We, who at this hour find ourselves standing on the
threshold of the last decade of the first century of the Bahá'í era,
might well pause to reflect upon the mysterious dispensations of so
august, so momentous a Revelation. How vast, how entrancing the
panorama which the revolution of four score years and ten unrolls
before our eyes! Its towering grandeur well-nigh overwhelms us.
To merely contemplate this unique spectacle, to visualize, however
dimly, the circumstances attending the birth and gradual unfoldment of this supreme Theophany, to recall even in their barest outline the woeful struggles that proclaimed its rise and accelerated its
march, will suffice to convince every unbiased observer of those
eternal truths that motivate its life and which must continue to
impel it forward until it achieves its destined ascendancy.

Dominating the entire range of this fascinating spectacle towers
the incomparable figure of Bahá'u'lláh, transcendental in His
majesty, serene, awe-inspiring, unapproachably glorious. Allied,
though subordinate in rank, and invested with the authority of
presiding with Him over the destinies of this supreme Dispensation,
there shines upon this mental picture the youthful glory of the Báb,
infinite in His tenderness, irresistible in His charm, unsurpassed in
His heroism, matchless in the dramatic circumstances of His short
yet eventful life. And finally there emerges, though on a plane of
its own and in a category entirely apart from the one occupied by
the twin Figures that preceded Him, the vibrant, the magnetic personality of 'Abdu'l-Bahá, reflecting to a degree that no man, how-

97

ever exalted his station, can hope to rival, the glory and power with which They who are the Manifestations of God are alone endowed.

With 'Abdu'l-Bahá's ascension, and more particularly with the passing of His well-beloved and illustrious sister the Most Exalted Leaf—the last survivor of a glorious and heroic age—there draws to a close the first and most moving chapter of Bahá'í history, marking the conclusion of the Primitive, the Apostolic Age of the Faith of Bahá'u'lláh. It was 'Abdu'l-Bahá Who, through the provisions of His weighty Will and Testament, has forged the vital link which must for ever connect the age that has just expired with the one we now live in—the Transitional and Formative period of the Faith—a stage that must in the fullness of time reach its blossom and yield its fruit in the exploits and triumphs that are to herald the Golden Age of the Revelation of Bahá'u'lláh.

Dearly-beloved friends! The onrushing forces so miraculously released through the agency of two independent and swiftly successive Manifestations are now under our very eyes and through the care of the chosen stewards of a far-flung Faith being gradually mustered and disciplined. They are slowly crystallizing into institutions that will come to be regarded as the hall-mark and glory of the age we are called upon to establish and by our deeds immortalize. For upon our present-day efforts, and above all upon the extent to which we strive to remodel our lives after the pattern of sublime heroism associated with those gone before us, must depend the efficacy of the instruments we now fashion—instruments that must erect the structure of that blissful Commonwealth which must signalize the Golden Age of our Faith.

It is not my purpose, as I look back upon these crowded years of heroic deeds, to attempt even a cursory review of the mighty events that have transpired since 1844 until the present day. Nor have I any intention to undertake an analysis of the forces that have precipitated them, or to evaluate their influence upon peoples and institutions in almost every continent of the globe. The authentic record of the lives of the first believers of the primitive period of our Faith, together with the assiduous research which competent Bahá'í historians will in the future undertake, will combine to transmit to posterity such masterly exposition of the history of that age as my own efforts can never hope to accomplish. My chief concern at this challenging period of Bahá'í history is rather to call the attention of those who are destined to be the champion-builders of the Administrative Order of Bahá'u'lláh to certain fundamental verities the elucidation of which must tremendously assist them in the effective prosecution of their mighty enterprise.

The international status which the Religion of God has thus far achieved, moreover, imperatively demands that its root principles be now definitely clarified. The unprecedented impetus which the illustrious deeds of the American believers have lent to the onward march of the Faith; the intense interest which the first Mashriqu'l-Adhkár of the West is fast awakening among divers races and nations; the rise and steady consolidation of Bahá'í institutions in no less than forty of the most advanced countries of the world; the dissemination of Bahá'í literature in no fewer than twenty-five of the most widely-spoken languages; the success that has recently attended the nation-wide efforts of the Persian believers in the preliminary steps they have taken for the establishment, in the outskirts of the capital-city of their native land, of the third Mashriqu'l-Adhkár of the Bahá'í world; the measures that are being taken for the immediate formation of their first National Spiritual Assembly representing the interests of the overwhelming majority of Bahá'í adherents; the projected erection of yet another pillar of the Universal House of Justice, the first of its kind, in the Southern Hemisphere; the testimonies, both verbal and written, that a struggling Faith has obtained from Royalty, from governmental institutions, international tribunals, and ecclesiastical dignitaries; the publicity it has received from the charges which unrelenting enemies, both new and old, have hurled against it; the formal enfranchisement of a section of its followers from the fetters of Muslim orthodoxy in a country that may be regarded as the most enlightened among Islamic nations—these afford ample proof of the growing momentum with which the invincible community of the Most Great Name is marching forward to ultimate victory.

Dearly-beloved friends! I feel it incumbent upon me, by virtue of the obligations and responsibilities which as Guardian of the Faith of Bahá'u'lláh I am called upon to discharge, to lay special stress, at a time when the light of publicity is being increasingly focussed upon us, upon certain truths which lie at the basis of our Faith and the integrity of which it is our first duty to safeguard. These verities, if valiantly upheld and properly assimilated, will, I am convinced, powerfully reinforce the vigor of our spiritual life and greatly assist in counteracting the machinations of an implacable and vigilant enemy.

To strive to obtain a more adequate understanding of the significance of Bahá'u'lláh's stupendous Revelation must, it is my unalterable conviction, remain the first obligation and the object of the constant endeavor of each one of its loyal adherents. An exact and thorough comprehension of so vast a system, so sublime a revelation, so sacred a trust, is for obvious reasons beyond the reach and ken of our finite minds. We can, however, and it is our bounden duty to seek to derive fresh inspiration and added sustenance as we labor for the propagation of His Faith through a clearer apprehension of the truths it enshrines and the principles on which it is based.

In a communication addressed to the American believers I have in the course of my explanation of the station of the Báb made a passing reference to the incomparable greatness of the Revelation of which He considered Himself to be the humble Precursor. He Whom Bahá'u'lláh has acclaimed in the Kitáb-i-Íqán as that promised Qá'im Who has manifested no less than twenty-five out of the twenty-seven letters which all the Prophets were destined to reveal—so great a Revealer has Himself testified to the preëminence of that superior Revelation that was soon to supersede His own. *"The germ,"* the Báb asserts in the Persian Bayán, *"that holds within itself the potentialities of the Revelation that is to come is endowed with a potency superior to the combined forces of all those who follow me."* *"Of all the tributes,"* He again affirms, *"I have paid to Him Who is to come after Me, the greatest is this, My written confession, that no words of Mine can adequately describe Him, nor can any reference to Him in My Book, the Bayán, do justice to His Cause."* *"The Bayán,"* He in that same Book categorically declares, *"and whosoever is therein revolve round the saying of 'Him Whom God shall make manifest,' even as the Alif* (the Gospel) *and whosoever was therein revolved round the saying of Muḥammad, the Apostle of God."* *"A thousand perusals of the Bayán,"* He further remarks, *"cannot equal the perusal of a single verse to be revealed by 'Him Whom God shall make manifest.' . . . Today the Bayán is in the stage of seed; at the beginning of the manifestation of 'Him Whom God shall make manifest' its ultimate perfection will become apparent. . . . The Bayán and such as are believers therein yearn more ardently after Him than the yearning of any lover after his beloved. . . . The Bayán deriveth all its glory from*

'Him Whom God shall make manifest.' All blessing be upon him who believeth in Him and woe betide him that rejecteth His truth."

Addressing Siyyid Yaḥyáy-i-Dárábí surnamed Vaḥíd, the most learned, the most eloquent and influential among His followers, the Báb utters this warning: *"By the righteousness of Him Whose power causeth the seed to germinate and Who breatheth the spirit of life into all things, were I to be assured that in the day of His manifestation thou wilt deny Him, I would unhesitatingly disown thee and repudiate thy faith. . . . If, on the other hand, I be told that a Christian, who beareth no allegiance to My Faith, will believe in Him, the same will I regard as the apple of Mine Eye."*

In one of His prayers He thus communes with Bahá'u'lláh: *"Exalted art Thou, O my Lord the Omnipotent! How puny and contemptible my word and all that pertaineth unto me appear unless they be related to Thy great glory. Grant that through the assistance of Thy grace whatsoever pertaineth unto me may be acceptable in Thy sight."*

In the Qayyúmu'l-Asmá'—the Báb's commentary on the Súrih of Joseph—characterized by the Author of the Íqán as *"the first, the greatest and mightiest"* of the books revealed by the Báb, we read the following references to Bahá'u'lláh: *"Out of utter nothingness, O great and omnipotent Master, Thou hast, through the celestial potency of Thy might, brought me forth and raised me up to proclaim this Revelation. I have made none other but Thee my trust; I have clung to no will but Thy will . . . O Thou Remnant of God! I have sacrificed myself wholly for Thee: I have accepted curses for Thy sake, and have yearned for naught but martyrdom in the path of Thy love. Sufficient witness unto me is God, the Exalted, the Protector, the Ancient of Days." "And when the appointed hour hath struck,"* He again addresses Bahá'u'lláh in that same commentary, *"do Thou, by the leave of God, the All-Wise, reveal from the heights of the Most Lofty and Mystic Mount a faint, an infinitesimal glimmer of Thy impenetrable Mystery, that they who have recognized the radiance of the Sinaic Splendor may faint away and die as they catch a lightening glimpse of the fierce and crimson Light that envelops Thy Revelation."*

As a further testimony to the greatness of the Revelation identified with Bahá'u'lláh may be cited the following extracts from a Tablet addressed by 'Abdu'l-Bahá to an eminent Zoroastrian follower of the Faith: *"Thou hadst written that in the sacred books of the followers of Zoroaster it is written that in the latter days, in three separate Dispensations, the sun must needs be brought to a standstill. In the first Dispensation, it is predicted, the sun will remain motionless for ten days; in the second for twice that time; in the third for no less than one whole month. The interpretation of this prophecy is this: the first Dispensation to which it refers is the Muhammadan Dispensation during which the Sun of Truth stood still for ten days. Each day is reckoned as one century. The Muhammadan Dispensation must have, therefore, lasted no less than one thousand years, which is precisely the period that has elapsed from the setting of the Star of the Imamate to the advent of the Dispensation proclaimed by the Báb. The second Dispensation referred to in this prophecy is the one inaugurated by the Báb Himself, which began in the year 1260 A.H. and was brought to a close in the year 1280 A.H. As to the third Dispensation—the Revelation proclaimed by Bahá'u'lláh—inasmuch as the Sun of Truth when attaining that station shineth in the plenitude of its meridian splendor its duration hath been fixed for a period of one whole month, which is the maximum time taken by the sun to pass through a sign of the Zodiac. From this thou canst imagine the magnitude of the Bahá'í cycle—a cycle that must extend over a period of at least five hundred thousand years."*

From the text of this explicit and authoritative interpretation of so ancient a prophecy it is evident how necessary it is for every faithful follower of the Faith to accept the divine origin and uphold the independent status of the Muhammadan Dispensation. The validity of the Imamate is, moreover, implicitly recognized in these same passages—that divinely-appointed institution of whose most distinguished member the Báb Himself was a lineal descendant, and which continued for a period of no less than two hundred and sixty years to be the chosen recipient of the guidance of the Almighty and the repository of one of the two most precious legacies of Islám.

This same prophecy, we must furthermore recognize, attests the independent character of the Bábí Dispensation and corroborates indirectly the truth that in accordance with the principle of progressive revelation every Manifestation of God must needs vouchsafe to the peoples of His day a measure of divine guidance ampler than any which a preceding and less receptive age could have received or appreciated. For this reason, and not for any superior merit which the Bahá'í Faith may be said to inherently possess, does this prophecy bear witness to the unrivaled power and glory with which the Dispensation of Bahá'u'lláh has been invested—a Dispensation the potentialities of which we are but beginning to perceive and the full range of which we can never determine.

The Faith of Bahá'u'lláh should indeed be regarded, if we wish to be faithful to the tremendous implications of its message, as the culmination of a cycle, the final stage in a series of successive, of preliminary and progressive revelations. These, beginning with Adam and ending with the Báb, have paved the way and anticipated with an ever-increasing emphasis the advent of that Day of Days in which He Who is the Promise of All Ages should be made manifest.

To this truth the utterances of Bahá'u'lláh abundantly testify. A mere reference to the claims which, in vehement language and with compelling power, He Himself has repeatedly advanced cannot but fully demonstrate the character of the Revelation of which He was the chosen bearer. To the words that have streamed from His pen—the fountainhead of so impetuous a Revelation—we should, therefore, direct our attention if we wish to obtain a clearer understanding of its importance and meaning. Whether in His assertion of the unprecedented claim He has advanced, or in His allusions to the mysterious forces He has released, whether in such passages as extol the glories of His long-awaited Day, or magnify the station which they who have recognized its hidden virtues will attain, Bahá'u'lláh and, to an almost equal extent, the Báb and 'Abdu'l-Bahá, have bequeathed to posterity mines of such inestimable wealth as none of us who belong to this generation can befittingly estimate. Such testimonies bearing on this theme are impregnated with such power and reveal such beauty as only those who are versed in the languages in which they were originally revealed can claim to have sufficiently appreciated. So numerous are these testimonies that a whole volume would be required to be written in order to compile the most outstanding among them. All I can venture to attempt at present is to share with you only such passages as I have been able to glean from His voluminous writings.

"I testify before God," proclaims Bahá'u'lláh, "to the greatness, the inconceivable greatness of this Revelation. Again and again have We in most of Our Tablets borne witness to this truth, that mankind may be roused from its heedlessness." "In this most mighty Revelation," He unequivocally announces, "all the Dispensations of the past have attained their highest, their final consummation." "That which hath been made manifest in this preëminent, this most exalted Revelation, stands unparalleled in the annals of the past, nor

will future ages witness its like." "He it is," referring to Himself
He further proclaims, *"Who in the Old Testament hath been named
Jehovah, Who in the Gospel hath been designated as the Spirit of
Truth, and in the Qur'án acclaimed as the Great Announcement."
"But for Him no Divine Messenger would have been invested with
the robe of prophethood, nor would any of the sacred scriptures
have been revealed. To this bear witness all created things." "The
word which the one true God uttereth in this day, though that word
be the most familiar and commonplace of terms, is invested with
supreme, with unique distinction." "The generality of mankind is
still immature. Had it acquired sufficient capacity We would have
bestowed upon it so great a measure of Our knowledge that all who
dwell on earth and in heaven would have found themselves, by
virtue of the grace streaming from Our pen, completely independent
of all knowledge save the knowledge of God, and would have been
securely established upon the throne of abiding tranquillity." "The
Pen of Holiness, I solemnly affirm before God, hath writ upon My
snow-white brow and in characters of effulgent glory these glowing,
these musk-scented and holy words: 'Behold ye that dwell on earth,
and ye denizens of heaven, bear witness, He in truth is your Well-
Beloved. He it is Whose like the world of creation hath not seen, He
Whose ravishing beauty hath delighted the eye of God, the Ordainer,
the All-Powerful, the Incomparable!' "*

"Followers of the Gospel," Bahá'u'lláh addressing the whole of
Christendom exclaims, *"behold the gates of heaven are flung open.
He that had ascended unto it is now come. Give ear to His voice
calling aloud over land and sea, announcing to all mankind the
advent of this Revelation—a Revelation through the agency of
which the Tongue of Grandeur is now proclaiming: 'Lo, the sacred
Pledge hath been fulfilled, for He, the Promised One, is come!' "
"The voice of the Son of Man is calling aloud from the sacred vale:
'Here am I, here am I, O God my God!' . . . whilst from the Burning Bush breaketh forth the cry: 'Lo, the Desire of the world is made
manifest in His transcendent glory!' The Father hath come. That
which ye were promised in the Kingdom of God is fulfilled. This is
the Word which the Son veiled when He said to those around Him
that at that time they could not bear it . . . Verily the Spirit of
Truth is come to guide you unto all truth . . . He is the One Who
glorified the Son and exalted His Cause . . ." "The Comforter
Whose advent all the scriptures have promised is now come that He*

may reveal unto you all knowledge and wisdom. Seek Him over the entire surface of the earth, haply ye may find Him."

"*Call out to Zion, O Carmel,*" writes Bahá'u'lláh, "*and announce the joyful tidings: 'He that was hidden from mortal eyes is come! His all-conquering sovereignty is manifest; His all-encompassing splendor is revealed . . . Hasten forth and circumambulate the City of God that hath descended from heaven—the celestial Kaaba round which have circled in adoration the favored of God, the pure in heart and the company of the most exalted angels.'*" "*I am the One,*" He in another connection affirms, "*Whom the tongue of Isaiah hath extolled, the One with Whose name both the Torah and the Evangel were adorned.*" "*The glory of Sinai hath hastened to circle round the Day-Spring of this Revelation, while from the heights of the Kingdom the voice of the Son of God is heard proclaiming: 'Bestir yourselves, ye proud ones of the earth, and hasten ye towards Him.' Carmel hath in this day hastened in longing adoration to attain His court, whilst from the heart of Zion there cometh the cry: 'The promise of all ages is now fulfilled. That which had been announced in the holy writ of God, the Beloved, the Most High, is made manifest.'*" "*Ḥijáz is astir by the breeze announcing the tidings of joyous reunion. 'Praise be to Thee,' We hear her exclaim, 'O my Lord, the Most High. I was dead through my separation from Thee; the breeze laden with the fragrance of Thy presence hath brought me back to life. Happy is he that turneth unto Thee, and woe betide the erring.'*" "*By the one true God, Elijah hath hastened unto My court and hath circumambulated in the day-time and in the night-season My throne of glory.*" "*Solomon in all his majesty circles in adoration around Me in this day, uttering this most exalted word: 'I have turned my face towards Thy face, O Thou omnipotent Ruler of the world! I am wholly detached from all things pertaining unto me, and yearn for that which Thou dost possess.'*" "*Had Muḥammad, the Apostle of God, attained this Day,*" Bahá'u'lláh writes in a Tablet revealed on the eve of His banishment to the penal colony of 'Akká, "*He would have exclaimed: 'I have truly recognized Thee, O Thou the Desire of the Divine Messengers!' Had Abraham attained it, He too, falling prostrate upon the ground, and in the utmost lowliness before the Lord thy God, would have cried: 'Mine heart is filled with peace, O Thou Lord of all that is in heaven and on earth! I testify that Thou hast unveiled before mine eyes all the glory of Thy power and the full majesty of Thy law!' . . . Had Moses Himself attained it, He, likewise, would have raised His voice saying: 'All praise be to Thee for having lifted upon me the light of Thy countenance and enrolled me among them that have been privileged to behold Thy face!' " "North and South both vibrate to the call announcing the advent of our Revelation. We can hear the voice of Mecca acclaiming: 'All praise be to Thee, O Lord my God, the All-Glorious, for having wafted over me the breath redolent with the fragrance of Thy presence!' Jerusalem, likewise, is calling aloud: 'Lauded and magnified art Thou, O Beloved of earth and heaven, for having turned the agony of my separation from Thee into the joy of a life-giving reunion!' "*

"By the righteousness of God," Bahá'u'lláh wishing to reveal the full potency of His invincible power asserts, *"should a man, all alone, arise in the name of Bahá and put on the armor of His love, him will the Almighty cause to be victorious, though the forces of earth and heaven be arrayed against him." "By God besides Whom is none other God! Should any one arise for the triumph of our Cause, him will God render victorious though tens of thousands of enemies be leagued against him. And if his love for Me wax stronger, God will establish his ascendancy over all the powers of earth and heaven. Thus have We breathed the spirit of power into all regions."*

"This is the King of Days," He thus extols the age that has witnessed the advent of His Revelation, *"the Day that hath seen the coming of the Best-beloved, Him Who through all eternity hath been acclaimed the Desire of the World." "The world of being shineth in this Day with the resplendency of this Divine Revelation. All created things extol its saving grace and sing its praises. The universe is wrapt in an ecstasy of joy and gladness. The Scriptures of past Dispensations celebrate the great jubilee that must needs greet this most great Day of God. Well is it with him that hath lived to see this Day and hath recognized its station." "Were mankind to give heed in a befitting manner to no more than one word of such a praise it would be so filled with delight as to be overpowered and lost in wonder. Entranced, it would then shine forth resplendent above the horizon of true understanding."*

"Be fair, ye peoples of the world," He thus appeals to mankind, *"is it meet and seemly for you to question the authority of one Whose presence 'He Who conversed with God' (Moses) hath longed to attain, the beauty of Whose countenance 'God's Well-beloved' (Muḥammad) had yearned to behold, through the potency of Whose love the 'Spirit of God' (Jesus) ascended to heaven, for Whose sake*

the 'Primal Point' (the Báb) *offered up His life?" "Seize your chance,"* He admonishes His followers, *"inasmuch as a fleeting moment in this Day excelleth centuries of a bygone age . . . Neither sun nor moon hath witnessed a day such as this . . . It is evident that every age in which a Manifestation of God hath lived is divinely ordained and may, in a sense, be characterized as God's appointed Day. This Day, however, is unique and is to be distinguished from those that have preceded it. The designation 'Seal of the Prophets' fully reveals and demonstrates its high station."*

Expatiating on the forces latent in His Revelation Bahá'u'lláh reveals the following: *"Through the movement of Our Pen of glory We have, at the bidding of the omnipotent Ordainer, breathed a new life into every human frame and instilled into every word a fresh potency. All created things proclaim the evidences of this world-wide regeneration." "This is,"* He adds, *"the most great, the most joyful tidings imparted by the pen of this wronged One to mankind." "How great,"* He in another passage exclaims, *"is the Cause! How staggering the weight of its message! This is the Day of which it hath been said: 'O my son! verily God will bring everything to light though it were but the weight of a grain of mustard seed, and hidden in a rock, or in the heavens or in the earth; for God is subtle, informed of all.' " "By the righteousness of the one true God! If one speck of a jewel be lost and buried beneath a mountain of stones, and lie hidden beyond the seven seas, the Hand of Omnipotence will assuredly reveal it in this day, pure and cleansed from dross." "He that partaketh of the waters of My Revelation will taste all the incorruptible delights ordained by God from the beginning that hath no beginning to the end that hath no end." "Every single letter proceeding from Our mouth is endowed with such regenerative power as to enable it to bring into existence a new creation—a creation the magnitude of which is inscrutable to all save God. He verily hath knowledge of all things." "It is in Our power, should We wish it, to enable a speck of floating dust to generate, in less than the twinkling of an eye, suns of infinite, of unimaginable splendor, to cause a dewdrop to develop into vast and numberless oceans, to infuse into every letter such a force as to empower it to unfold all the knowledge of past and future ages." "We are possessed of such power which, if brought to light, will transmute the most deadly of poisons into a panacea of unfailing efficacy."*

Estimating the station of the true believer He remarks: *"By the sorrows which afflict the beauty of the All-Glorious! Such is the station ordained for the true believer that if to an extent smaller than a needle's eye the glory of that station were to be unveiled to mankind, every beholder would be consumed away in his longing to attain it. For this reason it hath been decreed that in this earthly life the full measure of the glory of his own station should remain concealed from the eyes of such a believer."* "If the veil be lifted," He similarly affirms, *"and the full glory of the station of those who have turned wholly towards God, and in their love for Him renounced the world, be made manifest, the entire creation would be dumbfounded."*

Stressing the superlative character of His Revelation as compared with the Dispensation preceding it, Bahá'u'lláh makes the following affirmation: *"If all the peoples of the world be invested with the powers and attributes destined for the Letters of the Living, the Báb's chosen disciples, whose station is ten thousand times more glorious than any which the apostles of old have attained, and if they, one and all, should, swift as the twinkling of an eye, hesitate to recognize the light of My Revelation, their faith shall be of no avail and they shall be accounted among the infidels."* "So tremendous is the outpouring of Divine grace in this Dispensation that if mortal hands could be swift enough to record them, within the space of a single day and night there would stream verses of such number as to be equivalent to the whole of the Persian Bayán."*

"Give heed to my warning, ye people of Persia," He thus addresses His countrymen, *"If I be slain at your hands, God will assuredly raise up one who will fill the seat made vacant through my death; for such is God's method carried into effect of old, and no change can ye find in God's mode of dealing."* "Should they attempt to conceal His light on the continent, He will assuredly rear His head in the midmost heart of the ocean and, raising His voice, proclaim: 'I am the lifegiver of the world!' . . . And if they cast Him into a darksome pit, they will find Him seated on earth's loftiest heights calling aloud to all mankind: 'Lo, the Desire of the world is come in His majesty, His sovereignty, His transcendent dominion!' And if He be buried beneath the depths of the earth, His Spirit soaring to the apex of heaven shall peal the summons: 'Behold ye the coming of the Glory; witness ye the Kingdom of God, the most Holy, the Gracious, the All-Powerful!' "* "Within the throat of this Youth,"* is yet another astounding statement, *"there lie*

prisoned accents which, if revealed to mankind to an extent smaller than a needle's eye, would suffice to cause every mountain to crumble, the leaves of the trees to be discolored and their fruits to fall; would compel every head to bow down in worship and every face to turn in adoration towards this omnipotent Ruler Who, at sundry times and in diverse manners, appeareth as a devouring flame, as a billowing ocean, as a radiant light, as the tree which, rooted in the soil of holiness, lifteth its branches and spreadeth out its limbs as far as and beyond the throne of deathless glory."

Anticipating the System which the irresistible power of His Law was destined to unfold in a later age, He writes: *"The world's equilibrium hath been upset through the vibrating influence of this most great, this new World Order. Mankind's ordered life hath been revolutionized through the agency of this unique, this wondrous System—the like of which mortal eyes have never witnessed." "The Hand of Omnipotence hath established His Revelation upon an unassailable, an enduring foundation. Storms of human strife are powerless to undermine its basis, nor will men's fanciful theories succeed in damaging its structure."*

In the Súratu'l-Haykal, one of the most challenging works of Bahá'u'lláh, the following verses, each of which testifies to the resistless power infused into the Revelation proclaimed by its Author, have been recorded: *"Naught is seen in My temple but the Temple of God, and in My beauty but His Beauty, and in My being but His Being, and in My self but His Self, and in My movement but His Movement, and in My acquiescence but His Acquiescence, and in My pen but His Pen, the Mighty, the All-Praised. There hath not been in My soul but the Truth, and in Myself naught could be seen but God." "The Holy Spirit Itself hath been generated through the agency of a single letter revealed by this Most Great Spirit, if ye be of them that comprehend."* . . . *"Within the treasury of Our Wisdom there lies unrevealed a knowledge, one word of which, if we chose to divulge it to mankind, would cause every human being to recognize the Manifestation of God and to acknowledge His omniscience, would enable every one to discover the secrets of all the sciences, and to attain so high a station as to find himself wholly independent of all past and future learning. Other knowledges We do as well possess, not a single letter of which We can disclose, nor do We find humanity able to hear even the barest reference to their meaning. Thus have We informed you of the knowledge of God, the All-Knowing, the All-Wise." "The day is approaching when God will have, by an act of His Will, raised up a race of men the nature of which is inscrutable to all save God, the All-Powerful, the Self-Subsisting." "He will, ere long, out of the Bosom of Power draw forth the Hands of Ascendancy and Might—Hands who will arise to win victory for this Youth and who will purge mankind from the defilement of the outcast and the ungodly. These Hands will gird up their loins to champion the Faith of God, and will, in My name the self-subsistent, the mighty, subdue the peoples and kindreds of the earth. They will enter the cities and will inspire with fear the hearts of all their inhabitants. Such are the evidences of the might of God; how fearful, how vehement is His might!"*

Such is, dearly-beloved friends, Bahá'u'lláh's own written testimony to the nature of His Revelation. To the affirmations of the Báb, each of which reinforces the strength, and confirms the truth, of these remarkable statements, I have already referred. What remains for me to consider in this connection are such passages in the writings of 'Abdu'l-Bahá, the appointed Interpreter of these same utterances, as throw further light upon and amplify various features of this enthralling theme. The tone of His language is indeed as emphatic and His tribute no less glowing than that of either Bahá'u'lláh or the Báb.

"Centuries, nay ages, must pass away," He affirms in one of His earliest Tablets, *"ere the Day-Star of Truth shineth again in its mid-summer splendor, or appeareth once more in the radiance of its vernal glory . . . How thankful must we be for having been made in this Day the recipients of so overwhelming a favor! Would that we had ten thousand lives that we might lay them down in thanksgiving for so rare a privilege, so high an attainment, so priceless a bounty!"* *"The mere contemplation,"* He adds, *"of the Dispensation inaugurated by the Blessed Beauty would have sufficed to overwhelm the saints of bygone ages—saints who longed to partake for one moment of its great glory."* *"The holy ones of past ages and centuries have, each and all, yearned with tearful eyes to live, though for one moment, in the Day of God. Their longings unsatisfied, they repaired to the Great Beyond. How great, therefore, is the bounty of the Abhá Beauty Who, notwithstanding our utter unworthiness, hath through His grace and mercy breathed into us in this divinely-illumined century the spirit of life, hath gathered us beneath the standard of the Beloved of the world, and chosen to confer upon us a bounty for which the mighty ones of bygone ages had craved in vain."* *"The souls of the well-favored among the con-*

course on high," He likewise affirms, *"the sacred dwellers of the most exalted Paradise, are in this day filled with burning desire to return unto this world, that they may render such service as lieth in their power to the threshold of the Abhá Beauty."*

"The effulgence of God's splendrous mercy," He, in a passage alluding to the growth and future development of the Faith, declares, *"hath enveloped the peoples and kindreds of the earth, and the whole world is bathed in its shining glory . . . The day will soon come when the light of Divine unity will have so permeated the East and the West that no man dare any longer ignore it." "Now in the world of being the Hand of divine power hath firmly laid the foundations of this all-highest bounty and this wondrous gift. Whatsoever is latent in the innermost of this holy cycle shall gradually appear and be made manifest, for now is but the beginning of its growth and the dayspring of the revelation of its signs. Ere the close of this century and of this age, it shall be made clear and evident how wondrous was that springtide and how heavenly was that gift!"*

In confirmation of the exalted rank of the true believer, referred to by Bahá'u'lláh, He reveals the following: *"The station which he who hath truly recognized this Revelation will attain is the same as the one ordained for such prophets of the house of Israel as are not regarded as Manifestations 'endowed with constancy.' "*

In connection with the Manifestations destined to follow the Revelation of Bahá'u'lláh, 'Abdu'l-Bahá makes this definite and weighty declaration: *"Concerning the Manifestations that will come down in the future 'in the shadows of the clouds,' know verily that in so far as their relation to the source of their inspiration is concerned they are under the shadow of the Ancient Beauty. In their relation, however, to the age in which they appear, each and every one of them 'doeth whatsoever He willeth.' "*

"O my friend!" He thus addresses in one of His Tablets a man of recognized authority and standing, *"The undying Fire which the Lord of the Kingdom hath kindled in the midst of the holy Tree is burning fiercely in the midmost heart of the world. The conflagration it will provoke will envelop the whole earth. Its blazing flames will illuminate its peoples and kindreds. All the signs have been revealed; every prophetic allusion hath been manifested. Whatever hath been enshrined in all the Scriptures of the past hath been made evident. To doubt or hesitate is no more possible . . . Time is pressing. The Divine Charger is impatient, and can tarry no longer.*

Ours is the duty to rush forward and, ere it is too late, win the victory." And finally, is this most stirring passage which He, in one of His moments of exultation, was moved to address to one of His most trusted and eminent followers in the earliest days of His ministry: *"What more shall I say? What else can my pen recount? So loud is the call that reverberates from the Abhá Kingdom that mortal ears are well-nigh deafened with its vibrations. The whole creation, methinks, is being disrupted and is bursting asunder through the shattering influence of the Divine summons issued from the throne of glory. More than this I cannot write."*

Dearly-beloved friends! Enough has been said, and the quoted excerpts from the writings of the Báb, of Bahá'u'lláh and of 'Abdu'l-Bahá are sufficiently numerous and varied, to convince the conscientious reader of the sublimity of this unique cycle in the world's religious history. It would be utterly impossible to over-exaggerate its significance or to overrate the influence it has exerted and which it must increasingly exert as its great system unfolds itself amidst the welter of a collapsing civilization.

To whoever may read these pages a word of warning seems, however, advisable before I proceed further with the development of my argument. Let no one meditating, in the light of the afore-quoted passages, on the nature of the Revelation of Bahá'u'lláh, mistake its character or misconstrue the intent of its Author. The divinity attributed to so great a Being and the complete incarnation of the names and attributes of God in so exalted a Person should, under no circumstances, be misconceived or misinterpreted. The human temple that has been made the vehicle of so overpowering a Revelation must, if we be faithful to the tenets of our Faith, ever remain entirely distinguished from that "innermost Spirit of Spirits" and "eternal Essence of Essences"—that invisible yet rational God Who, however much we extol the divinity of His Mani-festations on earth, can in no wise incarnate His infinite, His unknowable, His incorruptible and all-embracing Reality in the concrete and limited frame of a mortal being. Indeed, the God Who could so incarnate His own reality would, in the light of the teach-ings of Bahá'u'lláh, cease immediately to be God. So crude and fantastic a theory of Divine incarnation is as removed from, and incompatible with, the essentials of Bahá'í belief as are the no less inadmissible pantheistic and anthropomorphic conceptions of God—

both of which the utterances of Bahá'u'lláh emphatically repudiate and the fallacy of which they expose.

He Who in unnumbered passages claimed His utterance to be the *"Voice of Divinity, the Call of God Himself"* thus solemnly affirms in the Kitáb-i-Íqán: *"To every discerning and illumined heart it is evident that God, the unknowable Essence, the Divine Being, is immeasurably exalted beyond every human attribute such as corporeal existence, ascent and descent, egress and regress . . . He is, and hath ever been, veiled in the ancient eternity of His Essence, and will remain in His Reality everlastingly hidden from the sight of men . . . He standeth exalted beyond and above all separation and union, all proximity and remoteness . . . 'God was alone; there was none else beside Him' is a sure testimony of this truth."*

"From time immemorial," Bahá'u'lláh, speaking of God, explains, *"He, the Divine Being, hath been veiled in the ineffable sanctity of His exalted Self, and will everlastingly continue to be wrapt in the impenetrable mystery of His unknowable Essence . . . Ten thousand Prophets, each a Moses, are thunderstruck upon the Sinai of their search at God's forbidding voice, 'Thou shalt never behold Me!'; whilst a myriad Messengers, each as great as Jesus, stand dismayed upon their heavenly thrones by the interdiction 'Mine Essence thou shalt never apprehend!' " "How bewildering to me, insignificant as I am,"* Bahá'u'lláh in His communion with God affirms, *"is the attempt to fathom the sacred depths of Thy knowledge! How futile my efforts to visualize the magnitude of the power inherent in Thine handiwork—the revelation of Thy creative power!" "When I contemplate, O my God, the relationship that bindeth me to Thee,"* He, in yet another prayer revealed in His own handwriting, testifies, *"I am moved to proclaim to all created things 'verily I am God!'; and when I consider my own self, lo, I find it coarser than clay!"*

"The door of the knowledge of the Ancient of Days," Bahá'u'-lláh further states in the Kitáb-i-Íqán, *"being thus closed in the face of all beings, He, the Source of infinite grace . . . hath caused those luminous Gems of Holiness to appear out of the realm of the spirit, in the noble form of the human temple, and be made manifest unto all men, that they may impart unto the world the mysteries of the unchangeable Being and tell of the subtleties of His imperishable Essence . . . All the Prophets of God, His well-favored, His holy and chosen Messengers are, without exception, the bearers of*

His names and the embodiments of His attributes . . . These Tabernacles of Holiness, these primal Mirrors which reflect the Light of unfading glory, are but expressions of Him Who is the Invisible of the Invisibles."

That Bahá'u'lláh should, notwithstanding the overwhelming intensity of His Revelation, be regarded as essentially one of these Manifestations of God, never to be identified with that invisible Reality, the Essence of Divinity itself, is one of the major beliefs of our Faith—a belief which should never be obscured and the integrity of which no one of its followers should allow to be compromised.

Nor does the Bahá'í Revelation, claiming as it does to be the culmination of a prophetic cycle and the fulfillment of the promise of all ages, attempt, under any circumstances, to invalidate those first and everlasting principles that animate and underlie the religions that have preceded it. The God-given authority, vested in each one of them, it admits and establishes as its firmest and ultimate basis. It regards them in no other light except as different stages in the eternal history and constant evolution of one religion, Divine and indivisible, of which it itself forms but an integral part. It neither seeks to obscure their Divine origin, nor to dwarf the admitted magnitude of their colossal achievements. It can countenance no attempt that seeks to distort their features or to stultify the truths which they instill. Its teachings do not deviate a hairbreadth from the verities they enshrine, nor does the weight of its message detract one jot or one tittle from the influence they exert or the loyalty they inspire. Far from aiming at the overthrow of the spiritual foundation of the world's religious systems, its avowed, its unalterable purpose is to widen their basis, to restate their fundamentals, to reconcile their aims, to reinvigorate their life, to demonstrate their oneness, to restore the pristine purity of their teachings, to coördinate their functions and to assist in the realization of their highest aspirations. These divinely-revealed religions, as a close observer has graphically expressed it, "are doomed not to die, but to be reborn . . . 'Does not the child succumb in the youth and the youth in the man; yet neither child nor youth perishes?' "

"They Who are the Luminaries of Truth and the Mirrors reflecting the light of Divine Unity," Bahá'u'lláh explains in the Kitáb-i-Íqán, *"in whatever age and cycle they are sent down from their invisible habitations of ancient glory unto this world to educate the souls of men and endue with grace all created things, are invariably*

endowed with an all-compelling power and invested with invincible
sovereignty . . . These sanctified Mirrors, these Day-Springs of
ancient glory are one and all the exponents on earth of Him Who
is the central Orb of the universe, its essence and ultimate purpose.
From Him proceed their knowledge and power; from Him is
derived their sovereignty. The beauty of their countenance is but a
reflection of His image, and their revelation a sign of His deathless
glory . . . Through them is transmitted a grace that is infinite,
and by them is revealed the light that can never fade . . . Human
tongue can never befittingly sing their praise, and human speech
can never unfold their mystery." "Inasmuch as these Birds of the
celestial Throne," He adds, *"are all sent down from the heaven of*
the Will of God, and as they all arise to proclaim His irresistible
Faith, they therefore are regarded as one soul and the same per-
son . . . They all abide in the same tabernacle, soar in the same
heaven, are seated upon the same throne, utter the same speech, and
proclaim the same Faith . . . They only differ in the intensity of
their revelation and the comparative potency of their light . . .
That a certain attribute of God hath not been outwardly manifested
by these Essences of Detachment doth in no wise imply that they
Who are the Day-Springs of God's attributes and the Treasuries
of His holy names did not actually possess it."

It should also be borne in mind that, great as is the power
manifested by this Revelation and however vast the range of the
Dispensation its Author has inaugurated, it emphatically repudiates
the claim to be regarded as the final revelation of God's will and
purpose for mankind. To hold such a conception of its character and
functions would be tantamount to a betrayal of its cause and a
denial of its truth. It must necessarily conflict with the fundamental
principle which constitutes the bedrock of Bahá'í belief, the principle
that religious truth is not absolute but relative, that Divine Revelation is orderly, continuous and progressive and not spasmodic or
final. Indeed, the categorical rejection by the followers of the Faith
of Bahá'u'lláh of the claim to finality which any religious system
inaugurated by the Prophets of the past may advance is as clear
and emphatic as their own refusal to claim that same finality for
the Revelation with which they stand identified. *"To believe that*
all revelation is ended, that the portals of Divine mercy are closed,
that from the daysprings of eternal holiness no sun shall rise
again, that the ocean of everlasting bounty is forever stilled, and
that out of the tabernacle of ancient glory the Messengers of God

have ceased to be made manifest" must constitute in the eyes of every follower of the Faith a grave, an inexcusable departure from one of its most cherished and fundamental principles.

A reference to some of the already quoted utterances of Bahá'u'lláh and 'Abdu'l-Bahá will surely suffice to establish, beyond the shadow of a doubt, the truth of this cardinal principle. Might not the following passage of the Hidden Words be, likewise, construed as an allegorical allusion to the progressiveness of Divine Revelation and an admission by its Author that the Message with which He has been entrusted is not the final and ultimate expression of the will and guidance of the Almighty? *"O Son of Justice! In the night-season the beauty of the immortal Being hath repaired from the emerald height of fidelity unto the Sadratu'l-Muntahá, and wept with such a weeping that the concourse on high and the dwellers of the realms above wailed at His lamenting. Whereupon there was asked, Why the wailing and weeping? He made reply: As bidden I waited expectant upon the hill of faithfulness, yet inhaled not from them that dwell on earth the fragrance of fidelity. Then summoned to return I beheld, and lo! certain doves of holiness were sore tried within the claws of the dogs of earth. Thereupon the Maid of heaven hastened forth unveiled and resplendent from Her mystic mansion, and asked of their names, and all were told but one. And when urged, the first letter thereof was uttered, whereupon the dwellers of the celestial chambers rushed forth out of their habitation of glory. And whilst the second letter was pronounced they fell down, one and all, upon the dust. At that moment a voice was heard from the inmost shrine: 'Thus far and no farther.' Verily We bear witness to that which they have done and now are doing."*

In a more explicit language Bahá'u'lláh testifies to this truth in one of His Tablets revealed in Adrianople: *"Know verily that the veil hiding Our countenance hath not been completely lifted. We have revealed Our Self to a degree corresponding to the capacity of the people of Our age. Should the Ancient Beauty be unveiled in the fullness of His glory mortal eyes would be blinded by the dazzling intensity of His revelation."*

In the Súriy-i-Ṣabr, revealed as far back as the year 1863, on the very first day of His arrival in the garden of Riḍván, He thus affirms: *"God hath sent down His Messengers to succeed to Moses and Jesus, and He will continue to do so till 'the end that hath no end'; so that His grace may, from the heaven of Divine bounty, be continually vouchsafed to mankind."*

"I am not apprehensive for My own self," Bahá'u'lláh still more explicitly declares, *"My fears are for Him Who will be sent down unto you after Me—Him Who will be invested with great sovereignty and mighty dominion."* And again He writes in the Súratu'l-Haykal: *"By those words which I have revealed, Myself is not intended, but rather He Who will come after Me. To it is witness God, the All-Knowing." "Deal not with Him,"* He adds, *"as ye have dealt with Me."*

In a more circumstantial passage the Báb upholds the same truth in His writings. *"It is clear and evident,"* He writes in the Persian Bayán, *"that the object of all preceding Dispensations hath been to pave the way for the advent of Muhammad, the Apostle of God. These, including the Muhammadan Dispensation, have had, in their turn, as their objective the Revelation proclaimed by the Qá'im. The purpose underlying this Revelation, as well as those that preceded it, has, in like manner, been to announce the advent of the Faith of Him Whom God will make manifest. And this Faith—the Faith of Him Whom God will make manifest—in its turn, together with all the Revelations gone before it, have as their object the Manifestation destined to succeed it. And the latter, no less than all the Revelations preceding it, prepare the way for the Revelation which is yet to follow. The process of the rise and setting of the Sun of Truth will thus indefinitely continue—a process that hath had no beginning and will have no end."*

"Know of a certainty," Bahá'u'lláh explains in this connection, *"that in every Dispensation the light of Divine Revelation has been vouchsafed to men in direct proportion to their spiritual capacity. Consider the sun. How feeble its rays the moment it appeareth above the horizon. How gradually its warmth and potency increase as it approacheth its zenith, enabling meanwhile all created things to adapt themselves to the growing intensity of its light. How steadily it declines until it reacheth its setting point. Were it all of a sudden to manifest the energies latent within it, it would no doubt cause injury to all created things . . . In like manner, if the Sun of Truth were suddenly to reveal, at the earliest stages of its manifestation, the full measure of the potencies which the providence of the Almighty hath bestowed upon it, the earth of human understanding would waste away and be consumed; for men's hearts would neither sustain the intensity of its revelation, nor be able to mirror forth the radiance of its light. Dismayed and overpowered, they would cease to exist."*

In the light of these clear and conclusive statements it is our clear duty to make it indubitably evident to every seeker after truth that from "the beginning that hath no beginning" the Prophets of the one, the unknowable God, including Bahá'u'lláh Himself, have all, as the channels of God's grace, as the exponents of His unity, as the mirrors of His light and the revealers of His purpose, been commissioned to unfold to mankind an ever-increasing measure of His truth, of His inscrutable will and Divine guidance, and will continue to "the end that hath no end" to vouchsafe still fuller and mightier revelations of His limitless power and glory.

We might well ponder in our hearts the following passages from a prayer revealed by Bahá'u'lláh which strikingly affirm, and are a further evidence of, the reality of the great and essential truth lying at the very core of His Message to mankind: *"Praise be to Thee, O Lord my God, for the wondrous revelations of Thine inscrutable decree and the manifold woes and trials Thou hast destined for myself. At one time Thou didst deliver me into the hands of Nimrod; at another Thou hast allowed Pharaoh's rod to persecute me. Thou alone canst estimate, through Thine all-encompassing knowledge and the operation of Thy Will, the incalculable afflictions I have suffered at their hands. Again Thou didst cast me into the prison-cell of the ungodly for no reason except that I was moved to whisper into the ears of the well-favored denizens of Thy kingdom an intimation of the vision with which Thou hadst, through Thy knowledge, inspired me and revealed to me its meaning through the potency of Thy might. And again Thou didst decree that I be beheaded by the sword of the infidel. Again I was crucified for having unveiled to men's eyes the hidden gems of Thy glorious unity, for having revealed to them the wondrous signs of Thy sovereign and everlasting power. How bitter the humiliations heaped upon me, in a subsequent age, on the plain of Karbilá! How lonely did I feel amidst Thy people; to what state of helplessness I was reduced in that land! Unsatisfied with such indignities, my persecutors decapitated me and carrying aloft my head from land to land paraded it before the gaze of the unbelieving multitude and deposited it on the seats of the perverse and faithless. In a later age I was suspended and my breast was made a target to the darts of the malicious cruelty of my foes. My limbs were riddled with bullets and my body was torn asunder. Finally, behold how in this day my treacherous enemies have leagued themselves against me, and are continually plotting to instill the venom of hate and malice into the souls of Thy servants. With all their might they are scheming to accomplish their purpose . . . Grievous as is my plight, O God, my Well-beloved, I render thanks unto Thee, and my spirit is grateful for whatsoever hath befallen me in the path of Thy good-pleasure. I am well pleased with that which Thou didst ordain for me, and welcome, however calamitous, the pains and sorrows I am made to suffer."*

THE BÁB

Dearly-beloved friends! That the Báb, the inaugurator of the Bábí Dispensation, is fully entitled to rank as one of the self-sufficient Manifestations of God, that He has been invested with sovereign power and authority, and exercises all the rights and prerogatives of independent Prophethood, is yet another fundamental verity which the Message of Bahá'u'lláh insistently proclaims and which its followers must uncompromisingly uphold. That He is not to be regarded merely as an inspired Precursor of the Bahá'í Revelation, that in His person, as He Himself bears witness in the Persian Bayán, the object of all the Prophets gone before Him has been fulfilled, is a truth which I feel it my duty to demonstrate and emphasize. We would assuredly be failing in our duty to the Faith we profess and would be violating one of its basic and sacred principles if in our words or by our conduct we hesitate to recognize the implications of this root principle of Bahá'í belief, or refuse to uphold unreservedly its integrity and demonstrate its truth. Indeed the chief motive actuating me to undertake the task of editing and translating Nabíl's immortal Narrative has been to enable every follower of the Faith in the West to better understand and more readily grasp the tremendous implications of His exalted station and to more ardently admire and love Him.

There can be no doubt that the claim to the twofold station ordained for the Báb by the Almighty, a claim which He Himself has so boldly advanced, which Bahá'u'lláh has repeatedly affirmed, and to which the Will and Testament of 'Abdu'l-Bahá has finally given the sanction of its testimony, constitutes the most distinctive feature of the Bahá'í Dispensation. It is a further evidence of its uniqueness, a tremendous accession to the strength, to the mysterious power and authority with which this holy cycle has been invested. Indeed the greatness of the Báb consists primarily, not in His being the divinely-appointed Forerunner of so transcendent a Revelation, but rather in His having been invested with the powers inherent in the inaugurator of a separate religious Dispensation, and in His wielding, to a degree unrivaled by the Messengers gone before Him, the scepter of independent Prophethood.

The short duration of His Dispensation, the restricted range within which His laws and ordinances have been made to operate, supply no criterion whatever wherewith to judge its Divine origin and to evaluate the potency of its message. *"That so brief a span,"* Bahá'u'lláh Himself explains, *"should have separated this most mighty and wondrous Revelation from Mine own previous Manifestation, is a secret that no man can unravel and a mystery such as no mind can fathom. Its duration had been foreordained, and no man shall ever discover its reason unless and until he be informed of the contents of My Hidden Book."* *"Behold,"* Bahá'u'lláh further explains in the Kitáb-i-Badí', one of His works refuting the arguments of the people of the Bayán, *"behold, how immediately upon the completion of the ninth year of this wondrous, this most holy and merciful Dispensation, the requisite number of pure, of wholly consecrated and sanctified souls had been most secretly consummated."*

The marvelous happenings that have heralded the advent of the Founder of the Bábí Dispensation, the dramatic circumstances of His own eventful life, the miraculous tragedy of His martyrdom, the magic of His influence exerted on the most eminent and powerful among His countrymen, to all of which every chapter of Nabíl's stirring narrative testifies, should in themselves be regarded as sufficient evidence of the validity of His claim to so exalted a station among the Prophets.

However graphic the record which the eminent chronicler of His life has transmitted to posterity, so luminous a narrative must pale before the glowing tribute paid to the Báb by the pen of Bahá'u'lláh. This tribute the Báb Himself has, by the clear assertion of His claim, abundantly supported, while the written testimonies of 'Abdu'l-Bahá have powerfully reinforced its character and elucidated its meaning.

Where else if not in the Kitáb-i-Íqán can the student of the Bábí Dispensation seek to find those affirmations that unmistakably attest the power and spirit which no man, except he be a Manifestation of God, can manifest? *"Could such a thing,"* exclaims Bahá'u'lláh, *"be made manifest except through the power of a Divine Revelation and the potency of God's invincible Will? By the righteousness of God! Were any one to entertain so great a Revelation in his heart the thought of such a declaration would alone confound him! Were the hearts of all men to be crowded into his heart, he would still hesitate to venture upon so awful an enterprise."* *"No eye,"* He in another passage affirms, *"hath beheld so great an outpouring of bounty, nor hath any ear heard of such a Revelation of loving-kindness . . . The Prophets 'endowed with constancy,' whose loftiness and glory shine as the sun, were each honored with a Book which all have seen, and the verses of which have been duly ascertained. Whereas the verses which have rained from this Cloud of divine mercy have been so abundant that none hath yet been able to estimate their number . . . How can they belittle this Revelation? Hath any age witnessed such momentous happenings?"*

Commenting on the character and influence of those heroes and martyrs whom the spirit of the Báb had so magically transformed Bahá'u'lláh reveals the following: *"If these companions be not the true strivers after God, who else could be called by this name? . . . If these companions, with all their marvelous testimonies and wondrous works, be false, who then is worthy to claim for himself the truth? . . . Has the world since the days of Adam witnessed such tumult, such violent commotion? . . . Methinks, patience was revealed only by virtue of their fortitude, and faithfulness itself was begotten only by their deeds."*

Wishing to stress the sublimity of the Báb's exalted station as compared with that of the Prophets of the past, Bahá'u'lláh in that same epistle asserts: *"No understanding can grasp the nature of His Revelation, nor can any knowledge comprehend the full measure of His Faith."* He then quotes, in confirmation of His argument, these prophetic words: *"Knowledge is twenty and seven letters. All that the Prophets have revealed are two letters thereof. No man thus far hath known more than these two letters. But when the Qá'im shall arise, He will cause the remaining twenty and five letters to be made manifest."* *"Behold,"* He adds, *"how great and lofty is His station! His rank excelleth that of all the Prophets and His Revelation transcendeth the comprehension and understanding of all their chosen ones."* *"Of His Revelation,"* He further adds, *"the Prophets of God, His saints and chosen ones, have either not been informed, or, in pursuance of God's inscrutable decree, they have not disclosed."*

Of all the tributes which Bahá'u'lláh's unerring pen has chosen to pay to the memory of the Báb, His "Best-Beloved," the most memorable and touching is this brief, yet eloquent passage which so greatly enhances the value of the concluding passages of that same epistle. *"Amidst them all,"* He writes, referring to the afflictive trials and dangers besetting him in the city of Baghdád, *"We stand life in hand wholly resigned to His Will, that perchance through God's loving kindness and grace, this revealed and manifest Letter* (Bahá'u'lláh) *may lay down His life as a sacrifice in the path of the Primal Point, the most exalted Word* (the Báb). *By*

Him, at Whose bidding the Spirit hath spoken, but for this yearning of Our soul, We would not, for one moment, have tarried any longer in this city."

Dearly-beloved friends! So resounding a praise, so bold an assertion issued by the pen of Bahá'u'lláh in so weighty a work, are fully re-echoed in the language in which the Source of the Bábí Revelation has chosen to clothe the claims He Himself has advanced. *"I am the Mystic Fane,"* the Báb thus proclaims His station in the Qayyúmu'l-Asmá', *"which the Hand of Omnipotence hath reared. I am the Lamp which the Finger of God hath lit within its niche and caused to shine with deathless splendor. I am the Flame of that supernal Light that glowed upon Sinai in the gladsome Spot, and lay concealed in the midst of the Burning Bush." "O Qurratu'l-'Ayn!"* He, addressing Himself in that same commentary, exclaims, *"I recognize in Thee none other except the 'Great Announcement'—the Announcement voiced by the Concourse on high. By this name, I bear witness, they that circle the Throne of Glory have ever known Thee." "With each and every Prophet, Whom We have sent down in the past,"* He further adds, *"We have established a separate Covenant concerning the 'Remembrance of God' and His Day. Manifest, in the realm of glory and through the power of truth, are the 'Remembrance of God' and His Day before the eyes of the angels that circle His mercy-seat." "Should it be Our wish,"* He again affirms, *"it is in Our power to compel, through the agency of but one letter of Our Revelation, the world and all that is therein to recognize, in less than the twinkling of an eye, the truth of Our Cause."*

"I am the Primal Point," the Báb thus addresses Muḥammad S͟háh from the prison-fortress of Máh-Kú, *"from which have been generated all created things . . . I am the Countenance of God Whose splendor can never be obscured, the light of God whose radiance can never fade . . . All the keys of heaven God hath chosen to place on My right hand, and all the keys of hell on My left . . . I am one of the sustaining pillars of the Primal Word of God. Whosoever hath recognized Me, hath known all that is true and right, and hath attained all that is good and seemly . . . The substance wherewith God hath created Me is not the clay out of which others have been formed. He hath conferred upon Me that which the worldly-wise can never comprehend, nor the faithful discover." "Should a tiny ant,"* the Báb, wishing to stress the limitless potentialities latent in His Dispensation, characteristically

affirms, *"desire in this day to be possessed of such power as to be able to unravel the abstrusest and most bewildering passages of the Qur'án, its wish will no doubt be fulfilled, inasmuch as the mystery of eternal might vibrates within the innermost being of all created things."* "If so helpless a creature," is 'Abdu'l-Bahá's comment on so startling an affirmation, *"can be endowed with so subtle a capacity, how much more efficacious must be the power released through the liberal effusions of the grace of Bahá'u'lláh!"*

To these authoritative assertions and solemn declarations made by Bahá'u'lláh and the Báb must be added 'Abdu'l-Bahá's own incontrovertible testimony. He, the appointed interpreter of the utterances of both Bahá'u'lláh and the Báb, corroborates, not by implication but in clear and categorical language, both in His Tablets and in His Testament, the truth of the statements to which I have already referred.

In a Tablet addressed to a Bahá'í in Mázindarán, in which He unfolds the meaning of a misinterpreted statement attributed to Him regarding the rise of the Sun of Truth in this century, He sets forth, briefly but conclusively, what should remain for all time our true conception of the relationship between the two Manifestations associated with the Bahá'í Dispensation. *"In making such a statement,"* He explains, *"I had in mind no one else except the Báb and Bahá'u'lláh, the character of whose Revelations it had been my purpose to elucidate. The Revelation of the Báb may be likened to the sun, its station corresponding to the first sign of the Zodiac— the sign Aries—which the sun enters at the Vernal Equinox. The station of Bahá'u'lláh's Revelation, on the other hand, is represented by the sign Leo, the sun's mid-summer and highest station. By this is meant that this holy Dispensation is illumined with the light of the Sun of Truth shining from its most exalted station, and in the plenitude of its resplendency, its heat and glory."*

"The Báb, the Exalted One," 'Abdu'l-Bahá more specifically affirms in another Tablet, *"is the Morn of Truth, the splendor of Whose light shineth throughout all regions. He is also the Harbinger of the Most Great Light, the Abhá Luminary. The Blessed Beauty is the One promised by the sacred books of the past, the revelation of the Source of light that shone upon Mount Sinai, Whose fire glowed in the midst of the Burning Bush. We are, one and all, servants of their threshold, and stand each as a lowly keeper at their door."* "Every proof and prophecy," is His still more emphatic warning, *"every manner of evidence, whether based on reason or*

on the text of the scriptures and traditions, are to be regarded as centered in the persons of Bahá'u'lláh and the Báb. In them is to be found their complete fulfillment."

And finally, in His Will and Testament, the repository of His last wishes and parting instructions, He in the following passage, specifically designed to set forth the guiding principles of Bahá'í belief, sets the seal of His testimony on the Báb's dual and exalted station: *"The foundation of the belief of the people of Bahá (may my life be offered up for them) is this: His holiness the exalted One (the Báb) is the Manifestation of the unity and oneness of God and the Forerunner of the Ancient Beauty (Bahá'u'lláh). His holiness, the Abhá Beauty (Bahá'u'lláh) (may my life be offered up as a sacrifice for His steadfast friends) is the supreme Manifestation of God and the Day-Spring of His most divine Essence."* "All others," He significantly adds, *"are servants unto Him and do His bidding."*

'ABDU'L-BAHÁ

Dearly-beloved friends! I have in the foregoing pages ventured to attempt an exposition of such truths as I firmly believe are implicit in the claim of Him Who is the Fountain-Head of the Bahá'í Revelation. I have moreover endeavored to dissipate such misapprehensions as may naturally **arise in** the mind of any one contemplating so superhuman a manifestation of the glory of God. I have striven to explain the meaning of the divinity with which He Who is the vehicle of so mysterious an energy must needs be invested. That the Message which so great a Being has, in this age, been commissioned by God to deliver to mankind recognizes the divine origin and upholds the first principles of every Dispensation inaugurated by the prophets of the past, and stands inextricably interwoven with each one of them, I have also to the best of my ability undertaken to demonstrate. That the Author of such a Faith, Who repudiates the claim to finality which leaders of various denominations uphold has, despite the vastness of His Revelation, disclaimed it for Himself I have, likewise, felt it necessary to prove and emphasize. That the Báb, notwithstanding the duration of His Dispensation, should be regarded primarily, not as the chosen Precursor of the Bahá'í Faith, but as One invested with the undivided authority assumed by each of the independent Prophets of the past, seemed to me yet another basic principle the elucidation of which would be extremely desirable at the present stage of the evolution of our Cause.

An attempt I strongly feel should now be made to clarify our minds regarding the station occupied by 'Abdu'l-Bahá and the significance of His position in this holy Dispensation. It would be indeed difficult for us, who stand so close to such a tremendous figure and are drawn by the mysterious power of so magnetic a personality, to obtain a clear and exact understanding of the rôle and character of One Who, not only in the Dispensation of Bahá'u'lláh but in the entire field of religious history, fulfills a unique function. Though moving in a sphere of His own and holding a rank radically different from that of the Author and the Forerunner of the Bahá'í Revelation, He, by virtue of the station ordained for Him through the Covenant of Bahá'u'lláh, forms together with them what may be termed the Three Central Figures of a Faith that stands unap-

131

proached in the world's spiritual history. He towers, in conjunction
with them, above the destinies of this infant Faith of God from
a level to which no individual or body ministering to its needs after
Him, and for no less a period than a full thousand years, can ever
hope to rise. To degrade His lofty rank by identifying His station
with or by regarding it as roughly equivalent to, the position of
those on whom the mantle of His authority has fallen would be an
act of impiety as grave as the no less heretical belief that inclines
to exalt Him to a state of absolute equality with either the central
Figure or Forerunner of our Faith. For wide as is the gulf that
separates 'Abdu'l-Bahá from Him Who is the Source of an independent Revelation, it can never be regarded as commensurate with
the greater distance that stands between Him Who is the Center
of the Covenant and His ministers who are to carry on His work,
whatever be their name, their rank, their functions or their future
achievements. Let those who have known 'Abdu'l-Bahá, who
through their contact with His magnetic personality have come to
cherish for Him so fervent an admiration, reflect, in the light of
this statement, on the greatness of One Who is so far above Him
in station.

That 'Abdu'l-Bahá is not a Manifestation of God, that, though
the successor of His Father, He does not occupy a cognate station,
that no one else except the Báb and Bahá'u'lláh can ever lay claim
to such a station before the expiration of a full thousand years—
are verities which lie embedded in the specific utterances of both
the Founder of our Faith and the Interpreter of His teachings.

"Whoso layeth claim to a Revelation direct from God," is the
express warning uttered in the Kitáb-i-Aqdas, *"ere the expiration of
a full thousand years, such a man is assuredly a lying impostor. We
pray God that He may graciously assist him to retract and repudiate
such claim. Should he repent, God will no doubt forgive him. If,
however, he persists in his error, God will assuredly send down one
who will deal mercilessly with him. Terrible indeed is God in punish-
ing!"* *"Whosoever,"* He adds as a further emphasis, *"interpreteth
this verse otherwise than its obvious meaning is deprived of the
Spirit of God and of His mercy which encompasseth all created
things."* *"Should a man appear,"* is yet another conclusive statement,
*"ere the lapse of a full thousand years—each year consisting of
twelve months according to the Qur'án, and of nineteen months of
nineteen days each, according to the Bayán—and if such a man
reveal to your eyes all the signs of God, unhesitatingly reject him!"*

'Abdu'l-Bahá's own statements, in confirmation of this warning, are no less emphatic and binding: *"This is,"* He declares, *"my firm, my unshakable conviction, the essence of my unconcealed and explicit belief—a conviction and belief which the denizens of the Abhá Kingdom fully share: The Blessed Beauty is the Sun of Truth, and His light the light of truth. The Báb is likewise the Sun of Truth, and His light the light of truth . . . My station is the station of servitude—a servitude which is complete, pure and real, firmly established, enduring, obvious, explicitly revealed and subject to no interpretation whatever . . . I am the Interpreter of the Word of God; such is my interpretation."*

Does not 'Abdu'l-Bahá in His own Will—in a tone and language that might well confound the most inveterate among the breakers of His Father's Covenant—rob of their chief weapon those who so long and so persistently had striven to impute to Him the charge of having tacitly claimed a station equal, if not superior, to that of Bahá'u'lláh? *"The foundation of the belief of the people of Bahá is this,"* thus proclaims one of the weightiest passages of that last document left to voice in perpetuity the directions and wishes of a departed Master, *"His Holiness the Exalted One* (the Báb) *is the Manifestation of the unity and oneness of God and the Forerunner of the Ancient Beauty. His Holiness the Abhá Beauty* (Bahá'u'lláh) *(may my life be a sacrifice for His steadfast friends) is the supreme Manifestation of God and the Day-Spring of His most divine Essence. All others are servants unto Him and do His bidding."*

From such clear and formally laid down statements, incompatible as they are with any assertion of a claim to Prophethood, we should not by any means infer that 'Abdu'l-Bahá is merely one of the servants of the Blessed Beauty, or at best one whose function is to be confined to that of an authorized interpreter of His Father's teachings. Far be it from me to entertain such a notion or to wish to instill such sentiments. To regard Him in such a light is a manifest betrayal of the priceless heritage bequeathed by Bahá'u'lláh to mankind. Immeasurably exalted is the station conferred upon Him by the Supreme Pen above and beyond the implications of these, His own written statements. Whether in the Kitáb-i-Aqdas, the most weighty and sacred of all the works of Bahá'u'lláh, or in the Kitáb-i-'Ahd, the Book of His Covenant, or in the Súriy-i-Ghusn (Tablet of the Branch), such references as have been recorded by the pen of Bahá'u'lláh—references which the Tablets of His Father addressed to Him mightily reinforce—invest 'Abdu'l-Bahá with a power, and surround Him with a halo, which the present generation can never adequately appreciate.

He is, and should for all time be regarded, first and foremost, as the Center and Pivot of Bahá'u'lláh's peerless and all-enfolding Covenant, His most exalted handiwork, the stainless Mirror of His light, the perfect Exemplar of His teachings, the unerring Interpreter of His Word, the embodiment of every Bahá'í ideal, the incarnation of every Bahá'í virtue, the Most Mighty Branch sprung from the Ancient Root, the Limb of the Law of God, the Being *"round Whom all names revolve,"* the Mainspring of the Oneness of Humanity, the Ensign of the Most Great Peace, the Moon of the Central Orb of this most holy Dispensation—styles and titles that are implicit and find their truest, their highest and fairest expression in the magic name 'Abdu'l-Bahá. He is, above and beyond these appellations, the *"Mystery of God"*—an expression by which Bahá'u'lláh Himself has chosen to designate Him, and which, while it does not by any means justify us to assign to Him the station of Prophethood, indicates how in the person of 'Abdu'l-Bahá the incompatible characteristics of a human nature and superhuman knowledge and perfection have been blended and are completely harmonized.

"When the ocean of My presence hath ebbed and the Book of My Revelation is ended," proclaims the Kitáb-i-Aqdas, *"turn your faces towards Him Whom God hath purposed, Who hath branched from this Ancient Root."* And again, *"When the Mystic Dove will have winged its flight from its Sanctuary of Praise and sought its far-off goal, its hidden habitation, refer ye whatsoever ye understand not in the Book to Him Who hath branched from this mighty Stock."*

In the Kitáb-i-'Ahd, moreover, Bahá'u'lláh solemnly and explicitly declares: *"It is incumbent upon the Aghṣán, the Afnán and My kindred to turn, one and all, their faces towards the Most Mighty Branch. Consider that which We have revealed in Our Most Holy Book: 'When the ocean of My presence hath ebbed and the Book of My Revelation is ended, turn your faces toward Him Whom God hath purposed, Who hath branched from this Ancient Root.' The object of this sacred verse is none other except the Most Mighty Branch ('Abdu'l-Bahá). Thus have We graciously revealed unto you our potent Will, and I am verily the Gracious, the All-Powerful."*

In the Súriy-i-Ghuṣn (Tablet of the Branch) the following

verses have been recorded: *"There hath branched from the Sadratu'l-Muntahá this sacred and glorious Being, this Branch of Holiness; well is it with him that hath sought His shelter and abideth beneath His shadow. Verily the Limb of the Law of God hath sprung forth from this Root which God hath firmly implanted in the Ground of His Will, and Whose Branch hath been so uplifted as to encompass the whole of creation. Magnified be He, therefore, for this sublime, this blessed, this mighty, this exalted Handiwork! . . . A Word hath, as a token of Our grace, gone forth from the Most Great Tablet—a Word which God hath adorned with the ornament of His own Self, and made it sovereign over the earth and all that is therein, and a sign of His greatness and power among its people . . . Render thanks unto God, O people, for His appearance; for verily He is the most great Favor unto you, the most perfect bounty upon you; and through Him every mouldering bone is quickened. Whoso turneth towards Him hath turned towards God, and whoso turneth away from Him hath turned away from My Beauty, hath repudiated My Proof, and transgressed against Me. He is the Trust of God amongst you, His charge within you, His manifestation unto you and His appearance among His favored servants . . . We have sent Him down in the form of a human temple. Blest and sanctified be God Who createth whatsoever He willeth through His inviolable, His infallible decree. They who deprive themselves of the shadow of the Branch, are lost in the wilderness of error, are consumed by the heat of worldly desires, and are of those who will assuredly perish."*

"O Thou Who art the apple of Mine eye!" Bahá'u'lláh, in His own handwriting, thus addresses 'Abdu'l-Bahá, *"My glory, the ocean of My loving-kindness, the sun of My bounty, the heaven of My mercy rest upon Thee. We pray God to illumine the world through Thy knowledge and wisdom, to ordain for Thee that which will gladden Thine heart and impart consolation to Thine eyes."* *"The glory of God rest upon Thee,"* He writes in another Tablet, *"and upon whosover serveth Thee and circleth around Thee. Woe, great woe, betide him that opposeth and injureth Thee. Well is it with him that sweareth fealty to Thee; the fire of hell torment him who is Thine enemy."* *"We have made Thee a shelter for all mankind,"* He, in yet another Tablet, affirms, *"a shield unto all who are in heaven and on earth, a stronghold for whosoever hath believed in God, the Incomparable, the All-Knowing. God grant that through Thee He may protect them, may enrich and sustain them, that He*

may inspire Thee with that which shall be a wellspring of wealth unto all created things, an ocean of bounty unto all men, and the dayspring of mercy unto all peoples."

"*Thou knowest, O my God,*" Bahá'u'lláh, in a prayer revealed in 'Abdu'l-Bahá's honor, supplicates, "*that I desire for Him naught except that which Thou didst desire, and have chosen Him for no purpose save that which Thou hadst intended for Him. Render Him victorious, therefore, through Thy hosts of earth and heaven . . . Ordain, I beseech Thee, by the ardor of My love for Thee and My yearning to manifest Thy Cause, for Him, as well as for them that love Him, that which Thou hast destined for Thy Messengers and the Trustees of Thy Revelation. Verily, Thou art the Almighty, the All-Powerful.*"

In a letter dictated by Bahá'u'lláh and addressed by Mírzá Áqá Ján, His amanuensis, to 'Abdu'l-Bahá while the latter was on a visit to Beirut, we read the following: "*Praise be to Him Who hath honored the Land of Bá* (Beirut) *through the presence of Him round Whom all names revolve. All the atoms of the earth have announced unto all created things that from behind the gate of the Prison-city there hath appeared and above its horizon there hath shone forth the Orb of the beauty of the great, the Most Mighty Branch of God—His ancient and immutable Mystery—proceeding on its way to another land. Sorrow, thereby, hath enveloped this Prison-city, whilst another land rejoiceth . . . Blessed, doubly blessed, is the ground which His footsteps have trodden, the eye that hath been cheered by the beauty of His countenance, the ear that hath been honored by hearkening to His call, the heart that hath tasted the sweetness of His love, the breast that hath dilated through His remembrance, the pen that hath voiced His praise, the scroll that hath borne the testimony of His writings.*"

'Abdu'l-Bahá, writing in confirmation of the authority conferred upon Him by Bahá'u'lláh, makes the following statement: "*In accordance with the explicit text of the Kitáb-i-Aqdas Bahá'u'lláh hath made the Center of the Covenant the Interpreter of His Word—a Covenant so firm and mighty that from the beginning of time until the present day no religious Dispensation hath produced its like.*"

Exalted as is the rank of 'Abdu'l-Bahá, and however profuse the praises with which in these sacred Books and Tablets Bahá'u'lláh has glorified His son, so unique a distinction must never be construed as conferring upon its recipient a station identical with, or equivalent to, that of His Father, the Manifestation Himself. To give such an interpretation to any of these quoted passages would at once, and for obvious reasons, bring it into conflict with the no less clear and authentic assertions and warnings to which I have already referred. Indeed, as I have already stated, those who over-estimate 'Abdu'l-Bahá's station are just as reprehensible and have done just as much harm as those who underestimate it. And this for no other reason except that by insisting upon an altogether unwarranted inference from Bahá'u'lláh's writings they are inadvertently justifying and continuously furnishing the enemy with proofs for his false accusations and misleading statements.

I feel it necessary, therefore, to state without any equivocation or hesitation that neither in the Kitáb-i-Aqdas nor in the Book of Bahá'u'lláh's Covenant, nor even in the Tablet of the Branch, nor in any other Tablet, whether revealed by Bahá'u'lláh or 'Abdu'l-Bahá, is there any authority whatever for the opinion that inclines to uphold the so-called "mystic unity" of Bahá'u'lláh and 'Abdu'l-Bahá, or to establish the identity of the latter with His Father or with any preceding Manifestation. This erroneous conception may, in part, be ascribed to an altogether extravagant interpretation of certain terms and passages in the Tablet of the Branch, to the introduction into its English translation of certain words that are either non-existent, misleading, or ambiguous in their connotation. It is, no doubt, chiefly based upon an altogether unjustified inference from the opening passages of a Tablet of Bahá'u'lláh, extracts of which, as reproduced in the "Bahá'í Scriptures," immediately precede, but form no part of, the said Tablet of the Branch. It should be made clear to every one reading those extracts that by the phrase "the Tongue of the Ancient" no one else is meant but God, and that the term "the Greatest Name" is an obvious reference to Bahá'u'lláh, and that "the Covenant" referred to is not the specific Covenant of which Bahá'u'lláh is the immediate Author and 'Abdu'l-Bahá the Center but that general Covenant which, as inculcated by the Bahá'í teaching, God Himself invariably establishes with mankind when He inaugurates a new Dispensation. "The Tongue" that "gives," as stated in those extracts, the "glad-tidings" is none other than the Voice of God referring to Bahá'u'lláh, and not Bahá'u'lláh referring to 'Abdu'l-Bahá.

Moreover, to maintain that the assertion "He is Myself," instead of denoting the mystic unity of God and His Manifestations, as explained in the Kitáb-i-Íqán, establishes the identity of Bahá'u'lláh with 'Abdu'l-Bahá, would constitute a direct violation of the oft-repeated principle of the oneness of God's Manifestations—a principle which the Author of these same extracts is seeking by implication to emphasize.

It would also amount to a reversion to those irrational and superstitious beliefs which have insensibly crept, in the first century of the Christian era, into the teachings of Jesus Christ, and by crystallizing into accepted dogmas have impaired the effectiveness and obscured the purpose of the Christian Faith.

"I affirm," is 'Abdu'l-Bahá's own written comment on the Tablet of the Branch, *"that the true meaning, the real significance, the innermost secret of these verses, of these very words, is my own servitude to the sacred Threshold of the Abhá Beauty, my complete self-effacement, my utter nothingness before Him. This is my resplendent crown, my most precious adorning. On this I pride myself in the kingdom of earth and heaven. Therein I glory among the company of the well-favored!"* *"No one is permitted,"* He warns us in the passage which immediately follows, *"to give these verses any other interpretation."* *"I am,"* He, in this same connection, affirms, *"according to the explicit texts of the Kitáb-i-Aqdas and the Kitáb-i-'Ahd the manifest Interpreter of the Word of God . . . Whoso deviates from my interpretation is a victim of his own fancy."*

Furthermore, the inescapable inference from the belief in the identity of the Author of our Faith with Him Who is the Center of His Covenant would be to place 'Abdu'l-Bahá in a position superior to that of the Báb, the reverse of which is the fundamental, though not as yet universally recognized, principle of this Revelation. It would also justify the charge with which, all throughout 'Abdu'l-Bahá's ministry, the Covenant-Breakers have striven to poison the minds and pervert the understanding of Bahá'u'lláh's loyal followers.

It would be more correct, and in consonance with the established principles of Bahá'u'lláh and the Báb, if instead of maintaining this fictitious identity with reference to 'Abdu'l-Bahá, we regard the Forerunner and the Founder of our Faith as identical in reality—a truth which the text of the Súratu'l-Haykal unmistakably affirms. *"Had the Primal Point* (the Báb) *been someone else beside Me as ye claim,"* is Bahá'u'lláh's explicit statement, *"and had attained My presence, verily He would have never allowed Himself to be separated from Me, but rather We would have had mutual delights with each other in My Days."* *"He Who now voiceth the Word of God,"*

Bahá'u'lláh again affirms, *"is none other except the Primal Point Who hath once again been made manifest." "He is,"* He thus refers to Himself in a Tablet addressed to one of the Letters of the Living, *"the same as the One Who appeared in the year sixty* (1260 A.H.). *This verily is one of His mighty signs." "Who,"* He pleads in the Súriy-i-Damm, *"will arise to secure the triumph of the Primal Beauty* (the Báb) *revealed in the countenance of His succeeding Manifestation?"* Referring to the Revelation proclaimed by the Báb He conversely characterizes it as *"My own previous Manifestation."*

That 'Abdu'l-Bahá is not a Manifestation of God, that He gets His light, His inspiration and sustenance direct from the Fountainhead of the Bahá'í Revelation; that He reflects even as a clear and perfect Mirror the rays of Bahá'u'lláh's glory, and does not inherently possess that indefinable yet all-pervading reality the exclusive possession of which is the hallmark of Prophethood; that His words are not equal in rank, though they possess an equal validity with the utterances of Bahá'u'lláh; that He is not to be acclaimed as the return of Jesus Christ, the Son Who will come "in the glory of the Father"—these truths find added justification, and are further reinforced, by the following statement of 'Abdu'l-Bahá, addressed to some believers in America, with which I may well conclude this section: *"You have written that there is a difference among the believers concerning the 'Second Coming of Christ.' Gracious God! Time and again this question hath arisen, and its answer hath emanated in a clear and irrefutable statement from the pen of 'Abdu'l-Bahá, that what is meant in the prophecies by the 'Lord of Hosts' and the 'Promised Christ' is the Blessed Perfection* (Bahá'u'lláh) *and His holiness the Exalted One* (the Báb). *My name is 'Abdu'l-Bahá. My qualification is 'Abdu'l-Bahá. My reality is 'Abdu'l-Bahá. My praise is 'Abdu'l-Bahá. Thraldom to the Blessed Perfection is my glorious and refulgent diadem, and servitude to all the human race my perpetual religion . . . No name, no title, no mention, no commendation have I, nor will ever have, except 'Abdu'l-Bahá. This is my longing. This is my greatest yearning. This is my eternal life. This is my everlasting glory."*

THE ADMINISTRATIVE ORDER

Dearly-beloved brethren in 'Abdu'l-Bahá! With the ascension of Bahá'u'lláh the Day-Star of Divine guidance which, as foretold by Shaykh Aḥmad and Siyyid Kázim, had risen in Shíráz, and, while pursuing its westward course, had mounted its zenith in Adrianople, had finally sunk below the horizon of 'Akká, never to rise again ere the complete revolution of one thousand years. The setting of so effulgent an Orb brought to a definite termination the period of Divine Revelation—the initial and most vitalizing stage in the Bahá'í era. Inaugurated by the Báb, culminating in Bahá'u'lláh, anticipated and extolled by the entire company of the Prophets of this great prophetic cycle, this period has, except for the short interval between the Báb's martyrdom and Bahá'u'lláh's shaking experiences in the Síyáh-Chál of Ṭihrán, been characterized by almost fifty years of continuous and progressive Revelation—a period which by its duration and fecundity must be regarded as unparalleled in the entire field of the world's spiritual history.

The passing of 'Abdu'l-Bahá, on the other hand, marks the closing of the Heroic and Apostolic Age of this same Dispensation —that primitive period of our Faith the splendors of which can never be rivaled, much less be eclipsed, by the magnificence that must needs distinguish the future victories of Bahá'u'lláh's Revelation. For neither the achievements of the champion-builders of the present-day institutions of the Faith of Bahá'u'lláh, nor the tumultuous triumphs which the heroes of its Golden Age will in the coming days succeed in winning, can measure with, or be included within the same category as, the wondrous works associated with the names of those who have generated its very life and laid its pristine foundations. That first and creative age of the Bahá'í era must, by its very nature, stand above and apart from the formative period into which we have entered and the golden age destined to succeed it.

'Abdu'l-Bahá, Who incarnates an institution for which we can find no parallel whatsoever in any of the world's recognized religious systems, may be said to have closed the Age to which He Himself belonged and opened the one in which we are now laboring. His Will and Testament should thus be regarded as the perpetual, the indissoluble link which the mind of Him Who is the Mystery of

God has conceived in order to insure the continuity of the three ages that constitute the component parts of the Bahá'í Dispensation. The period in which the seed of the Faith had been slowly germinating is thus intertwined both with the one which must witness its efflorescence and the subsequent age in which that seed will have finally yielded its golden fruit.

The creative energies released by the Law of Bahá'u'lláh, permeating and evolving within the mind of 'Abdu'l-Bahá, have, by their very impact and close interaction, given birth to an Instrument which may be viewed as the Charter of the New World Order which is at once the glory and the promise of this most great Dispensation. The Will may thus be acclaimed as the inevitable offspring resulting from that mystic intercourse between Him Who communicated the generating influence of His divine Purpose and the One Who was its vehicle and chosen recipient. Being the Child of the Covenant—the Heir of both the Originator and the Interpreter of the Law of God—the Will and Testament of 'Abdu'l-Bahá can no more be divorced from Him Who supplied the original and motivating impulse than from the One Who ultimately conceived it. Bahá'u'lláh's inscrutable purpose, we must ever bear in mind, has been so thoroughly infused into the conduct of 'Abdu'l-Bahá, and their motives have been so closely wedded together, that the mere attempt to dissociate the teachings of the former from any system which the ideal Exemplar of those same teachings has established would amount to a repudiation of one of the most sacred and basic truths of the Faith.

The Administrative Order, which ever since 'Abdu'l-Bahá's ascension has evolved and is taking shape under our very eyes in no fewer than forty countries of the world, may be considered as the framework of the Will itself, the inviolable stronghold wherein this new-born child is being nurtured and developed. This Administrative Order, as it expands and consolidates itself, will no doubt manifest the potentialities and reveal the full implications of this momentous Document—this most remarkable expression of the Will of One of the most remarkable Figures of the Dispensation of Bahá'u'lláh. It will, as its component parts, its organic institutions, begin to function with efficiency and vigor, assert its claim and demonstrate its capacity to be regarded not only as the nucleus but the very pattern of the New World Order destined to embrace in the fullness of time the whole of mankind.

It should be noted in this connection that this Administrative Order is fundamentally different from anything that any Prophet has previously established, inasmuch as Bahá'u'lláh has Himself revealed its principles, established its institutions, appointed the person to interpret His Word and conferred the necessary authority on the body designed to supplement and apply His legislative ordinances. Therein lies the secret of its strength, its fundamental distinction, and the guarantee against disintegration and schism. Nowhere in the sacred scriptures of any of the world's religious systems, nor even in the writings of the Inaugurator of the Bábí Dispensation, do we find any provisions establishing a covenant or providing for an administrative order that can compare in scope and authority with those that lie at the very basis of the Bahá'í Dispensation. Has either Christianity or Islám, to take as an instance two of the most widely diffused and outstanding among the world's recognized religions, anything to offer that can measure with, or be regarded as equivalent to, either the Book of Bahá'u'lláh's Covenant or to the Will and Testament of 'Abdu'l-Bahá? Does the text of either the Gospel or the Qur'án confer sufficient authority upon those leaders and councils that have claimed the right and assumed the function of interpreting the provisions of their sacred scriptures and of administering the affairs of their respective communities? Could Peter, the admitted chief of the Apostles, or the Imám 'Alí, the cousin and legitimate successor of the Prophet, produce in support of the primacy with which both had been invested written and explicit affirmations from Christ and Muḥammad that could have silenced those who either among their contemporaries or in a later age have repudiated their authority and, by their action, precipitated the schisms that persist until the present day? Where, we may confidently ask, in the recorded sayings of Jesus Christ, whether in the matter of succession or in the provision of a set of specific laws and clearly defined administrative ordinances, as distinguished from purely spiritual principles, can we find anything approaching the detailed injunctions, laws and warnings that abound in the authenticated utterances of both Bahá'u'lláh and 'Abdu'l-Bahá? Can any passage of the Qur'án, which in respect to its legal code, its administrative and devotional ordinances marks already a notable advance over previous and more corrupted Revelations, be construed as placing upon an unassailable basis the undoubted authority with which Muḥammad had, verbally and on several occasions, invested His successor? Can the Author of the Bábí Dispensation however much He may have succeeded through the provisions of the Persian Bayán in averting a schism as permanent and catastrophic as those that afflicted Christianity and Islám—can He be said to have produced instruments for the safeguarding of His Faith as definite and efficacious as those which must for all time preserve the unity of the organized followers of the Faith of Bahá'u'lláh?

Alone of all the Revelations gone before it this Faith has, through the explicit directions, the repeated warnings, the authenticated safeguards incorporated and elaborated in its teachings, succeeded in raising a structure which the bewildered followers of bankrupt and broken creeds might well approach and critically examine, and seek, ere it is too late, the invulnerable security of its world-embracing shelter.

No wonder that He Who through the operation of His Will has inaugurated so vast and unique an Order and Who is the Center of so mighty a Covenant should have written these words: *"So firm and mighty is this Covenant that from the beginning of time until the present day no religious Dispensation hath produced its like."* *"Whatsoever is latent in the innermost of this holy cycle,"* He wrote during the darkest and most dangerous days of His ministry, *"shall gradually appear and be made manifest, for now is but the beginning of its growth and the dayspring of the revelation of its signs."* *"Fear not,"* are His reassuring words foreshadowing the rise of the Administrative Order established by His Will, *"fear not if this Branch be severed from this material world and cast aside its leaves; nay, the leaves thereof shall flourish, for this Branch will grow after it is cut off from this world below, it shall reach the loftiest pinnacles of glory, and it shall bear such fruits as will perfume the world with their fragrance."*

To what else if not to the power and majesty which this Administrative Order—the rudiments of the future all-enfolding Bahá'í Commonwealth—is destined to manifest, can these utterances of Bahá'u'lláh allude: *"The world's equilibrium hath been upset through the vibrating influence of this most great, this new World Order. Mankind's ordered life hath been revolutionized through the agency of this unique, this wondrous System—the like of which mortal eyes have never witnessed."*

The Báb Himself, in the course of His references to "Him Whom God will make manifest" anticipates the System and glorifies the World Order which the Revelation of Bahá'u'lláh is destined to unfold. *"Well is it with him,"* is His remarkable statement in the third chapter of the Persian Bayán, *"who fixeth his gaze upon the Order of Bahá'u'lláh and rendereth thanks unto his Lord! For He will assuredly be made manifest. God hath indeed irrevocably ordained it in the Bayán."*

In the Tablets of Bahá'u'lláh where the institutions of the International and Local Houses of Justice are specifically designated and formally established; in the institution of the Hands of the Cause of God which first Bahá'u'lláh and then 'Abdu'l-Bahá brought into being; in the institution of both local and national Assemblies which in their embryonic stage were already functioning in the days preceding 'Abdu'l-Bahá's ascension; in the authority with which the Author of our Faith and the Center of His Covenant have in their Tablets chosen to confer upon them; in the institution of the Local Fund which operated according to 'Abdu'l-Bahá's specific injunctions addressed to certain Assemblies in Persia; in the verses of the Kitáb-i-Aqdas the implications of which clearly anticipate the institution of the Guardianship; in the explanation which 'Abdu'l-Bahá, in one of His Tablets, has given to, and the emphasis He has placed upon, the hereditary principle and the law of primogeniture as having been upheld by the Prophets of the past—in these we can discern the faint glimmerings and discover the earliest intimation of the nature and working of the Administrative Order which the Will of 'Abdu'l-Bahá was at a later time destined to proclaim and formally establish.

An attempt, I feel, should at the present juncture be made to explain the character and functions of the twin pillars that support this mighty Administrative Structure—the institutions of the Guardianship and of the Universal House of Justice. To describe in their entirety the diverse elements that function in conjunction with these institutions is beyond the scope and purpose of this general exposition of the fundamental verities of the Faith. To define with accuracy and minuteness the features, and to analyze exhaustively the nature of the relationships which, on the one hand, bind together these two fundamental organs of the Will of 'Abdu'l-Bahá and connect, on the other, each of them to the Author of the Faith and the Center of His Covenant is a task which future generations will no doubt adequately fulfill. My present intention is to elaborate certain salient features of this scheme which, however close we may stand to its colossal structure, are already so clearly defined that we find it inexcusable to either misconceive or ignore.

It should be stated, at the very outset, in clear and unambiguous language, that these twin institutions of the Administrative Order of Bahá'u'lláh should be regarded as divine in origin, essential in their functions and complementary in their aim and purpose. Their common, their fundamental object is to insure the continuity of that divinely-appointed authority which flows from the Source of our Faith, to safeguard the unity of its followers and to maintain the integrity and flexibility of its teachings. Acting in conjunction with each other these two inseparable institutions administer its affairs, coördinate its activities, promote its interests, execute its laws and defend its subsidiary institutions. Severally, each operates within a clearly defined sphere of jurisdiction; each is equipped with its own attendant institutions—instruments designed for the effective discharge of its particular responsibilities and duties. Each exercises, within the limitations imposed upon it, its powers, its authority, its rights and prerogatives. These are neither contradictory, nor detract in the slightest degree from the position which each of these institutions occupies. Far from being incompatible or mutually destructive, they supplement each other's authority and functions, and are permanently and fundamentally united in their aims.

Divorced from the institution of the Guardianship the World Order of Bahá'u'lláh would be mutilated and permanently deprived of that hereditary principle which, as 'Abdu'l-Bahá has written, has been invariably upheld by the Law of God. *"In all the Divine Dispensations,"* He states, in a Tablet addressed to a follower of the Faith in Persia, *"the eldest son hath been given extraordinary distinctions. Even the station of prophethood hath been his birthright."* Without such an institution the integrity of the Faith would be imperiled, and the stability of the entire fabric would be gravely endangered. Its prestige would suffer, the means required to enable it to take a long, an uninterrupted view over a series of generations would be completely lacking, and the necessary guidance to define the sphere of the legislative action of its elected representatives would be totally withdrawn.

Severed from the no less essential institution of the Universal House of Justice this same System of the Will of 'Abdu'l-Bahá would be paralyzed in its action and would be powerless to fill in those gaps which the Author of the Kitáb-i-Aqdas has deliberately left in the body of His legislative and administrative ordinances.

"He is the Interpreter of the Word of God," 'Abdu'l-Bahá, referring to the functions of the Guardian of the Faith, asserts, using

in His Will the very term which He Himself had chosen when refuting the argument of the Covenant-breakers who had challenged His right to interpret the utterances of Bahá'u'lláh. *"After him,"* He adds, *"will succeed the first-born of his lineal descendants." "The mighty stronghold,"* He further explains, *"shall remain impregnable and safe through obedience to him who is the Guardian of the Cause of God." "It is incumbent upon the members of the House of Justice, upon all the Aghṣán, the Afnán, the Hands of the Cause of God, to show their obedience, submissiveness and subordination unto the Guardian of the Cause of God."*

"It is incumbent upon the members of the House of Justice," Bahá'u'lláh, on the other hand, declares in the Eighth Leaf of the Exalted Paradise, *"to take counsel together regarding those things which have not outwardly been revealed in the Book, and to enforce that which is agreeable to them. God will verily inspire them with whatsoever He willeth, and He verily is the Provider, the Omniscient." "Unto the Most Holy Book"* (the Kitáb-i-Aqdas), 'Abdu'l-Bahá states in His Will, *"every one must turn, and all that is not expressly recorded therein must be referred to the Universal House of Justice. That which this body, whether unanimously or by a majority doth carry, that is verily the truth and the purpose of God Himself. Whoso doth deviate therefrom is verily of them that love discord, hath shown forth malice, and turned away from the Lord of the Covenant."*

Not only does 'Abdu'l-Bahá confirm in His Will Bahá'u'lláh's above-quoted statement, but invests this body with the additional right and power to abrogate, according to the exigencies of time, its own enactments, as well as those of a preceding House of Justice. *"Inasmuch as the House of Justice,"* is His explicit statement in His Will, *"hath power to enact laws that are not expressly recorded in the Book and bear upon daily transactions, so also it hath power to repeal the same . . . This it can do because these laws form no part of the divine explicit text."*

Referring to both the Guardian and the Universal House of Justice we read these emphatic words: *"The sacred and youthful Branch, the Guardian of the Cause of God, as well as the Universal House of Justice to be universally elected and established, are both under the care and protection of the Abhá Beauty, under the shelter and unerring guidance of the Exalted One* (the Báb) *(may my life be offered up for them both). Whatsoever they decide is of God."*

From these statements it is made indubitably clear and evident that the Guardian of the Faith has been made the Interpreter of the Word and that the Universal House of Justice has been invested with the function of legislating on matters not expressly revealed in the teachings. The interpretation of the Guardian, functioning within his own sphere, is as authoritative and binding as the enactments of the International House of Justice, whose exclusive right and prerogative is to pronounce upon and deliver the final judgment on such laws and ordinances as Bahá'u'lláh has not expressly revealed. Neither can, nor will ever, infringe upon the sacred and prescribed domain of the other. Neither will seek to curtail the specific and undoubted authority with which both have been divinely invested.

Though the Guardian of the Faith has been made the permanent head of so august a body he can never, even temporarily, assume the right of exclusive legislation. He cannot override the decision of the majority of his fellow-members, but is bound to insist upon a reconsideration by them of any enactment he conscientiously believes to conflict with the meaning and to depart from the spirit of Bahá'u'lláh's revealed utterances. He interprets what has been specifically revealed, and cannot legislate except in his capacity as member of the Universal House of Justice. He is debarred from laying down independently the constitution that must govern the organized activities of his fellow-members, and from exercising his influence in a manner that would encroach upon the liberty of those whose sacred right is to elect the body of his collaborators.

It should be borne in mind that the institution of the Guardianship has been anticipated by 'Abdu'l-Bahá in an allusion He made in a Tablet addressed, long before His own ascension, to three of His friends in Persia. To their question as to whether there would be any person to whom all the Bahá'ís would be called upon to turn after His ascension He made the following reply: *"As to the question ye have asked me, know verily that this is a well-guarded secret. It is even as a gem concealed within its shell. That it will be revealed is predestined. The time will come when its light will appear, when its evidences will be made manifest, and its secrets unraveled."*

Dearly-beloved friends! Exalted as is the position and vital as is the function of the institution of the Guardianship in the Administrative Order of Bahá'u'lláh, and staggering as must be the weight of responsibility which it carries, its importance must, whatever be the language of the Will, be in no wise over-emphasized. The Guardian of the Faith must not under any circumstances, and whatever his merits or his achievements, be exalted to the rank that will make him a co-sharer with 'Abdu'l-Bahá in the unique position which the Center of the Covenant occupies—much less to the station exclusively ordained for the Manifestation of God. So grave a departure from the established tenets of our Faith is nothing short of open blasphemy. As I have already stated, in the course of my references to 'Abdu'l-Bahá's station, however great the gulf that separates Him from the Author of a Divine Revelation it can never measure with the distance that stands between Him Who is the Center of Bahá'u'lláh's Covenant and the Guardians who are its chosen ministers. There is a far, far greater distance separating the Guardian from the Center of the Covenant than there is between the Center of the Covenant and its Author.

No Guardian of the Faith, I feel it my solemn duty to place on record, can ever claim to be the perfect exemplar of the teachings of Bahá'u'lláh or the stainless mirror that reflects His light. Though overshadowed by the unfailing, the unerring protection of Bahá'u'lláh and of the Báb, and however much he may share with 'Abdu'l-Bahá the right and obligation to interpret the Bahá'í teachings, he remains essentially human and cannot, if he wishes to remain faithful to his trust, arrogate to himself, under any pretense whatsoever, the rights, the privileges and prerogatives which Bahá'u'lláh has chosen to confer upon His Son. In the light of this truth to pray to the Guardian of the Faith, to address him as lord and master, to designate him as his holiness, to seek his benediction, to celebrate his birthday, or to commemorate any event associated with his life would be tantamount to a departure from those established truths that are enshrined within our beloved Faith. The fact that the Guardian has been specifically endowed with such power as he may need to reveal the purport and disclose the implications of the utterances of Bahá'u'lláh and of 'Abdu'l-Bahá does not necessarily confer upon him a station co-equal with those Whose words he is called upon to interpret. He can exercise that right and discharge this obligation and yet remain infinitely inferior to both of them in rank and different in nature.

To the integrity of this cardinal principle of our Faith the words, the deeds of its present and future Guardians must abundantly testify. By their conduct and example they must needs establish its truth upon an unassailable foundation and transmit to future generations unimpeachable evidences of its reality.

For my own part to hesitate in recognizing so vital a truth

or to vacillate in proclaiming so firm a conviction must constitute a shameless betrayal of the confidence reposed in me by 'Abdu'l-Bahá and an unpardonable usurpation of the authority with which He Himself has been invested.

A word should now be said regarding the theory on which this Administrative Order is based and the principle that must govern the operation of its chief institutions. It would be utterly misleading to attempt a comparison between this unique, this divinely-conceived Order and any of the diverse systems which the minds of men, at various periods of their history, have contrived for the government of human institutions. Such an attempt would in itself betray a lack of complete appreciation of the excellence of the handiwork of its great Author. How could it be otherwise when we remember that this Order constitutes the very pattern of that divine civilization which the almighty Law of Bahá'u'lláh is designed to establish upon earth? The divers and ever-shifting systems of human polity, whether past or present, whether originating in the East or in the West, offer no adequate criterion wherewith to estimate the potency of its hidden virtues or to appraise the solidity of its foundations.

The Bahá'í Commonwealth of the future, of which this vast Administrative Order is the sole framework, is, both in theory and practice, not only unique in the entire history of political institutions, but can find no parallel in the annals of any of the world's recognized religious systems. No form of democratic government; no system of autocracy or of dictatorship, whether monarchical or republican; no intermediary scheme of a purely aristocratic order; nor even any of the recognized types of theocracy, whether it be the Hebrew Commonwealth, or the various Christian ecclesiastical organizations, or the Imamate or the Caliphate in Islám—none of these can be identified or be said to conform with the Administrative Order which the master-hand of its perfect Architect has fashioned.

This new-born Administrative Order incorporates within its structure certain elements which are to be found in each of the three recognized forms of secular government, without being in any sense a mere replica of any one of them, and without introducing within its machinery any of the objectionable features which they inherently possess. It blends and harmonizes, as no government fashioned by mortal hands has as yet accomplished, the salutary truths which each of these systems undoubtedly contains without vitiating the integrity of those God-given verities on which it is ultimately founded.

The Administrative Order of the Faith of Bahá'u'lláh must in no wise be regarded as purely democratic in character inasmuch as the basic assumption which requires all democracies to depend fundamentally upon getting their mandate from the people is altogether lacking in this Dispensation. In the conduct of the administrative affairs of the Faith, in the enactment of the legislation necessary to supplement the laws of the Kitáb-i-Aqdas, the members of the Universal House of Justice, it should be borne in mind, are not, as Bahá'u'lláh's utterances clearly imply, responsible to those whom they represent, nor are they allowed to be governed by the feelings, the general opinion, and even the convictions of the mass of the faithful, or of those who directly elect them. They are to follow, in a prayerful attitude, the dictates and promptings of their conscience. They may, indeed they must, acquaint themselves with the conditions prevailing among the community, must weigh dispassionately in their minds the merits of any case presented for their consideration, but must reserve for themselves the right of an unfettered decision. *"God will verily inspire them with whatsoever He willeth,"* is Bahá'u'lláh's incontrovertible assurance. They, and not the body of those who either directly or indirectly elect them, have thus been made the recipients of the divine guidance which is at once the life-blood and ultimate safeguard of this Revelation. Moreover, he who symbolizes the hereditary principle in this Dispensation has been made the interpreter of the words of its Author, and ceases consequently, by virtue of the actual authority vested in him, to be the figurehead invariably associated with the prevailing systems of constitutional monarchies.

Nor can the Bahá'í Administrative Order be dismissed as a hard and rigid system of unmitigated autocracy or as an idle imitation of any form of absolutistic ecclesiastical government, whether it be the Papacy, the Imamate or any other similar institution, for the obvious reason that upon the international elected representatives of the followers of Bahá'u'lláh has been conferred the exclusive right of legislating on matters not expressly revealed in the Bahá'í writings. Neither the Guardian of the Faith nor any institution apart from the International House of Justice can ever usurp this vital and essential power or encroach upon that sacred right. The abolition of professional priesthood with its accompanying sacraments of baptism, of communion and of confession of sins, the laws requiring the election by universal suffrage of all local, national, and international Houses of Justice, the total absence of episcopal authority with its attendant privileges, corruptions and bureaucratic tendencies, are further evidences of the non-autocratic character of the Bahá'í Administrative Order and of its inclination to democratic methods in the administration of its affairs.

Nor is this Order identified with the name of Bahá'u'lláh to be confused with any system of purely aristocratic government in view of the fact that it upholds, on the one hand, the hereditary principle and entrusts the Guardian of the Faith with the obligation of interpreting its teachings, and provides, on the other, for the free and direct election from among the mass of the faithful of the body that constitutes its highest legislative organ.

Whereas this Administrative Order cannot be said to have been modeled after any of these recognized systems of government, it nevertheless embodies, reconciles and assimilates within its framework such wholesome elements as are to be found in each one of them. The hereditary authority which the Guardian is called upon to exercise, the vital and essential functions which the Universal House of Justice discharges, the specific provisions requiring its democratic election by the representatives of the faithful—these combine to demonstrate the truth that this divinely revealed Order, which can never be identified with any of the standard types of government referred to by Aristotle in his works, embodies and blends with the spiritual verities on which it is based the beneficent elements which are to be found in each one of them. The admitted evils inherent in each of these systems being rigidly and permanently excluded, this unique Order, however long it may endure and however extensive its ramifications, cannot ever degenerate into any form of despotism, of oligarchy, or of demagogy which must sooner or later corrupt the machinery of all man-made and essentially defective political institutions.

Dearly-beloved friends! Significant as are the origins of this mighty administrative structure, and however unique its features, the happenings that may be said to have heralded its birth and signalized the initial stage of its evolution seem no less remarkable. How striking, how edifying the contrast between the process of slow and steady consolidation that characterizes the growth of its infant strength and the devastating onrush of the forces of disintegration that are assailing the outworn institutions, both religious and secular, of present-day society!

The vitality which the organic institutions of this great, this ever-expanding Order so strongly exhibit; the obstacles which the high courage, the undaunted resolution of its administrators have already surmounted; the fire of an unquenchable enthusiasm that glows with undiminished fervor in the hearts of its itinerant teachers; the heights of self-sacrifice which its champion-builders are now attaining; the breadth of vision, the confident hope, the creative joy, the inward peace, the uncompromising integrity, the exemplary discipline, the unyielding unity and solidarity which its stalwart defenders manifest; the degree to which its moving Spirit has shown itself capable of assimilating the diversified elements within its pale, of cleansing them of all forms of prejudice and of fusing them with its own structure—these are evidences of a power which a disillusioned and sadly shaken society can ill afford to ignore.

Compare these splendid manifestations of the spirit animating this vibrant body of the Faith of Bahá'u'lláh with the cries and agony, the follies and vanities, the bitterness and prejudices, the wickedness and divisions of an ailing and chaotic world. Witness the fear that torments its leaders and paralyzes the action of its blind and bewildered statesmen. How fierce the hatreds, how false the ambitions, how petty the pursuits, how deep-rooted the suspicions of its peoples! How disquieting the lawlessness, the corruption, the unbelief that are eating into the vitals of a tottering civilization!

Might not this process of steady deterioration which is insidiously invading so many departments of human activity and thought be regarded as a necessary accompaniment to the rise of this almighty Arm of Bahá'u'lláh? Might we not look upon the momentous happenings which, in the course of the past twenty years, have so deeply agitated every continent of the earth, as ominous signs simultaneously proclaiming the agonies of a disintegrating civilization and the birthpangs of that World Order—that Ark of human salvation —that must needs arise upon its ruins?

The catastrophic fall of mighty monarchies and empires in the European continent, allusions to some of which may be found in the prophecies of Bahá'u'lláh; the decline that has set in, and is still continuing, in the fortunes of the Shí'ih hierarchy in His own native land; the fall of the Qájár dynasty, the traditional enemy of His Faith; the overthrow of the Sultanate and the Caliphate, the sustaining pillars of Sunní Islám, to which the destruction of Jerusalem in the latter part of the first century of the Christian era offers a striking parallel; the wave of secularization which is invading the Muḥammadan ecclesiastical institutions in Egypt and sapping the loyalty of its staunchest supporters; the humiliating blows that have afflicted some of the most powerful Churches of Christendom in Russia, in Western Europe and Central America; the dissemination of those subversive doctrines that are undermining the foundations and overthrowing the structure of seemingly impregnable strongholds in the political and social spheres of human activity; the signs of an impending catastrophe, strangely reminiscent of the Fall of the Roman Empire in the West, which threatens to engulf the whole structure of present-day civilization—all witness to the tumult which the birth of this mighty Organ of the Religion of Bahá'u'lláh has cast into the world—a tumult which will grow in scope and in intensity as the implications of this constantly evolving Scheme are more fully understood and its ramifications more widely extended over the surface of the globe.

A word more in conclusion. The rise and establishment of this Administrative Order—the shell that shields and enshrines so precious a gem—constitutes the hall-mark of this second and formative age of the Bahá'í era. It will come to be regarded, as it recedes farther and farther from our eyes, as the chief agency empowered to usher in the concluding phase, the consummation of this glorious Dispensation.

Let no one, while this System is still in its infancy, misconceive its character, belittle its significance or misrepresent its purpose. The bedrock on which this Administrative Order is founded is God's immutable Purpose for mankind in this day. The Source from which it derives its inspiration is no one less than Bahá'u'lláh Himself. Its shield and defender are the embattled hosts of the Abhá Kingdom. Its seed is the blood of no less than twenty thousand martyrs who have offered up their lives that it may be born and flourish. The axis round which its institutions revolve are the authentic provisions of the Will and Testament of 'Abdu'l-Bahá. Its guiding principles are the truths which He Who is the unerring Interpreter of the teachings of our Faith has so clearly enunciated in His public addresses throughout the West. The laws that govern its operation and limit its functions are those which have been expressly ordained in the Kitáb-i-Aqdas. The seat round which its spiritual, its humanitarian and administrative activities will cluster are the Mashriqu'l-Adhkár and its Dependencies. The pillars that sustain its authority and buttress its structure are the twin institutions of the Guardianship and of the Universal House of Justice. The central, the underlying aim which animates it is the establishment of the New World Order as adumbrated by Bahá'u'lláh. The methods it employs, the standard it inculcates, incline it to neither East nor West, neither Jew nor Gentile, neither rich nor poor, neither white nor colored. Its watchword is the unification of the human race; its standard the "Most Great Peace"; its consummation the advent of that golden millennium—the Day when the kingdoms of this world shall have become the Kingdom of God Himself, the Kingdom of Bahá'u'lláh.

SHOGHI.

Haifa, Palestine,
February 8, 1934.

THE UNFOLDMENT OF WORLD CIVILIZATION

THE UNFOLDMENT OF WORLD
CIVILIZATION

*To the beloved of God and the handmaids of the Merciful through-
out the West.*

Friends and fellow-heirs of the grace of Bahá'u'lláh:

As your co-sharer in the building up of the New World Order
which the mind of Bahá'u'lláh has visioned, and whose features the
pen of 'Abdu'l-Bahá, its perfect Architect, has delineated, I pause to
contemplate with you the scene which the revolution of well-nigh
fifteen years after His passing unfolds before us.

The contrast between the accumulating evidences of steady consolidation that accompany the rise of the Administrative Order of
the Faith of God, and the forces of disintegration which batter at
the fabric of a travailing society, is as clear as it is arresting. Both
within and outside the Bahá'í world the signs and tokens which, in
a mysterious manner, are heralding the birth of that World Order,
the establishment of which must signalize the Golden Age of the
Cause of God, are growing and multiplying day by day. No fair-
minded observer can any longer fail to discern them. He cannot be
misled by the painful slowness characterizing the unfoldment of the
civilization which the followers of Bahá'u'lláh are laboring to establish. Nor can he be deluded by the ephemeral manifestations of returning prosperity which at times appear to be capable of checking
the disruptive influence of the chronic ills afflicting the institutions
of a decaying age. The signs of the times are too numerous and
compelling to allow him to mistake their character or to belittle their
significance. He can, if he be fair in his judgment, recognize in the
chain of events which proclaim on the one hand the irresistible
march of the institutions directly associated with the Revelation of
Bahá'u'lláh and foreshadow on the other the downfall of those
powers and principalities that have either ignored or opposed it—he
can recognize in them all evidences of the operation of God's all-
pervasive Will, the shaping of His perfectly ordered and world-
embracing Plan.

"*Soon,*" Bahá'u'lláh's own words proclaim it, "*will the present
day Order be rolled up, and a new one spread out in its stead.
Verily, thy Lord speaketh the truth and is the Knower of things unseen.*" "*By Myself,*" He solemnly asserts, "*the day is approaching*

when We will have rolled up the world and all that is therein, and spread out a new Order in its stead. He, verily, is powerful over all things." "The world's equilibrium," He explains, *"hath been upset through the vibrating influence of this Most Great, this new World Order. Mankind's ordered life hath been revolutionized through the agency of this unique, this wondrous System, the like of which mortal eyes have never witnessed." "The signs of impending convulsions and chaos,"* He warns the peoples of the world, *"can now be discerned, inasmuch as the prevailing Order appeareth to be lamentably defective."*

Dearly-beloved friends! This New World Order, whose promise is enshrined in the Revelation of Bahá'u'lláh, whose fundamental principles have been enunciated in the writings of the Center of His Covenant, involves no less than the complete unification of the entire human race. This unification should conform to such principles as would directly harmonize with the spirit that animates, and the laws that govern the operation of, the institutions that already constitute the structural basis of the Administrative Order of His Faith.

No machinery falling short of the standard inculcated by the Bahá'í Revelation, and at variance with the sublime pattern ordained in His teachings, which the collective efforts of mankind may yet devise can ever hope to achieve anything above or beyond that *"Lesser Peace"* to which the Author of our Faith has Himself alluded in His writings. *"Now that ye have refused the Most Great Peace,"* He, admonishing the kings and rulers of the earth, has written, *"hold ye fast unto this the Lesser Peace, that haply ye may in some degree better your own condition and that of your dependents."* Expatiating on this Lesser Peace, He thus addresses in that same Tablet the rulers of the earth: *"Be reconciled among yourselves, that ye may need no more armaments save in a measure to safeguard your territories and dominions . . . Be united, O kings of the earth, for thereby will the tempest of discord be stilled amongst you, and your peoples find rest, if ye be of them that comprehend. Should any one among you take up arms against another, rise ye all against him, for this is naught but manifest justice."*

The Most Great Peace, on the other hand, as conceived by Bahá'u'lláh—a peace that must inevitably follow as the practical consequence of the spiritualization of the world and the fusion of all its races, creeds, classes and nations—can rest on no other basis, and can be preserved through no other agency, except the divinely appointed ordinances that are implicit in the World Order that stands associated with His Holy Name. In His Tablet, revealed almost seventy years ago to Queen Victoria, Bahá'u'lláh, alluding to this Most Great Peace, has declared: *"That which the Lord hath ordained as the sovereign remedy and mightiest instrument for the healing of all the world is the union of all its peoples in one universal Cause, one common Faith. This can in no wise be achieved except through the power of a skilled, an all-powerful and inspired Physician. This, verily, is the truth, and all else naught but error . . . Consider these days in which the Ancient Beauty, He Who is the Most Great Name, hath been sent down to regenerate and unify mankind. Behold how with drawn swords they rose against Him, and committed that which caused the Faithful Spirit to tremble. And whenever We said unto them: 'Lo, the World Reformer is come,' they made reply: 'He, in truth, is one of the stirrers of mischief.'"* *"It beseemeth all men in this Day,"* He, in another Tablet, asserts, *"to take firm hold on the Most Great Name, and to establish the unity of all mankind. There is no place to flee to, no refuge that any one can seek, except Him."*

Humanity's Coming of Age

The Revelation of Bahá'u'lláh, whose supreme mission is none other but the achievement of this organic and spiritual unity of the whole body of nations, should, if we be faithful to its implications, be regarded as signalizing through its advent the *coming of age of the entire human race*. It should be viewed not merely as yet another spiritual revival in the ever-changing fortunes of mankind, not only as a further stage in a chain of progressive Revelations, nor even as the culmination of one of a series of recurrent prophetic cycles, but rather as marking the last and highest stage in the stupendous evolution of man's collective life on this planet. The emergence of a world community, the consciousness of world citizenship, the founding of a world civilization and culture—all of which must synchronize with the initial stages in the unfoldment of the Golden Age of the Bahá'í Era—should, by their very nature, be regarded, as far as this planetary life is concerned, as the furthermost limits in the organization of human society, though man, as an individual, will, nay must indeed as a result of such a consummation, continue indefinitely to progress and develop.

That mystic, all-pervasive, yet indefinable change, which we associate with the stage of maturity inevitable in the life of the individual and the development of the fruit must, if we would correctly apprehend the utterances of Bahá'u'lláh, have its counterpart in the evolution of the organization of human society. A similar stage must sooner or later be attained in the collective life of mankind, producing an even more striking phenomenon in world relations, and endowing the whole human race with such potentialities of well-being as shall provide, throughout the succeeding ages, the chief incentive required for the eventual fulfillment of its high destiny. Such a stage of maturity in the process of human government must, for all time, if we would faithfully recognize the tremendous claim advanced by Bahá'u'lláh, remain identified with the Revelation of which He was the Bearer.

In one of the most characteristic passages He Himself has revealed, He testifies in a language that none can mistake to the truth of this distinguishing principle of Bahá'í belief: *"It hath been decreed by Us that the Word of God and all the potentialities thereof shall be manifested unto men in strict conformity with such conditions as have been foreordained by Him Who is the All-Knowing, the All-Wise . . . Should the Word be allowed to release suddenly all the energies latent within it, no man could sustain the weight of so mighty a revelation . . . Consider that which hath been sent down unto Muḥammad, the Apostle of God. The measure of the Revelation of which He was the Bearer had been clearly foreordained by Him Who is the Almighty, the All-Powerful. They that heard Him, however, could apprehend His purpose only to the extent of their station and spiritual capacity. He, in like manner, uncovered the Face of Wisdom in proportion to their ability to sustain the burden of His Message. No sooner had mankind attained the stage of maturity, than the Word revealed to men's eyes the latent energies with which it had been endowed—energies which manifested themselves in the plenitude of their glory when the Ancient Beauty appeared, in the year sixty, in the person of 'Alí-Muḥammad, the Báb."*

'Abdu'l-Bahá, elucidating this fundamental verity, has written: *"All created things have their degree or stage of maturity. The period of maturity in the life of a tree is the time of its fruit-bearing . . . The animal attains a stage of full growth and completeness, and in the human kingdom man reaches his maturity when the light of his intelligence attains its greatest power and development . . . Similarly there are periods and stages in the collective life of humanity. At one time it was passing through its stage of child-*

hood, at another its period of youth, but now it has entered its long-predicted phase of maturity, the evidences of which are everywhere apparent . . . That which was applicable to human needs during the early history of the race can neither meet nor satisfy the demands of this day, this period of newness and consummation. Humanity has emerged from its former state of limitation and preliminary training. Man must now become imbued with new virtues and powers, new moral standards, new capacities. New bounties, perfect bestowals, are awaiting and already descending upon him. The gifts and blessings of the period of youth, although timely and sufficient during the adolescence of mankind, are now incapable of meeting the requirements of its maturity."

The Process of Integration

Such a unique and momentous crisis in the life of organized mankind may, moreover, be likened to the culminating stage in the political evolution of the great American Republic—the stage which marked the emergence of a unified community of federated states. The stirring of a new national consciousness, and the birth of a new type of civilization, infinitely richer and nobler than any which its component parts could have severally hoped to achieve, may be said to have proclaimed the coming of age of the American people. Within the territorial limits of this nation, this consummation may be viewed as the culmination of the process of human government. The diversified and loosely related elements of a divided community were brought together, unified and incorporated into one coherent system. Though this entity may continue gaining in cohesive power, though the unity already achieved may be further consolidated, though the civilization to which that unity could alone have given birth may expand and flourish, yet the machinery essential to such an unfoldment may be said to have been, in its essential structure, erected, and the impulse required to guide and sustain it may be regarded as having been fundamentally imparted. No stage above and beyond this consummation of national unity can, within the geographical limits of that nation, be imagined, though the highest destiny of its people, as a constituent element in a still larger entity that will embrace the whole of mankind, may still remain unfulfilled. Considered as an isolated unit, however, this process of integration may be said to have reached its highest and final consummation.

Such is the stage to which an evolving humanity is collectively approaching. The Revelation entrusted by the Almighty Ordainer to Bahá'u'lláh, His followers firmly believe, has been endowed with such potentialities as are commensurate with the maturity of the human race—the crowning and most momentous stage in its evolution from infancy to manhood.

The successive Founders of all past Religions Who, from time immemorial, have shed, with ever-increasing intensity, the splendor of one common Revelation at the various stages which have marked the advance of mankind towards maturity may thus, in a sense, be regarded as preliminary Manifestations, anticipating and paving the way for the advent of that Day of Days when the whole earth will have fructified and the tree of humanity will have yielded its destined fruit.

Incontrovertible as is this truth, its challenging character should never be allowed to obscure the purpose, or distort the principle, underlying the utterances of Bahá'u'lláh—utterances that have established for all time the absolute oneness of all the Prophets, Himself included, whether belonging to the past or to the future. Though the mission of the Prophets preceding Bahá'u'lláh may be viewed in that light, though the measure of Divine Revelation with which each has been entrusted must, as a result of this process of evolution, necessarily differ, their common origin, their essential unity, their identity of purpose, should at no time and under no circumstances be misapprehended or denied. That all the Messengers of God should be regarded as *"abiding in the same Tabernacle, soaring in the same Heaven, seated upon the same Throne, uttering the same Speech, and proclaiming the same Faith"* must, however much we may extol the measure of Divine Revelation vouchsafed to mankind at this crowning stage of its evolution, remain the unalterable foundation and central tenet of Bahá'í belief. Any variations in the splendor which each of these Manifestations of the Light of God has shed upon the world should be ascribed not to any inherent superiority involved in the essential character of any one of them, but rather to the progressive capacity, the ever-increasing spiritual receptiveness, which mankind, in its progress towards maturity, has invariably manifested.

The Final Consummation

Only those who are willing to associate the Revelation proclaimed by Bahá'u'lláh with the consummation of so stupendous an evolution in the collective life of the whole human race can grasp the significance of the words which He, while alluding to the glories of this promised Day and to the duration of the Bahá'í Era, has deemed fit to utter. *"This is the King of Days,"* He exclaims, *"the Day that hath seen the coming of the Best-Beloved, Him Who, through all eternity, hath been acclaimed the Desire of the World."* *"The Scriptures of past Dispensations,"* He further asserts, *"celebrate the great jubilee that must needs greet this most great Day of God. Well is it with him that hath lived to see this Day and hath recognized its station."* *"It is evident,"* He, in another passage explains, *"that every age in which a Manifestation of God hath lived is divinely-ordained, and may, in a sense, be characterized as God's appointed Day. This Day, however, is unique, and is to be distinguished from those that have preceded it. The designation 'Seal of the Prophets' fully revealeth its high station. The Prophetic Cycle hath verily ended. The Eternal Truth is now come. He hath lifted up the ensign of power, and is now shedding upon the world the unclouded splendor of His Revelation."* *"In this most mighty Revelation,"* He, in categorical language, declares, *"all the Dispensations of the past have attained their highest, their final consummation. That which hath been made manifest in this preëminent, this most exalted Revelation, standeth unparalleled in the annals of the past, nor will future age witness its like."*

'Abdu'l-Bahá's authentic pronouncements should, likewise, be recalled as confirming, in no less emphatic manner, the unexampled vastness of the Bahá'í Dispensation. *"Centuries,"* He affirms in one of His Tablets, *"nay, countless ages, must pass away ere the Day-Star of Truth shineth again in its mid-summer splendor, or appeareth once more in the radiance of its vernal glory . . . The mere contemplation of the Dispensation inaugurated by the Blessed Beauty would have sufficed to overwhelm the saints of bygone ages —saints who longed to partake, for one moment, of its great glory."* *"Concerning the Manifestations that will come down in the future 'in the shadows of the clouds,'"* He, in a still more definite language, affirms, *"know, verily, that in so far as their relation to the Source of their inspiration is concerned, they are under the shadow of the Ancient Beauty. In their relation, however, to the age in which they appear, each and every one of them 'doeth whatsoever He willeth.'"* *"This holy Dispensation,"* He, alluding to the Revelation of Bahá'u'lláh, explains, *"is illumined with the light of the*

Sun of Truth shining from its most exalted station, and in the pleni-tude of its resplendency, its heat and glory."

Pangs of Death and Birth

Dearly-beloved friends: Though the Revelation of Bahá'u'lláh has been delivered, the World Order which such a Revelation must needs beget is as yet unborn. Though the Heroic Age of His Faith is passed, the creative energies which that Age has released have not as yet crystallized into that world society which, in the fullness of time, is to mirror forth the brightness of His glory. Though the framework of His Administrative Order has been erected, and the Formative Period of the Bahá'í Era has begun, yet the promised Kingdom into which the seed of His institutions must ripen remains as yet uninaugurated. Though His Voice has been raised, and the ensigns of His Faith have been lifted up in no less than forty countries of both the East and the West, yet the wholeness of the human race is as yet unrecognized, its unity unproclaimed, and the standard of its Most Great Peace unhoisted.

"The heights," Bahá'u'lláh Himself testifies, *"which, through the most gracious favor of God, mortal man can attain in this Day are as yet unrevealed to his sight. The world of being hath never had, nor doth it yet possess, the capacity for such a revelation. The day, however, is approaching when the potentialities of so great a favor will, by virtue of His behest, be manifested unto men."*

For the revelation of so great a favor a period of intense turmoil and wide-spread suffering would seem to be indispensable. Resplendent as has been the Age that has witnessed the inception of the Mission with which Bahá'u'lláh has been entrusted, the interval which must elapse ere that Age yields its choicest fruit must, it is becoming increasingly apparent, be overshadowed by such moral and social gloom as can alone prepare an unrepentant humanity for the prize she is destined to inherit.

Into such a period we are now steadily and irresistibly moving. Amidst the shadows which are increasingly gathering about us we can faintly discern the glimmerings of Bahá'u'lláh's unearthly sovereignty appearing fitfully on the horizon of history. To us, the "generation of the half-light," living at a time which may be designated as the period of the incubation of the World Commonwealth envisaged by Bahá'u'lláh, has been assigned a task whose high privilege we can never sufficiently appreciate, and the arduousness of which we can as yet but dimly recognize. We may well believe, we who are called upon to experience the operation of the dark forces destined to unloose a flood of agonizing afflictions, that the darkest hour that must precede the dawn of the Golden Age of our Faith has not yet struck. Deep as is the gloom that already encircles the world, the afflictive ordeals which that world is to suffer are still in preparation, nor can their blackness be as yet imagined. We stand on the threshold of an age whose convulsions proclaim alike the death-pangs of the old order and the birth-pangs of the new. Through the generating influence of the Faith announced by Bahá'-u'lláh this New World Order may be said to have been conceived. We can, at the present moment, experience its stirrings in the womb of a travailing age—an age waiting for the appointed hour at which it can cast its burden and yield its fairest fruit.

"The whole earth," writes Bahá'u'lláh, "is now in a state of pregnancy. The day is approaching when it will have yielded its noblest fruits, when from it will have sprung forth the loftiest trees, the most enchanting blossoms, the most heavenly blessings. Immeasurably exalted is the breeze that wafteth from the garment of thy Lord, the Glorified! For lo, it hath breathed its fragrance and made all things new! Well is it with them that comprehend." "The on-rushing winds of the grace of God," He, in the Súratu'l-Haykal, proclaims, "have passed over all things. Every creature hath been endowed with all the potentialities it can carry. And yet the peoples of the world have denied this grace! Every tree hath been endowed with the choicest fruits, every ocean enriched with the most luminous gems. Man, himself, hath been invested with the gifts of understanding and knowledge. The whole creation hath been made the recipient of the revelation of the All-Merciful, and the earth the repository of things inscrutable to all except God, the Truth, the Knower of things unseen. The time is approaching when every created thing will have cast its burden. Glorified be God Who hath vouchsafed this grace that encompasseth all things, whether seen or unseen!"

"The Call of God," 'Abdu'l-Bahá has written, "when raised, breathed a new life into the body of mankind, and infused a new spirit into the whole creation. It is for this reason that the world hath been moved to its depths, and the hearts and consciences of men been quickened. Erelong the evidences of this regeneration will be revealed, and the fast asleep will be awakened."

Universal Fermentation

As we view the world around us, we are compelled to observe the manifold evidences of that universal fermentation which, in every continent of the globe and in every department of human life, be it religious, social, economic or political, is purging and reshaping humanity in anticipation of the Day when the wholeness of the human race will have been recognized and its unity established. A two-fold process, however, can be distinguished, each tending, in its own way and with an accelerated momentum, to bring to a climax the forces that are transforming the face of our planet. The first is essentially an integrating process, while the second is fundamentally disruptive. The former, as it steadily evolves, unfolds a System which may well serve as a pattern for that world polity towards which a strangely-disordered world is continually advancing; while the latter, as its disintegrating influence deepens, tends to tear down, with increasing violence, the antiquated barriers that seek to block humanity's progress towards its destined goal. The constructive process stands associated with the nascent Faith of Bahá'u'lláh, and is the harbinger of the New World Order that Faith must erelong establish. The destructive forces that characterize the other should be identified with a civilization that has refused to answer to the expectation of a new age, and is consequently falling into chaos and decline.

A titanic, a spiritual struggle, unparalleled in its magnitude yet unspeakably glorious in its ultimate consequences, is being waged as a result of these opposing tendencies, in this age of transition through which the organized community of the followers of Bahá'u'lláh and mankind as a whole are passing.

The Spirit that has incarnated itself in the institutions of a rising Faith has, in the course of its onward march for the redemption of the world, encountered and is now battling with such forces as are, in most instances, the very negation of that Spirit, and whose continued existence must inevitably hinder it from achieving its purpose. The hollow and outworn institutions, the obsolescent doctrines and beliefs, the effete and discredited traditions which these forces represent, it should be observed, have, in certain instances, been undermined by virtue of their senility, the loss of their cohesive power, and their own inherent corruption. A few have been swept away by the onrushing forces which the Bahá'í Faith has, at the hour of its birth, so mysteriously released. Others, as a direct result of a vain and feeble resistance to its rise in the initial stages of its development, have died out and been utterly discredited. Still others, fearful of the pervasive influence of the institutions in which that same Spirit had, at a later stage, been embodied, had mobilized their forces and launched their attack, destined to sustain, in their turn, after a brief and illusory success, an ignominious defeat.

This Age of Transition

It is not my purpose to call to mind, much less to attempt a detailed analysis of, the spiritual struggles that have ensued, or to note the victories that have redounded to the glory of the Faith of Bahá'u'lláh since the day of its foundation. My chief concern is not with the happenings that have distinguished the First, the Apostolic Age of the Bahá'í Dispensation, but rather with the outstanding events that are transpiring in, and the tendencies which characterize, the formative period of its development, this Age of Transition, whose tribulations are the precursors of that Era of blissful felicity which is to incarnate God's ultimate purpose for all mankind.

To the catastrophic fall of mighty kingdoms and empires, on the eve of 'Abdu'l-Bahá's departure, Whose passing may be said to have ushered in the opening phase of the Age of Transition in which we now live, I have, in a previous communication, briefly alluded. The dissolution of the German Empire, the humiliating defeat inflicted upon its ruler, the successor and lineal descendant of the Prussian King and Emperor to whom Bahá'u'lláh had addressed His solemn and historic warning, together with the extinction of the Austro-Hungarian Monarchy, the remnant of the once-great Holy Roman Empire, were both precipitated by a war whose outbreak signalized the opening of the Age of Frustration destined to precede the establishment of the World Order of Bahá'u'lláh. Both of these momentous events may be viewed as the earliest occurrences of that turbulent Age, into the outer fringes of whose darkest phase we are now beginning to enter.

To the Conqueror of Napoleon III, the Author of our Faith had, on the morrow of the King's victory, addressed, in His Most Holy Book, this clear and ominous warning: *"O King of Berlin!* . . . *Take heed lest pride debar thee from recognizing the Day-Spring of Divine Revelation, lest earthly desires shut thee out, as by a veil, from the Lord of the Throne above and of the earth below. Thus counseleth thee the Pen of the Most High. He, verily, is the*

Most Gracious, the All-Bountiful. Do thou remember the one whose power transcended thy power (Napoleon III), *and whose station excelled thy station. Where is he? Whither are gone the things he possessed? Take warning, and be not of them that are fast asleep. He it was who cast the Tablet of God behind him, when We made known unto him what the hosts of tyranny had caused Us to suffer. Wherefore, disgrace assailed him from all sides, and he went down to dust in great loss. Think deeply, O King, concerning him, and concerning them who, like unto thee, have conquered cities and ruled over men. The All-Merciful brought them down from their palaces to their graves. Be warned, be of them who reflect."*

"O banks of the Rhine!" Bahá'u'lláh, in another passage of that same Book, prophesies, *"We have seen you covered with gore, inasmuch as the swords of retribution were drawn against you; and so you shall have another turn. And We hear the lamentations of Berlin, though she be today in conspicuous glory."*

Collapse of Islám

The collapse of the power of the Shí'ih hierarchy, in a land which had for centuries been one of the impregnable strongholds of Muslim fanaticism, was the inevitable consequence of that wave of secularization which, at a later time, was to invade some of the most powerful and conservative ecclesiastical institutions in both the European and American continents. Though not the direct outcome of the last war, this sudden trembling which had seized this hitherto immovable pillar of Islamic orthodoxy accentuated the problems and deepened the restlessness with which a war-weary world was being afflicted. Shí'ih Islám had lost once for all, in Bahá'u'lláh's native land and as the direct consequence of its implacable hostility to His Faith, its combative power, had forfeited its rights and privileges, had been degraded and demoralized, and was being condemned to hopeless obscurity and ultimate extinction. No less than twenty thousand martyrs, however, had to sacrifice their lives ere the Cause for which they had stood and died could register this initial victory over those who were the first to repudiate its claims and mow down its gallant warriors. "Vileness and poverty were stamped upon them, and they returned with wrath from God."

"Behold," writes Bahá'u'lláh, commenting on the decline of a fallen people, *"how the sayings and doings of Shí'ih Islám have dulled the joy and fervor of its early days, and tarnished the pristine*

brilliancy of its light. In its primitive days, whilst they still adhered to the precepts associated with the name of their Prophet, the Lord of mankind, their career was marked by an unbroken chain of victories and triumphs. As they gradually strayed from the path of their Ideal Leader and Master, as they turned away from the light of God and corrupted the principle of His Divine unity, and as they increasingly centered their attention upon them who were only the revealers of the potency of His Word, their power was turned into weakness, their glory into shame, their courage into fear. Thou dost witness to what a pass they have come."

The downfall of the Qájár Dynasty, the avowed defender and the willing instrument of a decaying clergy, almost synchronized with the humiliation which the S̲h̲í‘ih ecclesiastical leaders had suffered. From Muḥammad S̲h̲áh down to the last and feeble monarch of that dynasty, the Faith of Bahá'u'lláh was denied the impartial consideration, the disinterested and fair treatment which its cause had rightly demanded. It had, on the contrary, been atrociously harassed, consistently betrayed and prosecuted. The martyrdom of the Báb; the banishment of Bahá'u'lláh; the confiscation of His earthly possessions; His incarceration in Mázindarán; the reign of terror that confined Him in the most pestilential of dungeons; the intrigues, the protests, and calumnies which thrice renewed His exile and led to His ultimate imprisonment in the most desolate of cities; the shameful sentences passed, with the connivance of the judicial and ecclesiastical authorities, against the person, the property, and the honor of His innocent followers—these stand out as among the blackest acts for which posterity will hold this blood-stained dynasty responsible. One more barrier that had sought to obstruct the forward march of the Faith was now removed.

Though Bahá'u'lláh had been banished from His native land, the tide of calamity which had swept with such fury over Him and over the followers of the Báb, was by no means receding. Under the jurisdiction of the Sultán of Turkey, the arch-enemy of His Cause, a new chapter in the history of His ever-recurring trials had opened. The overthrow of the Sultanate and the Caliphate, the twin pillars of Sunní Islám, can be regarded in no other light except as the inevitable consequence of the fierce, the sustained and deliberate persecution which the monarchs of the tottering House of ‘U̲thmán, the recognized successors of the Prophet Muḥammad, had launched against it. From the city of Constantinople, the traditional seat of both the Sultanate and the Caliphate, the rulers of Turkey had, for a period covering almost three quarters of a century, striven, with unabated zeal, to stem the tide of a Faith they feared and abhorred. From the time Bahá'u'lláh set foot on Turkish soil and was made a virtual prisoner of the most powerful potentate of Islám to the year of the Holy Land's liberation from Turkish yoke, successive Caliphs, and in particular the Sultáns 'Abdu'l-'Azíz and 'Abdu'l-Hamíd, had, in the full exercise of the spiritual and temporal authority which their exalted office had conferred upon them, afflicted both the Founder of our Faith and the Center of His Covenant with such pain and tribulation as no mind can fathom nor pen or tongue describe. They alone could have measured or borne them.

To these afflictive trials Bahá'u'lláh has repeatedly testified: *"By the righteousness of the Almighty! Were I to recount to thee the tale of the things that have befallen Me, the souls and minds of men would be incapable of sustaining its weight. God Himself beareth Me witness."* *"Twenty years have passed,"* He, addressing the kings of Christendom, has written, *"during which We have, each day, tasted the agony of a fresh tribulation. No one of them that were before Us hath endured the things We have endured. Would that ye could perceive it! They that rose up against us have put us to death, have shed our blood, have plundered our property, and violated our honor."* *"Recall to mind My sorrows,"* He, in another connection, has revealed, *"My cares and anxieties, My woes and trials, the state of My captivity, the tears that I have shed, the bitterness of Mine anguish, and now Mine imprisonment in this far-off land . . . Couldst thou be told what hath befallen the Ancient Beauty, thou wouldst flee into the wilderness, and weep with a great weeping . . . Every morning I arose from my bed, I discovered the hosts of countless afflictions massed behind My door; and every night when I lay down, lo, My heart was torn with agony at what it had suffered from the fiendish cruelty of its foes."*

The orders which these foes issued, the banishments they decreed, the indignities they inflicted, the plans they devised, the investigations they conducted, the threats they pronounced, the atrocities they were prepared to commit, the intrigues and baseness to which they, their ministers, their governors, and military chieftains had stooped, constitute a record which can hardly find a parallel in the history of any revealed religion. The mere recital of the most salient features of that sinister theme would suffice to fill a volume. They knew full well that the spiritual and administrative Center of the Cause they had striven to eradicate had now shifted to their dominion, that its leaders were Turkish citizens, and that whatever resources these could command were at their mercy. That for a period of almost three score years and ten, while still in the plenitude of its unquestioned authority, while reinforced by the endless machinations of the civil and ecclesiastical authorities of a neighboring nation, and assured of the support of those of Bahá'u'lláh's kindred who had rebelled against, and seceded from, His Cause, this despotism should have failed in the end to extirpate a mere handful of its condemned subjects must, to every unbelieving observer, remain one of the most intriguing and mysterious episodes of contemporary history.

The Cause of which Bahá'u'lláh was still the visible leader had, despite the calculations of a short-sighted enemy, undeniably triumphed. No unbiased mind, penetrating the surface of conditions surrounding the Prisoner of 'Akká, could any longer mistake or deny it. Though the tension which had been relaxed was, for a time, heightened after Bahá'u'lláh's ascension and the perils of a still unsettled situation were revived, it was becoming increasingly evident that the insidious forces of decay, which for many a long year were eating into the vitals of a diseased nation, were now moving towards a climax. A series of internal convulsions, each more devastating than the previous one, had already been unchained, destined to bring in their wake one of the most catastrophic occurrences of modern times. The murder of that arrogant despot in the year 1876; the Russo-Turkish conflict that soon followed in its wake; the wars of liberation which succeeded it; the rise of the Young Turk movement; the Turkish Revolution of 1909 that precipitated the downfall of 'Abdu'l-Hamíd; the Balkan wars with their calamitous consequences; the liberation of Palestine enshrining within its bosom the cities of 'Akká and Haifa, the world center of an emancipated Faith; the further dismemberment decreed by the Treaty of Versailles; the abolition of the Sultanate and the downfall of the House of 'Uthmán; the extinction of the Caliphate; the disestablishment of the State Religion; the annulment of the Sharí'ah Law and the promulgation of a universal Civil Code; the suppression of various orders, beliefs, traditions and ceremonials believed to be inextricably interwoven with the fabric of the Muslim Faith—these followed with an ease and swiftness that no man had dared envisage. In these devastating blows, administered by friend and foe alike, by Christian nations and professing Muslims, every follower of the persecuted Faith of Bahá'u'lláh recognized evidences of the directing

Hand of the departed Founder of his religion, Who, from the invisible Realm, was unloosing a flood of well-deserved calamities upon a rebellious religion and nation.

Compare the evidences of Divine visitation which befell the persecutors of Jesus Christ with these historic retributions which, in the latter part of the first century of the Bahá'í Era, have hurled to dust the chief adversary of the religion of Bahá'u'lláh. Had not the Roman Emperor, in the second half of the first century of the Christian Era, after a distressful siege of Jerusalem, laid waste the Holy City, destroyed the Temple, desecrated and robbed the Holy of Holies of its treasures, and transported them to Rome, reared a pagan colony on the mount of Zion, massacred the Jews, and exiled and dispersed the survivors?

Compare, moreover, these words which the persecuted Christ, as witnessed by the Gospel, addressed to Jerusalem, with Bahá'u'-lláh's apostrophe to Constantinople, revealed while He lay in His far-off Prison, and recorded in His Most Holy Book: *"O Jerusalem, Jerusalem, thou that killest the Prophets and stonest them which are sent unto thee, how often would I have gathered thy children together, even as a hen gathereth her chickens under her wings!"* And again, as He wept over the city: *"If thou hadst known, even thou, at least in this thy day, the things which belong unto thy peace! but now they are hid from thine eyes. For the days shall come upon thee, that thine enemies shall cast a trench about thee, and compass thee round, and keep thee in on every side, and shall lay thee even with the ground, and thy children within thee; and they shall not leave in thee one stone upon another; because thou knewest not the time of thy visitation."*

"O Spot that art situate on the shores of the two seas!" Bahá'u'-lláh thus apostrophizes the City of Constantinople, *"The throne of tyranny hath, verily, been established upon thee, and the flame of hatred hath been kindled within thy bosom, in such wise that the Concourse on high and they who circle around the Exalted Throne have wailed and lamented. We behold in thee the foolish ruling over the wise, and darkness vaunting itself against the light. Thou art indeed filled with manifest pride. Hath thine outward splendor made thee vainglorious? By Him Who is the Lord of mankind! It shall soon perish, and thy daughters and thy widows and all the kindreds that dwell within thee shall lament. Thus informeth thee the All-Knowing, the All-Wise."*

To Sultán 'Abdu'l-'Azíz, the monarch who decreed each of Bahá'u'lláh's three banishments, the Founder of our Faith, while a prisoner in the Sulṭán's capital, addressed these words: *"Hearken, O king, to the speech of Him that speaketh the truth, Him that doth not ask thee to recompense Him with the things God hath chosen to bestow upon thee, Him Who unerringly treadeth the Straight Path . . . Set before thine eyes God's unerring Balance and, as one standing in His presence, weigh in that Balance thine actions every day, every moment of thy life. Bring thyself to account ere thou art summoned to a reckoning, on the day when no man shall have strength to stand for fear of God, the day when the hearts of the heedless ones shall be made to tremble."*

To the Ministers of the Turkish State, He, in that same Tablet, revealed: *"It behooveth you, O Ministers of State, to keep the precepts of God, and to forsake your own laws and regulations, and to be of them who are guided aright . . . Ye shall, erelong, discover the consequences of that which ye shall have done in this vain life, and shall be repaid for them . . . How great the number of those who, in bygone ages, have committed the things ye have committed, and who, though superior to you in rank, have, in the end, returned unto dust, and been consigned to their inevitable doom! . . . Ye shall follow in their wake, and shall be made to enter a habitation wherein none shall be found to befriend or help you . . . The days of your life shall roll away, and all the things with which ye are occupied, and of which ye boast yourselves, shall perish, and ye shall, most certainly, be summoned by a company of His angels to appear at the spot where the limbs of the entire creation shall be made to tremble, and the flesh of every oppressor to creep . . . This is the day that shall inevitably come upon you, the hour that none can put back."*

To the inhabitants of Constantinople, while He lived the life of an exile in their midst, Bahá'u'lláh, in that same Tablet, addressed these words: *"Fear God, ye inhabitants of the City, and sow not the seeds of dissension amongst men . . . Your days shall pass away as have the days of them who were before you. To dust shall ye return, even as your fathers of old did return."* *"We found,"* He, moreover, remarks, *"upon Our arrival in the City its governors and elders as children gathered about and disporting themselves with clay . . . Our inner eye wept sore over them, and over their transgressions and their total disregard of the thing for which they were created . . . The day is approaching when God will have raised up a people who will call to remembrance Our days, who will tell the tale of Our trials, who will demand the restitution of Our rights from them that, without a tittle of evidence, have treated Us with manifest injustice. God assuredly dominateth the lives of them that wronged Us, and is well aware of their doings. He will, most certainly, lay hold on them for their sins. He, verily, is the fiercest of avengers." "Wherefore," He graciously exhorteth them, "hearken ye unto My speech, and return ye to God and repent, that He, through His grace, may have mercy upon you, may wash away your sins, and forgive your trespasses. The greatness of His mercy surpasseth the fury of His wrath, and His grace encompasseth all who have been called into being and been clothed with the robe of life, be they of the past or of the future."*

And, finally, in the Lawḥ-i-Ra'ís we find these prophetic words recorded: *"Hearken, O Chief . . . to the Voice of God, the Sovereign, the Help in Peril, the Self-Subsisting . . . Thou hast, O Chief, committed that which hath made Muḥammad, the Apostle of God, groan in the Most Exalted Paradise. The world hath made thee proud, so much so that thou hast turned away from the Face through Whose brightness the Concourse on high hath been illumined. Soon thou shalt find thyself in evident loss . . . The day is approaching when the Land of Mystery* (Adrianople) *and what is beside it shall be changed, and shall pass out of the hands of the King, and commotions shall appear, and the voice of lamentation shall be raised, and the evidences of mischief shall be revealed on all sides, and confusion shall spread by reason of that which hath befallen these captives at the hands of the hosts of oppression. The course of things shall be altered, and conditions shall wax so grievous, that the very sands on the desolate hills will moan, and the trees on the mountain will weep, and blood will flow out of all things. Then wilt thou behold the people in sore distress."*

Thirteen hundred years had to elapse from the death of the Prophet Muḥammad ere the illegitimacy of the institution of the Caliphate, the founders of which had usurped the authority of the lawful successors of the Apostle of God, could be fully and publicly demonstrated. An institution which in its inception had trampled upon so sacred a right and unchained the forces of so distressful a schism, an institution which, in the latter days, had dealt so grievous a blow to a Faith Whose Forerunner was Himself a descendant of the very Imáms whose authority that institution had repudiated, deserved full well the chastisement that had sealed its fate.

The text of certain Muḥammadan traditions, the authenticity of which Muslims themselves recognize, and which have been extensively quoted by eminent Oriental Bahá'í scholars and authors, will serve to corroborate the argument and illuminate the theme I have attempted to expound: *"In the latter days a grievous calamity shall befall My people at the hands of their ruler, a calamity such as no man ever heard to surpass it. So fierce will it be that none can find a shelter. God will then send down One of My descendants, One sprung from My family, Who will fill the earth with equity and justice, even as it hath been filled with injustice and tyranny."* And, again: *"A day shall be witnessed by My people whereon there will have remained of Islám naught but a name, and of the Qur'án naught but a mere appearance. The doctors of that age shall be the most evil the world hath ever seen. Mischief hath proceeded from them, and on them will it recoil."* And, again: *"At that hour His malediction shall descend upon you, and your curse shall afflict you, and your religion shall remain an empty word on your tongues. And when these signs appear amongst you, anticipate the day when the red-hot wind will have swept over you, or the day when ye will have been disfigured, or when stones will have rained upon you."*

"O people of the Qur'án," Bahá'u'lláh, addressing the combined forces of Sunní and Shí'ih Islám, significantly affirms, *"Verily, the Prophet of God, Muḥammad, sheddeth tears at the sight of your cruelty. Ye have assuredly followed your evil and corrupt desires, and turned away your face from the light of guidance. Erelong will ye witness the result of your deeds; for the Lord, My God, lieth in wait and is watchful of your behavior . . . O concourse of Muslim divines! By your deeds the exalted station of the people hath been abased, the standard of Islám hath been reversed, and its mighty throne hath fallen."*

Deterioration of Christian Institutions

So much for Islám and the crippling blows its leaders and institutions have received—and may yet receive—in this, the first century of the Bahá'í Era. If I have dwelt too long on this theme, if I have, to a disproportionate degree, quoted from the sacred writings in support of my argument, it is solely because of my firm conviction that these retributive calamities that have rained down upon the foremost oppressor of the Faith of Bahá'u'lláh should rank not only among the stirring occurrences of this Age of Transition, but as some of the most startling and significant events of contemporary history.

Both Sunní and Shí'ih Islám had, through the convulsions that had seized them, contributed to the acceleration of the disruptive process to which I have previously referred—a process which, by its very nature, is to pave the way for that complete reorganization and unification which the world, in every aspect of its life, must achieve. What of Christianity and of the denominations with which it stands identified? Can it be said that this process of deterioration that has attacked the fabric of the Religion of Muḥammad has failed to exert its baneful influence on the institutions associated with the Faith of Jesus Christ? Have these institutions already experienced the impact of these menacing forces? Are their foundations so secure and their vitality so great as to enable them to resist this on-slaught? Will they, as the confusion of a chaotic world spreads and deepens, fall in turn a prey to their violence? Have the more ortho-dox among them already arisen, and, if not, will they arise, to repel the onset of a Cause which, having pulled down the barriers of Muslim orthodoxy, is now advancing into the heart of Christen-dom, in both the European and American continents? Would such a resistance sow the seeds of further dissension and confusion, and consequently serve indirectly to hasten the advent of the promised Day?

To these queries we can but partly answer. Time alone can reveal the nature of the rôle which the institutions directly associ-ated with the Christian Faith are destined to assume in this, the Formative Period of the Bahá'í Era, this dark age of transition through which humanity as a whole is passing. Such events as have already transpired, however, are of such a nature as can indicate the direction in which these institutions are moving. We can, in some degree, appraise the probable effect which the forces operating both within the Bahá'í Faith and outside it will exert upon them.

That the forces of irreligion, of a purely materialistic philos-ophy, of unconcealed paganism have been unloosed, are now spread-ing, and, by consolidating themselves, are beginning to invade some of the most powerful Christian institutions of the western world, no unbiased observer can fail to admit. That these institutions are becoming increasingly restive, that a few among them are already dimly aware of the pervasive influence of the Cause of Bahá'u'lláh, that they will, as their inherent strength deteriorates and their dis-cipline relaxes, regard with deepening dismay the rise of His New

World Order, and will gradually determine to assail it, that such an opposition will in turn accelerate their decline, few, if any, among those who are attentively watching the progress of His Faith would be inclined to question.

"The vitality of men's belief in God," Bahá'u'lláh has testified, *"is dying out in every land; nothing short of His wholesome medicine can ever restore it. The corrosion of ungodliness is eating into the vitals of human society; what else but the Elixir of His potent Revelation can cleanse and revive it?"* "The world is in travail," He has further written, *"and its agitation waxeth day by day. Its face is turned towards waywardness and unbelief. Such shall be its plight that to disclose it now would not be meet and seemly."*

This menace of secularism that has attacked Islám and is undermining its remaining institutions, that has invaded Persia, has penetrated into India, and raised its triumphant head in Turkey, has already manifested itself in both Europe and America, and is, in varying degrees, and under various forms and designations, challenging the basis of every established religion, and in particular the institutions and communities identified with the Faith of Jesus Christ. It would be no exaggeration to say that we are moving into a period which the future historian will regard as one of the most critical in the history of Christianity.

Already a few among the protagonists of the Christian Religion admit the gravity of the situation that confronts them. "A wave of materialism is sweeping round the world"; is the testimony of its missionaries, as witnessed by the text of their official reports, "the drive and pressure of modern industrialism, which are penetrating even the forests of Central Africa and the plains of Central Asia, make men everywhere dependent on, and preoccupied with, material things. At home the Church has talked, perhaps too glibly, in pulpit or on platform of the menace of secularism; though even in England we can catch more than a glimpse of its meaning. But to the Church overseas these things are grim realities, enemies with which it is at grips . . . The Church has a new danger to face in land after land—determined and hostile attack. From Soviet Russia a definitely anti-religious Communism is pushing west into Europe and America, East into Persia, India, China and Japan. It is an economic theory, definitely harnessed to disbelief in God. It is a religious irreligion . . . It has a passionate sense of mission, and is carrying on its anti-God campaign at the Church's base at home, as well as launching its offensive against its front-line in non-Christian lands. Such a conscious, avowed, organized attack against religion in general and Christianity in particular is something new in history. Equally deliberate in some lands in its determined hostility to Christianity is another form of social and political faith—nationalism. But the nationalist attack on Christianity, unlike Communism, is often bound up with some form of national religion—with Islám in Persia and Egypt, with Buddhism in Ceylon, while the struggle for communal rights in India is allied with a revival both of Hinduism and Islám."

I need not attempt in this connection an exposition of the origin and character of those economic theories and political philosophies of the post-war period, that have directly and indirectly exerted, and are still exerting, their pernicious influence on the institutions and beliefs connected with one of the most widely-spread and best organized religious systems of the world. It is with their influence rather than with their origin that I am chiefly concerned. The excessive growth of industrialism and its attendant evils—as the aforementioned quotation bears witness—the aggressive policies initiated and the persistent efforts exerted by the inspirers and organizers of the Communist movement; the intensification of a militant nationalism, associated in certain countries with a systematized work of defamation against all forms of ecclesiastical influence, have no doubt contributed to the de-Christianization of the masses, and been responsible for a notable decline in the authority, the prestige and power of the Church. "The whole conception of God," the persecutors of the Christian Religion have insistently proclaimed, "is a conception derived from the ancient oriental despotisms. It is a conception quite unworthy of free men." "Religion," one of their leaders has asserted, "is an opiate of the people." "Religion," declares the text of their official publications, "is a brutalization of the people. Education must be so directed as to efface from the people's minds this humiliation and this idiocy."

The Hegelian philosophy which, in other countries, has, in the form of an intolerant and militant nationalism, insisted on deifying the state, has inculcated the war-spirit, and incited to racial animosity, has, likewise, led to a marked weakening of the Church and to a grave diminution of its spiritual influence. Unlike the bold offensive which an avowedly atheistic movement had chosen to launch against it, both within the Soviet union and beyond its confines, this nationalistic philosophy, which Christian rulers and governments have upheld, is an attack directed against the Church by those who were previously its professed adherents, a betrayal of its cause by its own kith and kin. It was being stabbed by an alien and militant atheism from without, and by the preachers of a heretical doctrine from within. Both of these forces, each operating in its own sphere and using its own weapons and methods, have moreover been greatly assisted and encouraged by the prevailing spirit of modernism, with its emphasis on a purely materialistic philosophy, which, as it diffuses itself, tends increasingly to divorce religion from man's daily life.

The combined effect of these strange and corrupt doctrines, these dangerous and treacherous philosophies, has, as was natural, been severely felt by those whose tenets inculcated an opposite and wholly irreconcilable spirit and principle. The consequences of the clash that inevitably ensued between these contending interests, were, in some cases, disastrous, and the damage that has been wrought irreparable. The disestablishment and dismemberment of the Greek Orthodox Church in Russia, following upon the blow which the Church of Rome had sustained as a result of the collapse of the Austro-Hungarian Monarchy; the commotion that subsequently seized the Catholic Church and culminated in its separation from the State in Spain; the persecution of the same Church in Mexico; the perquisitions, arrests, intimidation and terrorization to which Catholics and Lutherans alike are being subjected in the heart of Europe; the turmoil into which another branch of the Church has been thrown as a result of the military campaign in Africa; the decline that has set in the fortunes of Christian Missions, both Anglican and Presbyterian, in Persia, Turkey, and the Far East; the ominous signs that foreshadow serious complications in the equivocal and precarious relationships now existing between the Holy See and certain nations in the continent of Europe—these stand out as the most striking features of the reverses which, in almost every part of the world, the members and leaders of Christian ecclesiastical institutions have suffered.

That the solidarity of some of these institutions has been irretrievably shattered is too apparent for any intelligent observer to mistake or deny. The cleavage between the fundamentalists and the liberals among their adherents is continually widening. Their creeds and dogmas have been watered down, and in certain instances ignored and discarded. Their hold upon human conduct is loosening, and the personnel of their ministries is dwindling in number and in influence. The timidity and insincerity of their preachers are, in several instances, being exposed. Their endowments have, in some countries, disappeared, and the force of their religious training has declined. Their temples have been partly deserted and destroyed, and an oblivion of God, of His teachings and of His Purpose, has enfeebled and heaped humiliation upon them.

Might not this disintegrating tendency, from which Sunní and Shí'ih Islám have so conspicuously suffered, unloose, as it reaches its climax, still further calamities upon the various denominations of the Christian Church? In what manner and how rapidly this process, which has already set in, will develop the future alone can reveal. Nor can it, at the present time, be estimated to what extent will the attacks which a still powerful clergy may yet launch against the strongholds of the Faith of Bahá'u'lláh in the West accentuate this decline and widen the range of inescapable disasters.

If Christianity wishes and expects to serve the world in the present crisis, writes a minister of the Presbyterian Church in America, it must "cut back through Christianity to Christ, back through the centuries-old religion about Jesus to the original religion of Jesus." Otherwise, he significantly adds, "the spirit of Christ will live in institutions other than our own."

So marked a decline in the strength and cohesion of the elements constituting Christian society has led, in its turn, as we might well anticipate, to the emergence of an increasing number of obscure cults, of strange and new worships, of ineffective philosophies, whose sophisticated doctrines have intensified the confusion of a troubled age. In their tenets and pursuits they may be said to reflect and bear witness to the revolt, the discontent, and the confused aspirations of the disillusioned masses that have deserted the cause of the Christian churches and seceded from their membership.

A parallel might almost be drawn between these confused and confusing systems of thought that are the direct outcome of the helplessness and confusion afflicting the Christian Faith and the great variety of popular cults, of fashionable and evasive philosophies which flourished in the opening centuries of the Christian Era, and which attempted to absorb and pervert the state religion of that Roman people. The pagan worshipers who constituted, at that time, the bulk of the population of the Western Roman Empire, found themselves surrounded, and in certain instances menaced, by the prevailing sect of the Neo-Platonists, by the followers of nature religions, by Gnostic philosophers, by Philonism, Mithraism, the adherents of the Alexandrian cult, and a multitude of kindred sects and beliefs, in much the same way as the defenders of the Christian Faith, the preponderating religion of the western world, are realizing, in the first century of the Bahá'í Era, how their influence is being undermined by a flood of conflicting beliefs, practices and tendencies which their own bankruptcy had helped to create. It was, however, this same Christian Religion, which has now fallen into such a state of impotence, that eventually proved itself capable of sweeping away the institutions of paganism and of swamping and suppressing the cults that had flourished in that age.

Such institutions as have strayed far from the spirit and teachings of Jesus Christ must of necessity, as the embryonic World Order of Bahá'u'lláh takes shape and unfolds, recede into the background, and make way for the progress of the divinely-ordained institutions that stand inextricably interwoven with His teachings. The indwelling Spirit of God which, in the Apostolic Age of the Church, animated its members, the pristine purity of its teachings, the primitive brilliancy of its light, will, no doubt, be reborn and revived as the inevitable consequence of this redefinition of its fundamental verities, and the clarification of its original purpose.

For the Faith of Bahá'u'lláh—if we would faithfully appraise it—can never, and in no aspect of its teachings, be at variance, much less in conflict, with the purpose animating, or the authority invested in, the Faith of Jesus Christ. This glowing tribute which Bahá'u'lláh Himself has been moved to pay to the Author of the Christian Religion stands as sufficient testimony to the truth of this central principle of Bahá'í belief :—*"Know thou that when the Son of Man yielded up His breath to God, the whole creation wept with a great weeping. By sacrificing Himself, however, a fresh capacity was infused into all created things. Its evidences, as witnessed in all the peoples of the earth, are now manifest before thee. The deepest wisdom which the sages have uttered, the profoundest learning which any mind hath unfolded, the arts which the ablest hands have produced, the influence exerted by the most potent of rulers, are but manifestations of the quickening power released by His transcendent, His all-pervasive and resplendent Spirit. We testify that when He came into the world, He shed the splendor of His glory upon all created things. Through Him the leper recovered from the leprosy of perversity and ignorance. Through Him the unchaste and wayward were healed. Through His power, born of Almighty God, the eyes of the blind were opened, and the soul of the sinner sancti-*

fied . . . He it is Who purified the world. Blessed is the man who, with a face beaming with light, hath turned towards Him."

Signs of Moral Downfall

No more, I believe, need be said of the decline of religious institutions, the disintegration of which constitutes so important an aspect of the Formative Period of the Bahá'í Era. Islám had both as a result of the rising tide of secularism and in direct consequence of its declared and persistent hostility to the Faith of Bahá'u'lláh sunk to a depth of abasement rarely attained in its history. Christianity had, likewise, owing to causes not wholly dissimilar to those operating in the case of its sister Faith, steadily weakened, and was contributing, in an increasing measure, its share to the process of general disintegration—a process that must necessarily precede the fundamental reconstruction of human society.

The signs of moral downfall, as distinct from the evidences of decay in religious institutions, would appear to be no less noticeable and significant. The decline that has set in in the fortunes of Islamic and Christian institutions may be said to have had its counterpart in the life and conduct of the individuals that compose them. In whichever direction we turn our gaze, no matter how cursory our observation of the doings and sayings of the present generation, we can not fail to be struck by the evidences of moral decadence which, in their individual lives no less than in their collective capacity, men and women around us exhibit.

There can be no doubt that the decline of religion as a social force, of which the deterioration of religious institutions is but an external phenomenon, is chiefly responsible for so grave, so conspicuous an evil. *"Religion,"* writes Bahá'u'lláh, *"is the greatest of all means for the establishment of order in the world and for the peaceful contentment of all that dwell therein. The weakening of the pillars of religion hath strengthened the hands of the ignorant and made them bold and arrogant. Verily I say, whatsoever hath lowered the lofty station of religion hath increased the waywardness of the wicked, and the result cannot be but anarchy."* "Religion," He, in another Tablet, has stated, *"is a radiant light and an impregnable stronghold for the protection and welfare of the peoples of the world, for the fear of God impelleth man to hold fast to that which is good, and shun all evil. Should the lamp of religion be obscured, chaos and confusion will ensue, and the lights of fairness, of justice,*

of tranquillity and peace cease to shine." "Know thou," He, in yet
another connection, has written, *"that they who are truly wise have
likened the world unto the human temple. As the body of man
needeth a garment to clothe it, so the body of mankind must needs
be adorned with the mantle of justice and wisdom. Its robe is the
Revelation vouchsafed unto it by God."*

No wonder, therefore, that when, as a result of human perversity, the light of religion is quenched in men's hearts, and the
divinely appointed Robe, designed to adorn the human temple, is
deliberately discarded, a deplorable decline in the fortunes of humanity immediately sets in, bringing in its wake all the evils which
a wayward soul is capable of revealing. The perversion of human
nature, the degradation of human conduct, the corruption and dissolution of human institutions, reveal themselves, under such circumstances, in their worst and most revolting aspects. Human character is debased, confidence is shaken, the nerves of discipline are
relaxed, the voice of human conscience is stilled, the sense of de-
cency and shame is obscured, conceptions of duty, of solidarity, of
reciprocity and loyalty are distorted, and the very feeling of peace-
fulness, of joy and of hope is gradually extinguished.

Such, we might well admit, is the state which individuals and
institutions alike are approaching. *"No two men,"* Bahá'u'lláh, lamenting the plight of an erring humanity, has written, *"can be
found who may be said to be outwardly and inwardly united. The
evidences of discord and malice are apparent everywhere, though
all were made for harmony and union." "How long,"* He, in the
same Tablet, exclaims, *"will humanity persist in its waywardness?
How long will injustice continue? How long is chaos and confusion
to reign amongst men? How long will discord agitate the face of
society? The winds of despair are, alas, blowing from every direction, and the strife that divideth and afflicteth the human race is
daily increasing."*

The recrudescence of religious intolerance, of racial animosity,
and of patriotic arrogance; the increasing evidences of selfishness,
of suspicion, of fear and of fraud; the spread of terrorism, of lawlessness, of drunkenness and of crime; the unquenchable thirst for,
and the feverish pursuit after, earthly vanities, riches and pleasures;
the weakening of family solidarity; the laxity in parental control;
the lapse into luxurious indulgence; the irresponsible attitude
towards marriage and the consequent rising tide of divorce; the
degeneracy of art and music, the infection of literature, and the

corruption of the press; the extension of the influence and activities of those "prophets of decadence" who advocate companionate marriage, who preach the philosophy of nudism, who call modesty an intellectual fiction, who refuse to regard the procreation of children as the sacred and primary purpose of marriage, who denounce religion as an opiate of the people, who would, if given free rein, lead back the human race to barbarism, chaos, and ultimate extinction— these appear as the outstanding characteristics of a decadent society, a society that must either be reborn or perish.

Breakdown of Political and Economic Structure

Politically a similar decline, a no less noticeable evidence of disintegration and confusion, can be discovered in the age we live in— the age which a future historian might well recognize to have been the preamble to the Great Age, whose golden days we can as yet but dimly visualize.

The passionate and violent happenings that have, in recent years, strained to almost the point of complete breakdown the political and economic structure of society are too numerous and complex to attempt, within the limitations of this general survey, to arrive at an adequate estimate of their character. Nor have these tribulations, grievous as they have been, seemed to have reached their climax, and exerted the full force of their destructive power. The whole world, wherever and however we survey it, offers us the sad and pitiful spectacle of a vast, an enfeebled, and moribund organism, which is being torn politically and strangulated economically by forces it has ceased to either control or comprehend. The Great Depression, the aftermath of the severest ordeals humanity had ever experienced, the disintegration of the Versailles system, the recrudescence of militarism in its most menacing aspects, the failure of vast experiments and new-born institutions to safeguard the peace and tranquillity of peoples, classes and nations, have bitterly disillusioned humanity and prostrated its spirits. Its hopes are, for the most part, shattered, its vitality is ebbing, its life strangely disordered, its unity severely compromised.

On the continent of Europe inveterate hatreds and increasing rivalries are once more aligning its ill-fated peoples and nations into combinations destined to precipitate the most awful and implacable tribulations that mankind throughout its long record of martyrdom has suffered. On the North American continent economic distress, industrial disorganization, widespread discontent at the abortive experiments designed to readjust an ill-balanced economy, and restlessness and fear inspired by the possibility of political entanglements in both Europe and Asia, portend the approach of what may well prove to be one of the most critical phases of the history of the American Republic. Asia, still to a great extent in the grip of one of the severest trials she has, in her recent history, experienced, finds herself menaced on her eastern confines by the onset of forces that threaten to intensify the struggles which the growing nationalism and industrialization of her emancipated races must ultimately engender. In the heart of Africa, there blazes the fire of an atrocious and bloody war—a war which, whatever its outcome, is destined to exert, through its world-wide repercussions, a most disturbing influence on the races and colored nations of mankind.

With no less than ten million people under arms, drilled and instructed in the use of the most abominable engines of destruction that science has devised; with thrice that number chafing and fretting at the rule of alien races and governments; with an equally vast army of embittered citizens impotent to procure for themselves the material goods and necessities which others are deliberately destroying; with a still greater mass of human beings groaning under the burden of ever-mounting armaments, and impoverished by the virtual collapse of international trade—with evils such as these, humanity would seem to be definitely entering the outer fringes of the most agonizing phase of its existence.

Is it to be wondered at, that in the course of a recent statement made by one of the outstanding Ministers in Europe this warning should have been deliberately uttered: "If war should break out again on a major scale in Europe, it must bring the collapse of civilization as we know it in its wake. In the words of the late Lord Bryce, 'If you don't end war, war will end you.' " "Poor Europe is in a state of neurasthenia . . .", is the testimony of one of the most outstanding figures among its present-day dictators. "It has lost its recuperative power, the vital force of cohesion, of synthesis. Another war would destroy us." "It is likely," writes one of the most eminent and learned dignitaries of the Christian Church, "there will have to be one more great conflict in Europe to definitely establish once and for all an international authority. This conflict will be the most horrible of horribles, and possibly this generation will be called on to sacrifice hundreds of thousands of lives."

The disastrous failure of both the Disarmament and Economic

Conferences; the obstacles confronting the negotiations for the limitation of Naval armaments; the withdrawal of two of the most powerful and heavily armed nations of the world from the activities and membership of the League of Nations; the ineptitude of the parliamentary system of government as witnessed by recent developments in Europe and America; the inability of the leaders and exponents of the Communist movement to vindicate the much-vaunted principle of the Dictatorship of the Proletariat; the perils and privations to which the rulers of the Totalitarian states have, in recent years, exposed their subjects—all these demonstrate, beyond the shadow of a doubt, the impotence of present-day institutions to avert the calamities with which human society is being increasingly threatened. What else remains, a bewildered generation may well ask, that can repair the cleavage that is constantly widening, and which may, at any time, engulf it?

Beset on every side by the cumulative evidences of disintegration, of turmoil and of bankruptcy, serious-minded men and women, in almost every walk of life, are beginning to doubt whether society, as it is now organized, can, through its unaided efforts, extricate itself from the slough into which it is steadily sinking. Every system, short of the unification of the human race, has been tried, repeatedly tried, and been found wanting. Wars again and again have been fought, and conferences without number have met and deliberated. Treaties, pacts and covenants have been painstakingly negotiated, concluded and revised. Systems of government have been patiently tested, have been continually recast and superseded. Economic plans of reconstruction have been carefully devised, and meticulously executed. And yet crisis has succeeded crisis, and the rapidity with which a perilously unstable world is declining has been correspondingly accelerated. A yawning gulf threatens to involve in one common disaster both the satisfied and dissatisfied nations, democracies and dictatorships, capitalists and wage-earners, Europeans and Asiatics, Jew and Gentile, white and colored. An angry Providence, the cynic might well observe, has abandoned a hapless planet to its fate, and fixed irrevocably its doom. Sore-tried and disillusioned, humanity has no doubt lost its orientation, and would seem to have lost as well its faith and hope. It is hovering, unshepherded and visionless, on the brink of disaster. A sense of fatality seems to pervade it. An ever-deepening gloom is settling on its fortunes as she recedes further and further from the outer fringes of the darkest zone of its agitated life and penetrates its very heart.

And yet while the shadows are continually deepening, might we not claim that gleams of hope, flashing intermittently on the international horizon, appear at times to relieve the darkness that encircles humanity? Would it be untrue to maintain that in a world of unsettled faith and disturbed thought, a world of steadily mounting armaments, of unquenchable hatreds and rivalries, the progress, however fitful, of the forces working in harmony with the spirit of the age can already be discerned? Though the great outcry raised by post-war nationalism is growing louder and more insistent every day, the League of Nations is as yet in its embryonic state, and the storm clouds that are gathering may for a time totally eclipse its powers and obliterate its machinery, yet the direction in which the institution itself is operating is most significant. The voices that have been raised ever since its inception, the efforts that have been exerted, the work that has already been accomplished, foreshadow the triumphs which this presently constituted institution, or any other body that may supersede it, is destined to achieve.

Bahá'u'lláh's Principle of Collective Security

A general Pact on security has been the central purpose towards which these efforts have, ever since the League was born, tended to converge. The Treaty of Guarantee which, in the initial stages of its development, its members had considered and discussed; the debate on the Geneva Protocol, the discussion of which, at a later period, aroused among the nations, both within the League and outside it, such fierce controversy; the subsequent proposal for a United States of Europe and for the economic unification of that continent; and last but not least the policy of sanctions initiated by its members, may be regarded as the most significant landmarks in its checkered history. That no less than fifty nations of the world, all members of the League of Nations, should have, after mature deliberation, recognized and been led to pronounce their verdict against an act of aggression which in their judgment has been deliberately committed by one of their fellow-members, one of the foremost Powers of Europe; that they should have, for the most part, agreed to impose collectively sanctions on the condemned aggressor, and should have succeeded in carrying out, to a very great measure, their decision, is no doubt an event without parallel in human history. For the first time in the history of humanity the system of collective security, foreshadowed by Bahá'u'lláh and explained by 'Abdu'l-

Bahá, has been seriously envisaged, discussed and tested. For the first time in history it has been officially recognized and publicly stated that for this system of collective security to be effectively established strength and elasticity are both essential—strength involving the use of an adequate force to ensure the efficacy of the proposed system, and elasticity to enable the machinery that has been devised to meet the legitimate needs and aspirations of its aggrieved upholders. For the first time in human history tentative efforts have been exerted by the nations of the world to assume collective responsibility, and to supplement their verbal pledges by actual preparation for collective action. And again, for the first time in history, a movement of public opinion has manifested itself in support of the verdict which the leaders and representatives of nations have pronounced, and for securing collective action in pursuance of such a decision.

How clear, how prophetic, must sound the words uttered by Bahá'u'lláh in the light of recent international developments :—*"Be united, O concourse of the sovereigns of the world, for thereby will the tempest of discord be stilled amongst you, and your peoples find rest. Should any one among you take up arms against another, rise ye all against him, for this is naught but manifest justice." "The time must come,"* He, foreshadowing the tentative efforts that are now being made, has written, *"when the imperative necessity for the holding of a vast, an all-embracing assemblage of men will be universally realized. The rulers and kings of the earth must needs attend it, and, participating in its deliberations, must consider such ways and means as will lay the foundations of the world's Great Peace among men . . . Should any king take up arms against another, all should unitedly arise and prevent him."*

"The sovereigns of the world," writes 'Abdu'l-Bahá in elaboration of this theme, *"must conclude a binding treaty, and establish a covenant, the provisions of which shall be sound, inviolable and definite. They must proclaim it to all the world, and obtain for it the sanction of all the human race . . . All the forces of humanity must be mobilized to insure the stability and permanence of this Most Great Covenant . . . The fundamental principle underlying this solemn Pact should be so fixed that if any government later violate any one of its provisions, all the governments on earth should arise to reduce it to utter submission, nay the human race as a whole should resolve, with every power at its disposal, to destroy that government."*

There can be no doubt whatever that what has already been accomplished, significant and unexampled though it is in the history of mankind, still immeasurably falls short of the essential requirements of the system which these words foreshadow. The League of Nations, its opponents will observe, still lacks the universality which is the prerequisite of abiding success in the efficacious settlement of international disputes. The United States of America, its begetter, has repudiated it, and is still holding aloof, while Germany and Japan, who ranked among its most powerful supporters, have abandoned its cause and withdrawn from its membership. The decisions arrived at and the action thus far taken, others will maintain, should be regarded as no more than a magnificent gesture, rather than a conclusive evidence of international solidarity. Still others may contend that though such a verdict has been pronounced, and such pledges been given, collective action must, in the end, fail in its ultimate purpose, and that the League itself will perish and be submerged by the flood of tribulations destined to overtake the whole race. Be that as it may, the significance of the steps already taken cannot be ignored. Whatever the present status of the League or the outcome of its historic verdict, whatever the trials and reverses which, in the immediate future, it may have to face and sustain, the fact must be recognized that so important a decision marks one of the most distinctive milestones on the long and arduous road that must lead it to its goal, the stage at which the oneness of the whole body of nations will be made the ruling principle of international life.

This historic step, however, is but a faint glimmer in the darkness that envelops an agitated humanity. It may well prove to be no more than a mere flash, a fugitive gleam, in the midst of an ever-deepening confusion. The process of disintegration must inexorably continue, and its corrosive influence must penetrate deeper and deeper into the very core of a crumbling age. Much suffering will still be required ere the contending nations, creeds, classes and races of mankind are fused in the crucible of universal affliction, and are forged by the fires of a fierce ordeal into one organic commonwealth, one vast, unified, and harmoniously functioning system. Adversities unimaginably appalling, undreamed of crises and upheavals, war, famine, and pestilence, might well combine to engrave in the soul of an unheeding generation those truths and principles which it has disdained to recognize and follow. A paralysis more painful than any it has yet experienced must creep over and further

afflict the fabric of a broken society ere it can be rebuilt and re-
generated.

"The civilization," writes Bahá'u'lláh, *"so often vaunted by the
learned exponents of arts and sciences will, if allowed to overleap
the bounds of moderation, bring great evil upon men . . . If carried to excess, civilization will prove as prolific a source of evil as it
had been of goodness when kept within the restraints of moderation . . . The day is approaching when its flame will devour the
cities, when the Tongue of Grandeur will proclaim: 'The Kingdom
is God's, the Almighty, the All-Praised!' "* *"From the moment the
Súriy-i-Ra'ís* (Tablet to Ra'ís) *was revealed,"* He further explains,
*"until the present day, neither hath the world been tranquillized, nor
have the hearts of its peoples been at rest . . . Its sickness is approaching the stage of utter hopelessness, inasmuch as the true Physician is debarred from administering the remedy, whilst unskilled
practitioners are regarded with favor, and are accorded full freedom
to act. The dust of sedition hath clouded the hearts of men, and
blinded their eyes. Erelong they will perceive the consequences of
what their hands have wrought in the Day of God."* *"This is the
Day,"* He again has written, *"whereon the earth shall tell out her
tidings. The workers of iniquity are her burdens . . . The Crier
hath cried out, and men have been torn away, so great hath been
the fury of His wrath. The people of the left hand sigh and be-
moan. The people of the right abide in noble habitations: they quaff
the Wine that is life indeed from the hands of the All-Merciful, and
are, verily, the blissful."*

Community of the Most Great Name

Who else can be the blissful if not the community of the Most
Great Name, whose world-embracing, continually consolidating activities constitute the one integrating process in a world whose institutions, secular as well as religious, are for the most part dis-
solving? They indeed are *"the people of the right,"* whose *"noble
habitation"* is fixed on the foundations of the World Order of Bahá'u'lláh—the Ark of everlasting salvation in this most grievous
Day. Of all the kindreds of the earth they alone can recognize,
amidst the welter of a tempestuous age, the Hand of the Divine
Redeemer that traces its course and controls its destinies. They alone
are aware of the silent growth of that orderly world polity whose
fabric they themselves are weaving.

Conscious of their high calling, confident in the society-building power which their Faith possesses, they press forward, undeterred and undismayed, in their efforts to fashion and perfect the necessary instruments wherein the embryonic World Order of Bahá'u'lláh can mature and develop. It is this building process, slow and unobtrusive, to which the life of the world-wide Bahá'í Community is wholly consecrated, that constitutes the one hope of a stricken society. For this process is actuated by the generating influence of God's changeless Purpose, and is evolving within the framework of the Administrative Order of His Faith.

In a world the structure of whose political and social institutions is impaired, whose vision is befogged, whose conscience is bewildered, whose religious systems have become anemic and lost their virtue, this healing Agency, this leavening Power, this cementing Force, intensely alive and all-pervasive, has been taking shape, is crystallizing into institutions, is mobilizing its forces, and is preparing for the spiritual conquest and the complete redemption of mankind. Though the society which incarnates its ideals be small, and its direct and tangible benefits as yet inconsiderable, yet the potentialities with which it has been endowed, and through which it is destined to regenerate the individual and rebuild a broken world, are incalculable.

For well nigh a century it has, amid the noise and tumult of a distracted age, and despite the incessant persecutions to which its leaders, institutions, and followers have been subjected, succeeded in preserving its identity, in reinforcing its stability and strength, in maintaining its organic unity, in preserving the integrity of its laws and its principles, in erecting its defenses, and in extending and consolidating its institutions. Numerous and powerful have been the forces that have schemed, both from within and from without, in lands both far and near, to quench its light and abolish its holy name. Some have apostatized from its principles, and betrayed ignominiously its cause. Others have hurled against it the fiercest anathemas which the embittered leaders of any ecclesiastical institution are able to pronounce. Still others have heaped upon it the afflictions and humiliations which sovereign authority can alone, in the plentitude of its power, inflict.

The utmost its avowed and secret enemies could hope to achieve was to retard its growth and obscure momentarily its purpose. What they actually accomplished was to purge and purify its life, to stir it to still greater depths, to galvanize its soul, to prune its institutions, and cement its unity. A schism, a permanent cleavage in the vast body of its adherents, they could never create.

They who betrayed its cause, its lukewarm and faint-hearted supporters, withered away and dropped as dead leaves, powerless to cloud its radiance or to imperil its structure. Its most implacable adversaries, they who assailed it from without, were hurled from power, and, in the most astonishing fashion, met their doom. Persia had been the first to repress and oppose it. Its monarchs had miserably fallen, their dynasty had collapsed, their name was execrated, the hierarchy that had been their ally and had propped their declining state, had been utterly discredited. Turkey, which had thrice banished its Founder and inflicted on Him cruel and life-long imprisonment, had passed through one of the severest ordeals and far-reaching revolutions that its history has recorded, had shrunk from one of the most powerful empires to a tiny Asiatic republic, its Sultanate obliterated, its dynasty overthrown, its Caliphate, the mightiest institution of Islám, abolished.

Meanwhile the Faith that had been the object of such monstrous betrayals, and the target for such woeful assaults, was going from strength to strength, was forging ahead, undaunted and undivided by the injuries it had received. In the midst of trials it had inspired its loyal followers with a resolution that no obstacle, however formidable, could undermine. It had lighted in their hearts a faith that no misfortune, however black, could quench. It had infused into their hearts a hope that no force, however determined, could shatter.

A World Religion

Ceasing to designate to itself a movement, a fellowship and the like—designations that did grave injustice to its ever-unfolding system—dissociating itself from such appellations as Bábí sect, Asiatic cult, and offshoot of Shí'ih Islám, with which the ignorant and the malicious were wont to describe it, refusing to be labeled as a mere philosophy of life, or as an eclectic code of ethical conduct, or even as a new religion, the Faith of Bahá'u'lláh is now visibly succeeding in demonstrating its claim and title to be regarded as a World Religion, destined to attain, in the fullness of time, the status of a world-embracing Commonwealth, which would be at once the instrument and the guardian of the Most Great Peace announced by its Author. Far from wishing to add to the number of the religious systems, whose conflicting loyalties have for so many generations disturbed the peace of mankind, this Faith is instilling into each of its adherents a new love for, and a genuine appreciation of the unity underlying, the various religions represented within its pale.

"It is like a wide embrace," such is the testimony of Royalty to its claim and position, "gathering together all those who have long searched for words of hope. It accepts all great Prophets gone before it, destroys no other creeds, and leaves all doors open." "The Bahá'í teaching," she has further written, "brings peace to the soul and hope to the heart. To those in search of assurance the words of the Father are as a fountain in the desert after long wandering." "Their writings," she, in another statement referring to Bahá'u'lláh and 'Abdu'l-Bahá, has testified, "are a great cry toward peace, reaching beyond all limits of frontiers, above all dissension about rites and dogmas . . . It is a wondrous message that Bahá'u'lláh and His son 'Abdu'l-Bahá have given us. They have not set it up aggressively knowing that the germ of eternal truth which lies at its core cannot but take root and spread." "If ever the name of Bahá'-u'lláh or 'Abdu'l-Bahá," is her concluding plea, "comes to your attention, do not put their writings from you. Search out their Books, and let their glorious, peace-bringing, love-creating words and lessons sink into your hearts as they have into mine."

The Faith of Bahá'u'lláh has assimilated, by virtue of its creative, its regulative and ennobling energies, the varied races, nationalities, creeds and classes that have sought its shadow, and have pledged unswerving fealty to its cause. It has changed the hearts of its adherents, burned away their prejudices, stilled their passions, exalted their conceptions, ennobled their motives, coördinated their efforts, and transformed their outlook. While preserving their patriotism and safeguarding their lesser loyalties, it has made them lovers of mankind, and the determined upholders of its best and truest interests. While maintaining intact their belief in the Divine origin of their respective religions, it has enabled them to visualize the underlying purpose of these religions, to discover their merits, to recognize their sequence, their interdependence, their wholeness and unity, and to acknowledge the bond that vitally links them to itself. This universal, this transcending love which the followers of the Bahá'í Faith feel for their fellow-men, of whatever race, creed, class or nation, is neither mysterious nor can it be said to have been artificially stimulated. It is both spontaneous and genuine. They whose hearts are warmed by the energizing influence of God's creative love cherish His creatures for His sake, and recognize in every human face a sign of His reflected glory.

Of such men and women it may be truly said that to them "every foreign land is a fatherland, and every fatherland a foreign land." For their citizenship, it must be remembered, is in the Kingdom of Bahá'u'lláh. Though willing to share to the utmost the temporal benefits and the fleeting joys which this earthly life can confer, though eager to participate in whatever activity that conduces to the richness, the happiness and peace of that life, they can, at no time, forget that it constitutes no more than a transient, a very brief stage of their existence, that they who live it are but pilgrims and wayfarers whose goal is the Celestial City, and whose home the Country of never-failing joy and brightness.

Though loyal to their respective governments, though profoundly interested in anything that affects their security and welfare, though anxious to share in whatever promotes their best interests, the Faith with which the followers of Bahá'u'lláh stand identified is one which they firmly believe God has raised high above the storms, the divisions, and controversies of the political arena. Their Faith they conceive to be essentially non-political, supra-national in character, rigidly non-partisan, and entirely dissociated from nationalistic ambitions, pursuits, and purposes. Such a Faith knows no division of class or of party. It subordinates, without hesitation or equivocation, every particularistic interest, be it personal, regional, or national, to the paramount interests of humanity, firmly convinced that in a world of inter-dependent peoples and nations the advantage of the part is best to be reached by the advantage of the whole, and that no abiding benefit can be conferred upon the component parts if the general interests of the entity itself are ignored or neglected.

Small wonder if by the Pen of Bahá'u'lláh these pregnant words, written in anticipation of the present state of mankind, should have been revealed: *"It is not for him to pride himself who loveth his own country, but rather for him who loveth the whole world. The earth is but one country, and mankind its citizens."* And again, *"That one indeed is a man who today dedicateth himself to the service of the entire human race."* *"Through the power released by these exalted words,"* He explains, *"He hath lent a fresh impulse, and set a new direction, to the birds of men's hearts, and hath obliterated every trace of restriction and limitation from God's Holy Book."*

Their Faith, Bahá'ís firmly believe, is moreover undenominational, non-sectarian, and wholly divorced from every ecclesiastical system, whatever its form, origin, or activities. No ecclesiastical organization, with its creeds, its traditions, its limitations, and exclusive outlook, can be said (as is the case with all existing political factions, parties, systems and programs) to conform, in all its aspects, to the cardinal tenets of Bahá'í belief. To some of the principles and ideals animating political and ecclesiastical institutions every conscientious follower of the Faith of Bahá'u'lláh can, no doubt, readily subscribe. With none of these institutions, however, can he identify himself, nor can he unreservedly endorse the creeds, the principles and programs on which they are based.

How can a Faith, it should moreover be borne in mind, whose divinely-ordained institutions have been established within the jurisdiction of no less than forty different countries, the policies and interests of whose governments are continually clashing and growing more complex and confused every day—how can such a Faith, by allowing its adherents, whether individually or through its organized councils, to meddle in political activities, succeed in preserving the integrity of its teachings and in safeguarding the unity of its followers? How can it insure the vigorous, the uninterrupted and peaceful development of its expanding institutions? How can a Faith, whose ramifications have brought it into contact with mutually incompatible religious systems, sects and confessions, be in a position, if it permits its adherents to subscribe to obsolescent observances and doctrines, to claim the unconditional allegiance of those whom it is striving to incorporate into its divinely-appointed system? How can it avoid the constant friction, the misunderstandings and controversies which formal affiliation, as distinct from association, must inevitably engender?

These directing and regulating principles of Bahá'í belief the upholders of the Cause of Bahá'u'lláh feel bound, as their Administrative Order expands and consolidates itself, to assert and vigilantly apply. The exigencies of a slowly crystallizing Faith impose upon them a duty which they cannot shirk, a responsibility they cannot evade.

Nor are they unmindful of the imperative necessity of upholding and of executing the laws, as distinguished from the principles, ordained by Bahá'u'lláh, both of which constitute the warp and woof of the institutions upon which the structure of His World Order must ultimately rest. To demonstrate their usefulness and efficacy, to carry out and apply them, to safeguard their integrity, to grasp their implications, and to facilitate their propagation Bahá'í communities in the East, and recently in the West, are displaying the utmost effort and are willing, if necessary, to make whatever sacrifices may be demanded. The day may not be far distant when in certain countries of the East, in which religious communities exercise jurisdiction in matters of personal status, Bahá'í Assemblies may be called upon to assume the duties and responsibilities devolving upon officially constituted Bahá'í courts. They will be empowered, in such matters as marriage, divorce, and inheritance, to execute and apply, within their respective jurisdictions, and with the sanction of civil authorities, such laws and ordinances as have been expressly provided in their Most Holy Book.

The Faith of Bahá'u'lláh has, in addition to these tendencies and activities which its evolution is now revealing, demonstrated, in other spheres, and wherever the illumination of its light has penetrated, the force of its cohesive strength, of its integrating power, of its invincible spirit. In the erection and consecration of its House of Worship in the heart of the North American continent; in the construction and multiplication of its administrative headquarters in the land of its birth and in neighboring countries; in the fashioning of the legal instruments designed to safeguard and regulate the corporate life of its institutions; in the accumulation of adequate resources, material as well as cultural, in every continent of the globe; in the endowments which it has created for itself in the immediate surroundings of its Shrines at its world center; in the efforts that are being made for the collection, the verification, and the systematization of the writings of its Founders; in the measures that are being taken for the acquisition of such historical sites as are associated with the lives of its Forerunner and its Author, its heroes and martyrs; in the foundations that are being laid for the gradual formation and establishment of its educational, its cultural and humanitarian institutions; in the vigorous efforts that are being exerted to safeguard the character, stimulate the initiative and coordinate the world-wide activities of its youth; in the extraordinary vitality with which its valiant defenders, its elected representatives, its itinerant teachers and pioneer administrators are pleading its cause, extending its boundaries, enriching its literature, and strengthening the basis of its spiritual conquests and triumphs; in the recognition which civil authorities have, in certain instances, been induced to grant to the body of its local and national representatives, enabling them to incorporate their councils, establish their subsidiary institutions, and safeguard their endowments; in the facilities which these same authorities have consented to accord to its shrines, its consecrated edifices, and educational institutions; in the enthusiasm and determination with which certain communities that had been severely tested and harassed are resuming their activities; in the spontaneous tributes paid by royalty, princes, statesmen and scholars to the sublimity of its cause and the station of its Founders—in these, as in many others, the Faith of Bahá'u'-lláh is proving beyond doubt its virility and capacity to counteract the disintegrating influences to which religious systems, moral standards, and political and social institutions are being subjected.

From Iceland to Tasmania, from Vancouver to the China Sea spreads the radiance and extend the ramifications of this world-enfolding System, this many-hued and firmly-knit Fraternity, infusing into every man and woman it has won to its cause a faith, a hope, and a vigor that a wayward generation has long lost, and is powerless to recover. They who preside over the immediate destinies of this troubled world, they who are responsible for its chaotic state, its fears, its doubts, its miseries will do well, in their bewilderment, to fix their gaze and ponder in their hearts upon the evidences of this saving grace of the Almighty that lies within their reach— a grace that can ease their burden, resolve their perplexities, and illuminate their path.

Divine Retribution

The whole of mankind is groaning, is dying to be led to unity, and to terminate its age-long martyrdom. And yet it stubbornly refuses to embrace the light and acknowledge the sovereign authority of the one Power that can extricate it from its entanglements, and avert the woeful calamity that threatens to engulf it.

Ominous indeed is the voice of Bahá'u'lláh that rings through these prophetic words: *"O ye peoples of the world! Know, verily, that an unforeseen calamity followeth you, and grievous retribution awaiteth you. Think not that which ye have committed hath been effaced in My sight."* And again: *"We have a fixed time for you, O peoples. If ye fail, at the appointed hour, to turn towards God, He, verily, will lay violent hold on you, and will cause grievous afflictions to assail you from every direction. How severe, indeed, is the chastisement with which your Lord will then chastise you!"*

Must humanity, tormented as she now is, be afflicted with still severer tribulations ere their purifying influence can prepare her to enter the heavenly Kingdom destined to be established upon earth? Must the inauguration of so vast, so unique, so illumined an era in human history be ushered in by so great a catastrophe in human affairs as to recall, nay surpass, the appalling collapse of Roman civilization in the first centuries of the Christian Era? Must a series of profound convulsions stir and rock the human race ere Bahá'u'lláh can be enthroned in the hearts and consciences of the masses, ere His undisputed ascendancy is universally recognized, and the noble edifice of His World Order is reared and established?

The long ages of infancy and childhood, through which the human race had to pass, have receded into the background. Humanity is now experiencing the commotions invariably associated with the most turbulent stage of its evolution, the stage of adolescence, when the impetuosity of youth and its vehemence reach their climax, and must gradually be superseded by the calmness, the wisdom, and the maturity that characterize the stage of manhood. Then will the human race reach that stature of ripeness which will enable it to acquire all the powers and capacities upon which its ultimate development must depend.

World Unity the Goal

Unification of the whole of mankind is the hall-mark of the stage which human society is now approaching. Unity of family, of tribe, of city-state, and nation have been successively attempted and fully established. World unity is the goal towards which a harassed humanity is striving. Nation-building has come to an end. The anarchy inherent in state sovereignty is moving towards a climax. A world, growing to maturity, must abandon this fetish, recognize the oneness and wholeness of human relationships, and establish once for all the machinery that can best incarnate this fundamental principle of its life.

"*A new life,*" Bahá'u'lláh proclaims, "*is, in this age, stirring within all the peoples of the earth; and yet none hath discovered its cause, or perceived its motive.*" "*O ye children of men,*" He thus addresses His generation, "*the fundamental purpose animating the Faith of God and His Religion is to safeguard the interests and promote the unity of the human race . . . This is the straight path, the fixed and immovable foundation. Whatsoever is raised on this foundation, the changes and chances of the world can never impair its strength, nor will the revolution of countless centuries under-mine its structure." "The well-being of mankind,"* He declares, *"its peace and security are unattainable unless and until its unity is firmly established." "So powerful is the light of unity,"* is His fur-ther testimony, *"that it can illuminate the whole earth. The one true God, He Who knoweth all things, Himself testifieth to the truth of these words . . . This goal excelleth every other goal, and this as-piration is the monarch of all aspirations." "He Who is your Lord, the All-Merciful,"* He, moreover, has written, *"cherisheth in His heart the desire of beholding the entire human race as one soul and one body. Haste ye to win your share of God's good grace and mercy in this Day that eclipseth all other created days."*

The unity of the human race, as envisaged by Bahá'u'lláh, im-plies the establishment of a world commonwealth in which all na-tions, races, creeds and classes are closely and permanently united, and in which the autonomy of its state members and the personal freedom and initiative of the individuals that compose them are definitely and completely safeguarded. This commonwealth must, as far as we can visualize it, consist of a world legislature, whose members will, as the trustees of the whole of mankind, ultimately control the entire resources of all the component nations, and will enact such laws as shall be required to regulate the life, satisfy the needs and adjust the relationships of all races and peoples. A world executive, backed by an international Force, will carry out the deci-sions arrived at, and apply the laws enacted by, this world legisla-ture, and will safeguard the organic unity of the whole common-wealth. A world tribunal will adjudicate and deliver its compulsory and final verdict in all and any disputes that may arise between the various elements constituting this universal system. A mechanism of world inter-communication will be devised, embracing the whole planet, freed from national hindrances and restrictions, and func-tioning with marvellous swiftness and perfect regularity. A world metropolis will act as the nerve center of a world civilization, the focus towards which the unifying forces of life will converge and from which its energizing influences will radiate. A world language will either be invented or chosen from among the existing languages and will be taught in the schools of all the federated nations as an auxiliary to their mother tongue. A world script, a world literature, a uniform and universal system of currency, of weights and meas-ures, will simplify and facilitate intercourse and understanding among the nations and races of mankind. In such a world society, science and religion, the two most potent forces in human life, will be reconciled, will coöperate, and will harmoniously develop. The press will, under such a system, while giving full scope to the expression of the diversified views and convictions of mankind, cease to be mischievously manipulated by vested interests, whether private or public, and will be liberated from the influence of contending governments and peoples. The economic resources of the world will be organized, its sources of raw materials will be tapped and fully utilized, its markets will be coördinated and developed, and the distribution of its products will be equitably regulated.

National rivalries, hatreds, and intrigues will cease, and racial animosity and prejudice will be replaced by racial amity, understanding and coöperation. The causes of religious strife will be permanently removed, economic barriers and restrictions will be completely abolished, and the inordinate distinction between classes will be obliterated. Destitution on the one hand, and gross accumulation of ownership on the other, will disappear. The enormous energy dissipated and wasted on war, whether economic or political, will be consecrated to such ends as will extend the range of human inventions and technical development, to the increase of the productivity of mankind, to the extermination of disease, to the extension of scientific research, to the raising of the standard of physical health, to the sharpening and refinement of the human brain, to the exploitation of the unused and unsuspected resources of the planet, to the prolongation of human life, and to the furtherance of any other agency that can stimulate the intellectual, the moral, and spiritual life of the entire human race.

A world federal system, ruling the whole earth and exercising unchallengeable authority over its unimaginably vast resources, blending and embodying the ideals of both the East and the West, liberated from the curse of war and its miseries, and bent on the exploitation of all the available sources of energy on the surface of the planet, a system in which Force is made the servant of Justice, whose life is sustained by its universal recognition of one God and by its allegiance to one common Revelation—such is the goal towards which humanity, impelled by the unifying forces of life, is moving.

"One of the great events," affirms 'Abdu'l-Bahá, *"which is to occur in the Day of the manifestation of that incomparable Branch is the hoisting of the Standard of God among all nations. By this is meant that all nations and kindreds will be gathered together un-*

der the shadow of this Divine Banner, which is no other than the *Lordly Branch itself, and will become a single nation. Religious and sectarian antagonism, the hostility of races and peoples, and differences among nations, will be eliminated. All men will adhere to one religion, will have one common faith, will be blended into one race and become a single people. All will dwell in one common fatherland, which is the planet itself." "Now, in the world of being,"* He has moreover explained, *"the Hand of Divine power hath firmly laid the foundations of this all-highest bounty, and this wondrous gift. Whatsoever is latent in the innermost of this holy Cycle shall gradually appear and be made manifest, for now is but the beginning of its growth, and the dayspring of the revelation of its signs. Ere the close of this century and of this age, it shall be made clear and evident how wondrous was that spring-tide, and how heavenly was that gift."*

No less enthralling is the vision of Isaiah, the greatest of the Hebrew Prophets, predicting, as far back as twenty five hundred years ago, the destiny which mankind must, at its stage of maturity, achieve: *"And He* (the Lord) *shall judge among the nations, and shall rebuke many people: and they shall beat their swords into plowshares, and their spears into pruninghooks: nation shall not lift up sword against nation, neither shall they learn war any more . . . And there shall come forth a rod out of the stem of Jesse, and a Branch shall grow out of his roots . . . And he shall smite the earth with the rod of his mouth, and with the breath of his lips shall he slay the wicked. And righteousness shall be the girdle of his loins, and faithfulness the girdle of his reins. The wolf also shall dwell with the lamb, and the leopard shall lie down with the kid; and the calf and the young lion and the fatling together . . . And the sucking child shall play on the hole of the asp, and the weaned child shall put his hand on the cockatrice's den. They shall not hurt nor destroy in all my holy mountain: for the earth shall be full of the knowledge of the Lord, as the waters cover the sea."*

The writer of the Apocalypse, prefiguring the millenial glory which a redeemed, a jubilant humanity must witness, has similarly testified: *"And I saw a new heaven and a new earth: for the first heaven and the first earth were passed away; and there was no more sea. And I, John, saw the holy city, new Jerusalem, coming down from God out of heaven, prepared as a bride adorned for her husband. And I heard a great voice out of heaven saying, 'Behold, the tabernacle of God is with men, and he will dwell with them, and they shall be his people, and God himself shall be with them, and be their God. And God shall wipe away all tears from their eyes; and there shall be no more death, neither sorrow, nor crying, neither shall there be any more pain: for the former things are passed away.' "*

Who can doubt that such a consummation—the coming of age of the human race—must signalize, in its turn, the inauguration of a world civilization such as no mortal eye hath ever beheld or human mind conceived? Who is it that can imagine the lofty standard which such a civilization, as it unfolds itself, is destined to attain? Who can measure the heights to which human intelligence, liberated from its shackles, will soar? Who can visualize the realms which the human spirit, vitalized by the outpouring light of Bahá'u'lláh, shining in the plenitude of its glory, will discover?

What more fitting conclusion to this theme than these words of Bahá'u'lláh, written in anticipation of the golden age of His Faith—the age in which the face of the earth, from pole to pole, will mirror the ineffable splendors of the Abhá Paradise? *"This is the Day whereon naught can be seen except the splendors of the Light that shineth from the face of thy Lord, the Gracious, the Most Bountiful. Verily, We have caused every soul to expire by virtue of Our irresistible and all-subduing sovereignty. We have then called into being a new creation, as a token of Our grace unto men. I am, verily, the All-Bountiful, the Ancient of Days. This is the Day whereon the unseen world crieth out: 'Great is thy blessedness, O earth, for thou hast been made the foot-stool of thy God, and been chosen as the seat of His mighty throne!' The realm of glory exclaimeth: 'Would that my life could be sacrificed for thee, for He Who is the Beloved of the All-Merciful hath established His sovereignty upon thee, through the power of His name that hath been promised unto all things, whether of the past or of the future.' "*

SHOGHI.

Haifa, Palestine,
March 11, 1936.

INDEX

INDEX

Aqdas (see Kitáb-i-Aqdas)
Arch-Enemy of Faith, 81, 82, 173
Argentina, 87
Ark of salvation, 19, 84, 155, 194
Armaments, 32, 35, 37, 40, 162,
    189, 190, 191
Asceticism, 22
Asia, 31, 78, 181, 189
Atheism, 182, 183
Australia, 31, 78, 88
Austro-Hungarian Monarchy, down-
    fall of, 171, 183
Autonomy, national, essential, 41,
    203

Báb, 'Alí-Muhammad
    anticipated World Order of Bahá'-
        u'lláh, 146, 147
    apostles of, 55, 63, 108, 125
    attacks against, 72, 173
    characteristics, 97, 124
    descendant of Imáms, 102, 178
    Dispensation of, 61, 62, 102, 117,
        123-128, 143
    Forerunner of Bahá'u'lláh, 61, 72,
        100, 123, 128, 131, 132
    fulfilled prophecies, 123, 127, 143,
        179
    guides Guardian and Houses of
        Justice, 149
    identical in reality with Bahá'u'-
        lláh, 138, 139
    influence of, 103, 124, 125
    knowledge revealed by, 25, 62,
        100, 125, 143
    last preliminary Revelator, 103
    Manifestation of God, 61, 103,
        123, 124, 125, 126, 128, 131,
        133
    martyrdom, 56, 72, 101, 124,
        173, 178

Báb—Cont.
    oneness with Prophets of past,
        117, 126
    proclaims supremacy of Bahá'u'-
        lláh, 62, 100, 101
    Qá'im, 25, 62, 100, 117, 125
    quotations from (see Quotations)
    Revelation of, as sun in Aries, 127
    station, 97, 100, 102, 126, 131
    station attested by 'Abdu'l-Bahá,
        61, 123, 124, 127, 128, 133
    station attested by Bahá'u'lláh, 25,
        62, 125
    station revealed in Nabíl's "Dawn-
        Breakers," 123, 124
    titles of
        Ancient Beauty, 164
        Great Announcement, 126
        Mystic Fane, 126
        Primal Point, 107, 125, 126,
            138, 139
        Promised Christ, 139
        Sun of Truth, 133
        "Word," 125
    tomb of, 82, 84
    two-fold station, 123, 131
Bábís, patience and faithfulness of,
    125
Baghdád, 125
Baghdád, Bahá'í appeal to League of
    Nations, 93
Baghdád, house of Bahá'u'lláh, 26,
    92, 93
Bahá'í Administration (see Admin-
    istrative Order)
Bahá'í Assemblies, 6, 9, 18, 64, 99,
    147, 200
Bahá'í Assemblies of East, social
    jurisdiction, 200
Bahá'í Cause (see Faith of Bahá'u'-
    lláh)